The Dark Side of Our Digital World

The Dark Side of Our Digital World

And What You Can Do about It

ANDREW WEISS

ROWMAN & LITTLEFIELD
Lanham • Boulder • New York • London

Published by Rowman & Littlefield
An imprint of The Rowman & Littlefield Publishing Group, Inc.
4501 Forbes Boulevard, Suite 200, Lanham, Maryland 20706
www.rowman.com

86-90 Paul Street, London EC2A 4NE

British Library Cataloguing in Publication Information Available

Library of Congress Cataloging-in-Publication Data

Names: Weiss, Andrew, 1971– author.
Title: The dark side of our digital world : and what you can do about it /
   Andrew Weiss.
Description: Lanham : Rowman & Littlefield, [2020] | Series: Library
   Information Technology Association (LITA) guides | Includes
   bibliographical references and index. | Summary: "This book will help
   readers identify strategies to understand, avoid and handle fake news,
   misinformation, disinformation, information overload, surveillance and
   privacy loss, cyberbullying, hacking and other security flaws, and
   online and IT behavioral conditioning"— Provided by publisher.
Identifiers: LCCN 2019056383 (print) | LCCN 2019056384 (ebook)
Subjects: LCSH: Information behavior. | Information resources management. |
   Information technology—Management. | Electronic information resource
   literacy. | Privacy, Right of. | Social media—Psychological aspects.
Classification: LCC ZA3075 .W44 2020 (print) | LCC ZA3075 (ebook) | DDC
   025.5/24—dc23
LC record available at https://lccn.loc.gov/2019056383
LC ebook record available at https://lccn.loc.gov/2019056384

ISBN: 978-1-5381-1905-1 (cloth : alk. paper)
ISBN: 978-1-5381-9218-4 (pbk : alk. paper)
ISBN: 978-1-5381-1906-8 (ebook)

♾™ The paper used in this publication meets the minimum requirements of
American National Standard for Information Sciences—Permanence of Paper
for Printed Library Materials, ANSI/NISO Z39.48-1992.

To Akiko, Mia, and Cooper
for their love, support, and patience.
To my parents for their lifelong encouragement.

Contents

Figures

Preface

As a librarian, I have spent more than a decade working in libraries serving the people who use them. The stereotype of librarians is well-worn: quiet, mousy types in constant vigilance against noise while wearing what could be generously described as "comfortable clothes." It's a pervasive image in pop culture.

And it's completely wrong.

Although most of the work of libraries and librarians admittedly goes on behind the scenes, don't be fooled by the mostly placid surfaces, the quiet study spaces, or the well-tended bookshelves. For not only have libraries already changed from this stereotype—shushing is definitely "out," collaborative study is all the rage, and electronic books and journals are replacing the physical shelf—the library world also sits on the front lines of an ongoing conflict between gathering forces of ignorance, fear, and control and the bulwark defenses of open information, transparency, and knowledge creation. As a result, librarians have a front-row seat to the problems that we face as a society: ranging from the public librarians who have dealt with the opioid scourge in Philadelphia's suburbs to the school librarians that saved children's lives in Parkland and Sandy Hook. Lately the country has been concerned with the malicious actors of foreign governments attempting to manipulate public discourse through amplified divisions in social media. These problems are nothing new. Our library institutions, both public and private, have attempted to keep these problems at bay and provide clear information commons spaces for all to use, while providing safe harbors for people in need.

This book is both an exploration of the information problems that are impacting us so negatively and a call for more public action. To examine these ongoing problems, this book is broken into several sections, each taking on the issues raised by what I define as "information pathologies." The link to disease in the physical sense is deliberate, as we can only solve our problems if we have a clear understanding of not only the symptoms of what ails us but also the root causes (i.e., their disease vectors and mechanisms for spreading).

Part I of this book, "Information and the Weapons of Mass Distraction," defines information pathologies and provides the clearest frame and context possible for these ongoing issues in information, including the methods that contribute to distracting us from observing the world, such as behavioral conditioning, "nudging," and surveillance capitalism. Part II, "Drinking Directly from a Fire Hose," examines the concept of information overload, looks at the role of conspiracy theory in spreading false information, and concludes with a look at the way in which our digital cultures are being co-opted by specific for-profit interests. Part III, "Information and Power," focuses on the impact of excessive amounts of information being shared and collected and how it can impact a person's sense of well-being, autonomy, and overall privacy. It also examines how information itself can be used to actively harm and negatively impact someone's life. Finally, part IV, "Draining the Fever Swamp," attempts to provide some solutions to the problems described, especially with a look at how to protect user privacy, how to effectively fight Internet trolls and online bots, and how to develop a stronger digital commons and e-democracy.

On a final note, the fascinating part of writing this book has been the unfolding of events, often in real time, that hammered home many of the pathologies and problems I outline in each part. These events have only made it even more important that this book be completed and see the light of day. Real-world impacts from these pathologies affect us daily. The world is ours to protect, be it digital or physical, and it starts with ensuring that access to information and freedom from manipulation remain strong.

It starts with us.

Acknowledgments

I would like to acknowledge the following people and organizations for their generous cooperation in the creation of this book: LITA and the staff and volunteers at LITA Guides, the American Library Association, and Drs. Martin Hilbert and Shoshana Zuboff, whose works have had particular influence on me and on the direction that this book has taken. Special acknowledgment also goes to the editorial staff at Rowman & Littlefield for their help in shaping and developing this book, especially Charles Harmon. Among colleagues at CSUN, many thanks to Oviatt Library dean Mark Stover; Ahmed Alwan and Eric Garcia, for our research collaborations in fake news, misinformation, disinformation, and all that *jawn*, much of which informed chapter 9; and Luiz Mendes for his constant guidance and encouragement. Finally, a special acknowledgment to Akiko, for making sure I don't get too sidetracked on "barefoot doctors" and stay focused on the topic.

I

INFORMATION AND THE WEAPONS OF MASS DISTRACTION

1

Into the "Upside-Down"

Identifying Our Problem

THE FEVER SWAMP: A LOOK AT THE CURRENT PROBLEMS OF A LIFE SPENT ONLINE

Several years back, a man walked into a pizzeria with a semi-automatic weapon and opened fire. The motive? To rescue child victims of a sex-trafficking ring that worked out of this restaurant. The problem? It was completely false, the result of a conspiracy theory initially spread by liars and rumor-mongers, looking for any way possible to discredit Democrat Hillary Clinton's presidential campaign. Thankfully, no one was injured or killed from the gunfire. But the man's actions nevertheless showed he was completely convinced and serious, willing to bring the wicked to justice. He even saw himself as the hero of this story, a rescuer of abused children. While the man eventually came to understand that he was duped, this has still not been enough to dispel the lunatic fringe or the maliciously inclined. Even now there are people who still spread this particular lie.

Of course, the "Pizzagate" incident is merely one example of countless conspiracy theories, misinformation, disinformation, rumor-mongering, and propaganda that pass for factual information. These phenomena, though, are hardly new. They likely date back for as long as humans have been talking to each other. Indeed, the Ancient Greeks attributed these communication behaviors to the goddess Pheme (Fama to the Romans), who could be either benevolent by bestowing renown and fame upon someone or destructive by spreading lies and innuendo about them.

3

More recently, fake news, social media manipulation, and trolling are all the news. From Russian interference in America's presidential election to online hoaxes and the fever swamps of despicable conspiracy theories about the victims in the Parkland, Florida, high school shooting, the Internet seems uniquely capable of bringing out the very worst in people. The Internet's original utopian vision of open information has given way to something more exploitative. The early promise of the Internet's decentralized connections is now dominated by corporate visions of deregulated markets that rely on private data gathered from end-users. The early benefits of unlimited communication are now controlled by governments interested in surveilling their own citizens for the sake of safety instead of protecting constitutional or human rights.

And what of information itself? The idealistic, perhaps even unexamined, "promise" of information is that it leads us to truth and understanding. Information, one theory suggests, is one rung in a hierarchy that leads us from data, to informed facts (information), to knowledge, and ultimately to wisdom. Others see information as a building block of data, which are not just numbers or "information in the raw" but assertions that we make about understanding reality. In other words, through information and data, we assert that the world and the wider universe can be examined and understood outside of faith-based beliefs, gut feelings, or long-standing traditions.

Yet there are dark sides to this idealism as well, as the ancient Greeks and Romans suggest with the dual positive and negative natures of Pheme/Fama. What if our assumptions about information and the Internet are not as clearly positive as we would like to believe? What if information is not only a promise of leading us to truth, but something that can also lead us to a realization of incompleteness and despair? The positive benefit that we believe information provides us can easily be thwarted. There is for many of us a gap between the anticipated benefit of learning something new and the actual, less-than-ideal result. The mission of finding something out to make us more "informed"— and thus better people—is consistently thrown off the rails. In other ways, as information becomes central to this futuristic economy, it becomes a form of power, capable of helping as well as harming. In this sense, we must re-examine our assumptions about information and its unexamined blanket promise of betterment.

Most of us have likely dealt with information problems as creators, consumers, or users of information. We have all been confronted with, for example, a failed search, the frustration of reading an online troll's obnoxious response in an online forum, malware-infested software, the loss of privacy, or the anxiety that comes from too many choices. We will examine these and other ongoing problems found in information and information technology. It is hoped that once these information pathologies are identified, readers will begin to find solutions to alleviate or even eliminate them. Without a clear concept to describe what is happening to us, we may be doomed to repeat the same patterns of destructive behavior, manipulated by external forces and conditions into acting in predictable ways or becoming willing participants who give in to our own worst impulses.

WHAT IS INFORMATION?

First, some background on the modern development of information theory and its organization. The history of information science for the past fifty to sixty years is the result of a steady shift of removing information from physical containers, such as books, magazines, journals, and other paper-based materials, into electronic formats composed of digital data that can move nearly unhindered through borderless communication channels.

Obviously, the telegraph, telephone, and television are influential in the development of communications, and their progress has helped to shift the primary vehicle of information transmission from print to electronic methods. But this is only part of the story. The modern concept of information also stems from important research initiated by Claude Shannon of Bell Laboratories in the 1940s. Shannon "showed how the logical algebra of 19th-century mathematician George Boole could be implemented using electronic circuits of relays and switches" (Collins, 2002). The most basic architecture of a computer's design was broken down into binaries representing <true> and <false>, or <0> and <1>, in the physical form of open or closed electronic switches. These switches were then combined with electronic logic gates "to make decisions and to carry out arithmetic" (Collins, 2002). Shannon's revolutionary theory of information envisioned information as the number of *binary digits*, or *bits*, required to encode a message capable of being transmitted across multiple communications channels. It forever changed how information was conceptualized and removed it far from the physical constraints that traditionally bound it.

In a sense, for the first time in history, information could be reliably stripped from its physical container's properties to become an abstract, mathematical entity. Information would become nearly ethereal in its ability to transcend previous physical boundaries. It would also become nearly eternal in its ability to overcome time and transmission limitations. Our own terminology reflects this change, moving from printed books (the word *book* in English stems from a Germanic word for *beech* tree) to mainframes and computers to information highways and superconductors and on to clouds, fogs, and mists. Combined with the realization that data itself is something without an essence of its own, the modern notion of information and information science springs into being.

As we all know, however, shifting to new technologies can come with a price, often subtly changing the user to fit the tool (i.e., when all you have is a hammer, everything looks like a nail, they say), adapting and incorporating new behaviors that were unintended, and generally phasing out prior practices. Only a select few technologies, such as vinyl LP records or Polaroid film, might make a legitimate comeback. Many technologies, though, do not rebound and are thrown onto the trash heap of history.

Yet, the more things change, the more they stay the same. Problems associated with information and its technologies have persisted for a long time and might be central to our own human natures and cognitive limits. As the Greeks and Romans point out, rumor and fame come from the kindness and wrath of the same goddess. But these impacts are based on real experiences. Lies and betrayal have real-world consequences. Failure to act on clear evidence can destroy us. Spying and misinformation can manipulate or control us. Too much information can lead to physical stress and indecision. New digital information technologies provide similar benefits and challenges that the scroll, the book, and the printing presses offered. The only differences now are the speed of their performance, the scope of their reach, and the scale of their impact. These information pathologies can more easily become pandemic in a more connected world, much like the flu travels much farther in a Boeing 777, but they are nevertheless deeply rooted in our cultures' long histories.

WHAT ARE INFORMATION PATHOLOGIES?

Information pathologies can be defined simply as breakdowns in the promise of "informing" and providing useful data to those who need it, blockages along pathways to knowledge. They demonstrate the fundamental weaknesses in the information systems and knowledge structures we have created. These breakdowns—whether they are recurrent or sporadic, universal or local—prevent users of information from fulfilling their desired goals and purposes, even if those goals and purposes are not fully understood or consciously decided upon by the users themselves.

In order to better examine these problems, I am proposing three distinct areas of information pathology: information architecture and research pathologies, information technology pathologies, and information usage pathologies. As we can see in figure 1.1, some of these pathologies, such as information overload and abandoning searches, are a direct result of human limitations in cognition, memory, bias, and imagination. Human nature is sometimes a questionable influence, with its compromised reliance on logical fallacies, faulty memories, and embellished remembrances of the past. These are evident in the persistence of conspiracy theories and the spread of disinformation (aka the "rumor mill"). Other pathologies, such as security vulnerabilities, hacking, and the loss of privacy, arise as a result of technological flaws and intentionally malicious applications of both IT and information

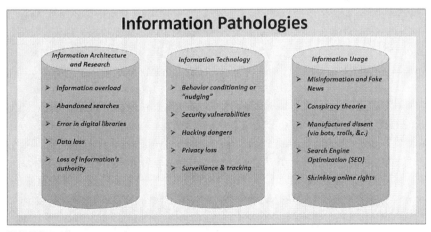

FIGURE 1.1
The main types of information pathologies. *Author*

sources. The next sections will outline these negative aspects of information more closely.

The Cracks in Information Architecture

The first set of information pathologies exists within the architecture of information itself. Information is not isolated. It needs to be described using metadata (literally data about data) to preserve its link to reality. It also needs to be stored in something and then reconstructed and transmitted into formats for people to comprehend it. In the case of books or magazines, you just have to open one and the information is accessible—provided you know how to read it (which requires a bit of cultural background knowledge itself). But obstacles to access inevitably occur. Communicability breaks down due to flaws within the infrastructure that conveys information.

This breakdown is not a new problem and has arguably existed for thousands of years. For example, the desire to collect things—especially books—is an ancient one. But this thirst for universal knowledge unbound also sets us up for failure. We eventually become overwhelmed by the tasks of organizing, finding, and then establishing meaning for all of this information—some of which winds up being contradictory. The term for this feeling of being overwhelmed is "information overload," which is the inability of users to make good decisions in the face of too much information, especially if it is disorganized. This information fatigue, as it is also called, is further characterized by people abandoning their searches, digging-in to their hardened opinions, or rejecting alternate views regardless of the evidence. In a more recent example, the large-scale collection of digital information has led to a magnification of errors and falseness. This has been apparent in the flaws found in massive digital libraries such as Google Books. Large amounts of metadata error creep in, "poisoning the well," so to speak, and undermining user trust. The results contribute to not only general user distrust but also to erroneous conclusions, overall poor scholarship, and incomplete or omitted results.

The loss of context with digital texts or media also has an uneven legacy. On one hand, digitalization allows for remixing, rehashing, or remaking works from the past. One could easily crop, copy, and paste images from a book and append them to another one. But one might also lose the background from which such images come. Completely loosening an item from its ties to a physical location, environment, or period of time compromises the knowledge—and the lessons derived from it—that we have generated over the centuries. This loss of context, or *provenance*, is characteristic of the web. "It's a feature, not a bug," as the saying goes.

Finally, the way in which science is conducted also changes based on the use of digital data and the development of algorithms that help to interpret it. While data-mining techniques are necessary to examine the terabytes of data many researchers now work with, it sometimes omits the human element. This will be a challenging time to make sure that data remains tethered to reality even as it moves beyond human scale to interpret it. We will increasingly rely on artificial intelligence (AI) and algorithms to derive meaning from the data we collect. However, as Clifford Lynch, Director of the Coalition for Networked Information (CNI), describes it, "Making important decisions entirely by algorithm is a profound abdication of responsibility; there needs to be a way to also bring human judgment, intuition and empathy to the situation" (Lynch, 2017). If our ability to decide what is relevant to us is left to machines, then we risk losing not only our physical control of future actions but also our most essential of human qualities: the ability to imagine change itself through our own sense of responsibility to each other.

How IT Makes Us Vulnerable

The second set of information pathologies is concerned with the breakdown in our ability to securely and safely use information technologies. One of the major problems with information technology for the past seventy years has been with ensuring privacy of users. In particular, the development of a post-WWII and Cold War surveillance system in the United States—especially with the post-9/11 PATRIOT Act—has severely compromised our ability to maintain privacy and ensure the confidentiality of collected information.

Technology in the era of "big data" has morphed into tools designed for mass surveillance and now erodes what little privacy people have left to hold onto. The so-called grand bargain of surveillance capitalism trades user privacy and confidentiality for the "free" use of online software and services. This unequal bargain promises to erode the private sphere even further. Unfortunately, nearly all online organizations have wittingly or unwittingly become pillars of the surveillance state. Documentation of mass surveillance in various sources, including WikiLeaks, demonstrates the extent to which the NSA, CIA, and FBI (not to mention foreign intelligence organizations) are capable of tracking information usage online. It has come to the point that if you are online, you must assume that you are being surveilled by some*one* or some*thing* some*where*. People need to be aware of this participation in the surveillance state and allowed to take appropriate measures to ensure privacy. At the very least, people need to be aware of how surveillance directly impacts their own lives!

Another concerning problem with online behavior is the way in which technology companies "nudge" their users into making choices they might not make in real life. It has been noted that Apple and other smart phone makers try to condition their users into using the devices as much as possible, using conditioning techniques similar to the pigeon's food pellet in a Skinner Box. Instead of the Internet, we are using the *Skinnernet*, a tool used to condition its users by manipulating basic human psychology. The likes and dislike buttons on a Facebook page are an obvious example of this ongoing attempt at conditioning human behavior. It has been shown that people are more likely to comply with rules if they are given constant feedback about what they are doing. In the same way that setting up a sign along the road indicating your current speed helps to curb speeding, so too does constant data feedback modify a user's behavior in real time. While this could be a helpful application in the case of exercise regimens and diets, it is downright creepy when it points out how and what to think of certain topics, or when it targets ads and videos at users in an attempt to shape opinions and attitudes. The purchases of Facebook ads by the Kremlin-backed Internet Research Agency—as outlined in Robert Mueller's February 16, 2018, indictment and the March 2019 report to Congress—provide clear evidence of the negative consequences of allowing public opinion to be swayed by foreign agents with deep pockets and malicious intent.

Finally, vulnerabilities are also found within information systems themselves. The spate of hacking incidents and their scope is astounding. All three billion—yes three *billion!*—of Yahoo!'s e-mail accounts were compromised in the August 2013 data breach. Additionally, it was recently announced that there are fundamental security weaknesses in *all* Intel computer chips due to the so-called Meltdown and Spectre vulnerabilities. As Glenn Greenberg describes it, Meltdown is "[a] bug in Intel chips [that] allows low-privilege processes to access memory in the computer's kernel, the machine's most privileged inner sanctum. Theoretical attacks that exploit that bug, based on quirks in features Intel has implemented for faster processing, could allow malicious software to spy deeply into other processes and data on the target computer or smartphone" (Greenberg, 2018a). Although IT companies have attempted to downplay the potential for hacking and data breaches, it is clear that *connected* computers are likely *compromised* computers, and "one malicious virtual machine could peer deeply into the secrets of its neighbors" (Greenberg, 2018b). The immediate impact of this is that many computers may need to be redesigned from the ground up if they are to be fully secure in a world that is just now on the brink of artificial intelligence, quantum computing, and full-scale adoption of the Internet of Things. But when no one's information is safe, no one's livelihood is safe. Anyone can now potentially be compromised if secrets about a person are known to a malicious party or a bad actor.

The problem of security is not isolated to just computers. Amazon in 2017 added to the issues of vulnerability and privacy in physical homes with their offering of Amazon Key. This service allows Amazon delivery staff "keyless" access to a person's home in order to safely deliver packages. Several issues have already been pointed out with the service, however. The tradeoff for the peace of mind to prevent packages theft seems hardly worth the trouble that Amazon could cause by being able to track all of your actions from within your own home. Though many rights are given up voluntarily, much of this privacy loss occurs inadvertently and surreptitiously. The lesson to be learned is simple. In exchange for "security," by controlling access to your house, Amazon controls which services, products, and utilities might eventually be adopted by the dweller in the house. Amazon-dominated smart homes could become aligned with any number of vested, corporate interests, further eroding personal choice and privacy for the sake of nominally better services. This is an all-encompassing vision of control over a person's life choices and represents an ability for companies to nudge personal preferences in ways that profit them. Perhaps reduced rents in these units might be offered to people, but the tradeoff comes at a steep price in privacy and autonomy.

This confluence of conditioning and surveillance will only grow, too, as the Internet of Things becomes more widespread, conceivably capable of monitoring the lives of *all* people. Vizio, a manufacturer of smart TVs, for example, was recently caught illegally surveilling and tracking the behaviors of their users. Though this is small in scale, one can easily imagine it growing in scale to include "smart" homes and "smart" cities, which would be just as vulnerable to illegal tracking as televisions. It remains to be seen how people would react to such a digital fishbowl once it becomes more widespread. Will people see this constant monitoring as the payoff necessary to lead a life of convenience where all needs are anticipated and met? Or will they see it as being incarcerated in a life of pseudo-freedom that lacks personal choice and no relief from observation?

The Use and Misuse of Information

Similar to the vulnerabilities found within information technology systems, people can also be victimized by the use and abuse of information. These pathologies concern the breakdowns in the behavioral norms of communication and information use. The social contracts and long-established rules established by societies and their subcultures are disrupted by malicious online users and their devices—either trolls, bots, or other ill-meaning third-party agents and actors. The increase in fake news, misinformation, disinformation, and other types of propaganda and weaponized information is turning the Internet into a nearly unusable wasteland, where clicks, likes, dissent, and paranoia are the new "coins of the realm." People are goaded and twisted by various agents into irrational acts or beliefs, making them easier targets for later long-term manipulation.

In addition to the outright faking of information, there is a tendency to emphasize division and, with apologies to Noam Chomsky, "manufacture *dissent*." Under the cover of seemingly neutral third-party digital platforms, trolls, bots, and other disruptive agents find ways to stir up controversies, especially in relation to political movements, elections, and current news events. German Marshall Fund and Alliance for Securing Democracy's Hamilton 68 online dashboard tracks Russian propagandists whose aim appears to be sowing such dissent in times of extreme trouble (dashboard.se curingdemocracy.org/). As seen in figure 1.2, the site displays the top hashtags used by Kremlin-linked accounts on Twitter; this screenshot, showing the top hashtags "#americanpridett45" and "#parklandstudentsspeak," was captured on February 22, 2018, eight days after the Parkland, Florida, shooting. It shows how easily dissent and chaos can be manufactured through social media platforms.

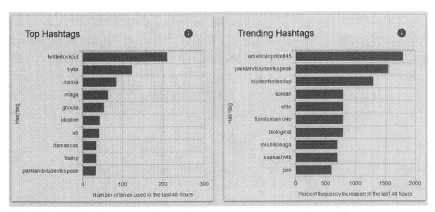

FIGURE 1.2
The top and trending hashtags promoted by Russian-linked online propagandists as tracked by Hamilton 68 on February 22, 2018. *Hamilton 68*

Search results, which many users assume to be a transparent and neutral activity, have also been increasingly tweaked by the highest payers through black hat SEO (search engine optimization). These techniques mislead users by taking them down paths they had not intended to go down, using fake businesses, redirecting links to different sites, or the wholesale stealing of content from legitimate sites in order to hide malicious code or invisible text. The negative impact of these manipulations should not be underestimated, for they contribute to widespread mistrust in the online environment, increase security vulnerabilities, and waste the time and effort of online users.

Finally, no discussion of online behavior would be complete without mentioning digital rights, copyright, and personal agency. Corporations routinely make ownership claims on their users' online content and personal information. Boilerplate website and software license agreements have become notable objects of concern among legal rights experts. Most of us, myself included, skim over these long and confusing rights and usage agreements when we sign up for online services or software. But the fine print of many of these agreements often severely curtails our rights to legal action or significantly compromises our privacy.

The breach of personal information held by the credit rating company Equifax is a good example of this problem. After the hack of nearly 143 million consumers—nearly 30 percent of the U.S. population—Equifax argued that the data they collected was "a proprietary byproduct" of customers using their service (Gressin, 2017). In plain English, this means they believe your data about you is *their* property. The somewhat overused expression "If you are not paying for it, you're not the customer; you're the *product being sold*," actually holds some water in this situation. Making matters worse, Equifax also denies that they violated privacy regulations because in their eyes there was no customer privacy to begin with! The possibility of abuse beyond the data hack and subsequent leak should make all people pause about the supposed benefits of the new online information economy—especially if courts determine regular people have no pathway to reparation or justice.

TOWARD WORKABLE SOLUTIONS: VANQUISHING THE INTERNET'S HIDDEN MONSTERS

One can argue that each of these information pathologies contributes to the current state of the online world. For every benefit that comes from digital information and technology usage, there are just as many drawbacks. It would be easy for us to take Google and other major IT companies at face value and assume that they truly do have our best interests in mind when they create these products for us. However, it has become increasingly clear that their "Don't Be Evil" (Google), "Think Different" (Apple), or "Empowering Us All" (Microsoft) slogans are merely ruses. These corporations are instead looking for ways to dominate and control us both culturally and politically, especially through the funneling of money into government with lobbying and campaign contributions.

Jean-Noël Jeanneney's early warning in 2004 about Google Books in his book *Google and the Myth of Universal Knowledge: A View from Europe* is coming back to haunt us. Even though Google eventually prevailed in the ten-year-long *Authors Guild* lawsuit, unresolved issues regarding the ownership and control of our culture remain. If Google or any other company can claim proprietary ownership of the data set from the millions of books they have digitized, what happens to our culture if this control is used in restrictive or exploitative ways? We must ask ourselves why we are denying our own culture to ourselves and what long-term effects this will have on us. A culture needs to be cultivated by real people, not corporations that gather and then limit access to digital copies of our representative works.

I am confident, though, that singling out these areas where information pathologies are common can help us to cope with the changing times and our dominant technologies. For a long time, librarians like myself have assumed the best in our users, allowing them free and open access to use, create, and pursue their interests with a light touch. However, it is clear that people online are being manipulated and conditioned into exhibiting or allowing clearly self-destructive and negative behaviors. We would all be well-advised to find ways to help ourselves identify and then address these behaviors. Assisting others while simultaneously creating online safe havens, we can surely create a better world both online and off; a world that values truth and fact, reason and discussion; a world that appeals to and promotes our "better angels"; one that diminishes our worst tendencies lurking at the center of the online labyrinth.

REFERENCES

Collins, G. (2002). Claude E. Shannon: Founder of information theory. *Scientific American*. www.scientificamerican.com/article/claude-e-shannon-founder/.

Greenberg, A. (2018a). A critical Intel flaw breaks basic security for most computers. *Wired*. www.wired.com/story/critical-intel-flaw-breaks-basic-security-for-most -computers/?mbid=BottomRelatedStories.

———. (2018b). Triple meltdown: How so many researchers found a 20-year-old chip flaw at the same time. *Wired*. www.wired.com/story/meltdown-spectre-bug -collision-intel-chip-flaw-discovery/.

Gressin, S. (2017). The Equifax data breach: What to do. Federal Trade Commission. www.consumer.ftc.gov/blog/2017/09/equifax-data-breach-what-do.

Lynch, C. (2017). Stewardship in the age of algorithms. First Monday. firstmonday .org/ojs/index.php/fm/article/view/8097/6583.

2

Online Behavioral Conditioning

WHY IS IT SO HARD TO QUIT FACEBOOK?

If you're like me and another two billion people all over the world, you've probably got a Facebook account. It's always there, ubiquitous in the modern world, like the constant hum of that electric transformer in your neighborhood. But despite its near-universal adoption, I rarely use it. When I first set up an account about ten years ago in 2009, I immediately found and re-friended about thirty people from my distant and not-so-distant past. This includes former high school friends and classmates, coworkers from a previous career, and some of their spouses or significant others. For a few months, I tried to keep it up, diligently replying and responding to posts and other requests. Until, that is, a couple things happened. First, one person in particular started to send overtly religious-toned messages and "deep thoughts for the day" to *all* his connections. Second, I kept receiving updates on how well another friend was doing on the then-popular game Farmville. It became so annoying that I abruptly stopped and have not really been back. Every now and then I'd pop in, see what was happening, and then immediately head back underground like Punxsutawney Phil. But for the most part it's silent, dead, unused, yet weighing on me like a procrastinator's unfinished chore.

So why, you might ask, don't I just delete it? I've certainly tried. I've even reached the point of going through the deletion protocols that Facebook has set up. Yet it has been harder than I expected. I'm finding it difficult to sever the strange attachment I have to the page, but I can't quite pinpoint the source of my hesitation. "Why," I keep asking myself after I've shelved my latest attempt at deleting the account, "should it be so difficult to just cut off something I don't even use?"

I have some speculations as to why this is the case, though I won't run through all the reasons right now. But a few ideas come to mind:

1. I seem to be unable to let go of the past, and the Facebook page somehow has come to represent those personal connections—even if I had already broken decades ago, voluntarily or involuntarily, 99 percent of the bonds with the people on that page.
2. It feels like I'm throwing away a favorite sweater, one with holes, that's a little scratchy and smells mildly of mildew and sweat but is oddly comforting.
3. There's a feeling that I'm throwing something away that's integral to my past, like a long-held love letter, a high school yearbook, or a college notebook full of doodles and half-heard lecture notes.

So how does a digital environment comprised of 0s and 1s that has no real impact on my current life nevertheless find a way to control me? Partly it is to be found in the unintended consequences of these attachments and relationships in "digital form," so to speak, but there are also more direct causes of this attachment stemming directly from the designers of the online platform itself. This chapter will examine the strange attachments we create and the not-quite-functional relationships we develop with a technology that often dissembles and hides its methods for controlling us.

SURFING THE "SKINNERNET"

Behavioral psychology is perhaps the best place to start. With a long history as *behaviorism*, the theory was proposed that humans as well as animals could be understood in terms of their reflexes to external stimuli and behaviors predicted based on the right conditions. B. F. Skinner was one of the major pioneers of behavioral conditioning in the twentieth century and is most well-known for his invention the "Skinner box," also known by the charming name "Operant Conditioning Chamber." *Yikes.* Skinner used pigeons in his experiments to examine how physical deprivation and reward using food could alter an animal's behavior. He was able to demonstrate a couple of important conditioning techniques using the box. In the first technique, called continuous reinforcement, an animal would receive a pellet of food for every lever or button pressed. For the second, called partial reinforcement, the animal would receive a pellet of food at predetermined time intervals or after a requisite number of lever-pressings. Among these partial reinforcements, there could be fixed-ratio schedules, where the animal would receive something after, say, five pecks at the button/lever; there could be variable-interval schedules as well, which were merely randomly determined rewards. The last one was very effective at making animals anxious, especially if positive reinforcements were replaced with random punishments. The most effective of these, as one would predict, was the continuous reinforcement.

Extending that principle to humans, we can also be seen as the conditioned products of our environments, both physical as well as cultural. The long literature of behavioral conditioning hints that reinforcement is a strong influencer of human actions. In the popular parlance, positive reinforcement has become a clear theme in the dealings with children and education. Positive reinforcement can be seen in the ubiquitous Facebook <Likes>, which satisfy, much like the pellet, the "reward center" in the brain. Of course, the opposite then also holds, to a limited degree, and negative reinforcement encourages people to alter their behavior to avoid punishments.

While behavior modification is one notorious example of how we are being nudged to behave online, there are other tricks that online social media platforms employ to keep users from quitting and even to get them addicted. As one researcher suggests, "All interactive media . . . provide us with new possibilities for interaction on the platform that can satisfy some of our innate human cravings" (Sundar et al., 2018).

Let's explore these in more detail.

Nurturing Our Friendships: Keeping the Wheel Spinning

Aleksandr Solzhenitsyn in his lesser-known and not-so-uplifting novel *Cancer Ward* once described friendship as keeping a spinning wheel rolling, where both people need to perform just enough action on that wheel to keep it from toppling over. Once tipped over, meaning if either side let it fall to the wayside, the friendship was effectively over. We all know of the stunting that time, distance, and inertia can play on the growth and sustainment of friendships. Often, for example, when we graduate from high school, we lose touch until finally we just send cards once a Christmas and meet at reunions every five years (if at all). Our lives are often filled with these regrets of lost friendships as we move on to greener or browner pastures.

Facebook, as well as other networking sites such as LinkedIn, provide us with the illusion that we are still linked in a significant way to people we have likely not seen in three or even thirty years. These platforms provide us with the subjective feeling that the little actions here and there that we conduct online (e.g., clicking a "like" button for a friend's uploaded baby photo; commenting on a post about the hot weather) are somehow, now, impactful events, significant expenditures of social capital, or signals of genuine care and concern for others. We imagine ourselves—returning to that dour Russian author's visualization—virtually keeping that wheel rolling, even as our actions are little more than just slightly above the very least we could ever do. It's only "this-shy" of nothing at all. Online "friending" certainly helps to alleviate some of the feelings of shame and cognitive dissonance that build up over years or even decades of procrastination as we let the wheels of friendship topple over! This is a powerful urge and emotion that Facebook has stumbled upon. It has found a way to help people cope with these feelings, it's true, but it also monetizes and manipulates them.

Empowerment and Deceit: Who Do You Want to *Be* Online?

When I was a teenager, stuck in a high school experience that felt like it would go on forever, I imagined what it would be like to go to a new place where no one knew who I was. There'd be such great things to come from this, I thought. No one would know, for instance, that in fifth grade I wore thick glasses with plastic brown frames, corduroy pants my mom picked out, and a really dorky Philadelphia Eagles jacket from McDonald's. No one would know I got a concussion playing basketball when another kid knocked me over. *Oh, the shame.* They would see me as I then saw my sixteen-year old self: as if I'd sprouted perfectly, fully formed from Zeus's big head.

Of course, that was a delusion. We all have incidents or past histories we'd rather forget. We all would prefer that everyone sees us in the best possible light, in every best possible angle, at all times. Online social media lets us do that. Everyone can forget, or never know, that the girl you liked said, *"Ewww"* when you asked her to the junior high dance that one time! Everyone can learn, to paraphrase Nick Hornby in *High Fidelity*, that you were always punk and always shaved your head like one. The point is that now, that illusion is everything. Social media allows for you to project a self-image to as large an audience as you desire, and the past need not interfere.

The root of this need to self-actualize is powerful, perhaps more powerful than anything in our lives, driving myths and religions, societies and governing, sex and reproduction, and overall human progress. In this manner, Facebook and other social media platforms tap into this need for self-actualization and self-image development. Certainly, if it helps people to reach self-actualization and attain a state of self-empowerment, that's a wonderful application for a tool that truly benefits our society.

Yet, there's also the potential to distort reality with these online tools. One way we can distort reality is through self-deception. We are all unable sometimes to see who we really are. In many ways, as studies have shown on the sources of incompetency in business management, it is perhaps the hardest to know our own limitations. Indeed, we are often the last to know our own flaws when they are evident to everyone else. We pretend or find ways to avoid confronting our flaws. The images we project online, then, can also contribute to this self-deception, stunting our growth and failing to let us become more than the illusions we inhabit. This cognitive dissonance we strive so hard to avoid is a true obstacle to self-awareness.

Additionally, we also find ways to deceive others through these tools. The images projected onto Facebook can be used to fool others into thinking that we are living charmed lives, even if the reality is something a little more normal or just plain boring. There is a documented effect, too, of people using Facebook that demonstrates the negative impact of such outward deceptions. People, seeing the wonderful news and daily successes of online "friends," can be susceptible to self-doubt, negative comparisons, and even depression. Usually the best antidote to this is to realize that everyone online is probably exaggerating their accomplishments. Everyone is likely projecting their best, happiest, most successful selves, even if they aren't feeling it.

Facebook and other social media companies likely know this. They encourage users to both project their best selves as well as communicate all the positive events in one's life, such as a job promotion, a birthday, a work anniversary, and the like. It's a perpetual party at *your* house! They also suggest further actions you can take to contribute to this "best self" projection: for example, wish someone a happy birthday, update a skill in your profile page, or find out who was looking at your profile. Of course, there are economic benefits to presenting a good, positive image of oneself online. This "signaling" allows us to project images as well as to gather potential resources to improve our social standing among peers and within our communities. It has been shown that the use of social networking platforms not only improves one's social standing, but it also provides clear economic benefits. As a result, leaving an activity that provides such a clear benefit to one's own social standing proves to be nearly impossible, even as the truth of your own life becomes obscured in the process.

The Peeping Tom Effect: Do Open Windows Equal Bared Souls?

People like to spy. They might never admit it, but people like to know what others are doing behind closed doors. Perhaps it lets us understand people better; perhaps it lets us understand ourselves better. Maybe it lets us off the hook for our own bad behaviors or ill thoughts that occur to us when no one is looking. Maybe it lets us justify these bad behaviors or helps us confirm the worst thoughts or suspicions that we have about others. On the other side of the coin, though, most people don't like to be spied upon. Even if we apparently have nothing to hide, the removal of that barrier protecting our inner thoughts and private actions can be quite unnerving.

Social media allows us to satisfy that strange urge to spy on others. Perhaps it's a phenomenon similar to gossip, where the thrill comes less from the actual information shared and more from transgressing conventions, boundaries, or trust. We can look into the window someone left open. It's not our fault if we happen to see them undressing, is it? The abuse of this is rampant, however. One-way surveillance is a problem that social media has yet to fully solve. Online stalking is a problem that can only be solved by blocking users, changing names and hiding identities, or dropping out of social media altogether.

Yet, there must at some point come the realization that the window itself may be dressed in such a way as to *seem* open, but that it is in reality angled to provide *just enough* to titillate but not enough to fully see the person, understand the motivations, or be completely empathetic with the subject in the window. This open window, like someone's carefully manicured Facebook page, is not a soul laid bare. It is something more complex, more compromising. It is closer in spirit to something like Marcel Duchamp's installation in the Philadelphia Museum, *Étant donnés: 1. La chute d'eau, 2. Le gaz d'éclairage (Given: 1. The Waterfall, 2. The Illuminating Gas)*. This art installation developed over two decades may be the most important piece of art for this digital era of eroding privacy. Eschewing video and other technologies, it nevertheless renders a literal three-dimensional scene into two dimensions, like so many of the screens in our lives. The peepholes in the door's installation let us see only a limited glimpse of a woman's body (possibly dead, but possibly not) lying in a field. As the Philadelphia Museum describes it:

> The unsuspecting viewer encounters a spectacular sight: a realistically constructed simulacrum of a naked woman lying spread-eagle on a bed of dead twigs and fallen leaves. In her left hand, this life-size mannequin holds aloft an old-fashioned illuminated gas lamp of the Bec Auer type, while behind her, in the far distance, a lush wooded landscape rises toward the horizon. (Philadelphia Museum of Art, 2018)

Duchamp shows us that *we* are the ones complicit in this spying, responsible as onlookers but also detached from the fate of this person, both unthinking as gawkers as well as helpless to impact the subject's life in a meaningful way. Or worse, we are unable to even understand what has come before and what will come next, looking at a literal dead end. Observing others on Facebook can take on a similarly desensitized distance that ultimately isolates us to our own fates, while rendering us helpless to fully assist in someone else's. It is one of the paradoxes of voyeurism: on one hand it informs us, satisfies a shallow need to know a secret about another person; but, at last, it also truly fails to confirm what we really need, which is the ultimate truth about another person or whether that person is even sincere. This truth is especially difficult to obtain if the person being spied upon is aware of it and plays to the expectations of the observer.

Bandwagoning and Enlarging "The Tribe"

Having grown up in southeastern Pennsylvania, I'm not *that* embarrassed to say that I'm a fan of Philadelphia sports teams. Even though I'm currently living in Los Angeles and have no outward animosity to this city's teams, I just can't get into another tribe of sports teams, try as I might. I will still wear my Phillies T-shirt in public, maybe to the mall or the swimming pool or something. It's a burden, I guess, especially if they're in another rebuilding (or underachieving) season. Well, the Philadelphia football team finally won their first Super Bowl in 2018. Suddenly, I started to notice more people in Los Angeles with Eagles hats, T-shirts, jerseys, car window decals, and the like. It's strange, but I have a sneaking suspicion that some might not have ties to the region. Oh, well. The next year a different team will crop up. Conversely, having also grown up as a fan of Penn State football (an inherited habit, some might say), ever since the Jerry Sandusky scandal, you'll almost *never* see a Penn State Jersey anywhere outside of the tristate area. But why is that?

Well, it's partly the old saw: *Success has many fathers while failure is an orphan.* Sports fandoms, and really fandoms of all stripes (be it music, artist, dance, or political parties), stem from our human tendencies to want to join in when someone is successful and opt-out when things are going bad. Die-hards, who see themselves as the true fans, call this "jumping on the bandwagon." They are being derisive when they say this, by the way, as faith in a bright future and unwavering fidelity in the dark present are the twin virtues of fandom. But, despite what the super-fans have to say about it, it's a common occurrence. It's so common that psychologists have noticed this and devised specific terms for it: *BIRG* and *CORF*. Before you close the book: these are actually acronyms, not names from a Klingon family registry. BIRG stands for *basking in reflected glory*, which happens whenever "we" win the Super Bowl; CORF stands for *cutting off reflected failure*, which is easily visible when your favorite team is in its fifth hundred-loss season in a row and the seats are empty. You, too, might consider wearing a paper bag on your head at the stadium, if you show up at all.

We see this phenomenon in social media, too, with users and their profiles. Fandom of all scales—from minor (my Twitter account had two people, one of which I suspect was a bot) to major (Kanye West has 28.5 million)—is dependent somewhat on the bandwagon effect. The more one does it, the more people will rally around you. You can form your base of admirers, as long as it is reflecting something about success to them and vice versa. The moment a scandal appears, though, people begin to waver in their support, and they will drop you.

Of course, the effect of seeing a million people follow you also appeals directly to your vanity and sense of self-worth. For that reason, social media platforms also want to keep you generating more and more content so that you are tied in a kind of spiraling dance of self-worth reinforced by your encouraging audience. In some cases, the more you create, the more users you'll gather. It is a strained relationship, though, between your audience and yourself, and one that sometimes can be dysfunctional. Sometimes people—especially celebrities stuck in their celebrity bubbles—begin to blur the distinction between the two, losing themselves to become trapped in their audience's perceived image of them, only to occasionally act out in strange or self-destructive ways as if to remind themselves that they were once real.

Expressing Yourself and Being Validated

Finally, the promise of being able to express your innermost thoughts and ardent opinions also spurs people to participate and remain participating in something like Facebook. We also come to crave the "like" or external validation that comes with that personal opinion or expression of ideas. Just as more commenting helps to gather followers and admirers there along for the ride, so too does more self-expression (and the audience's increased validation of that self-expression) appeal to the sense of self-worth. It's an entwined phenomenon that spirals upward. The more you do it, the more validation you can get from others externally, which also boosts internal validation from expressing oneself.

We begin to suspect that we are part of a wider movement. In politics, that can fuel a sense that the person is actually shaping policy or law and contributing to a national movement (or counter-movement). The #MeToo or #Occupy movements appear to be partly fueled by this. People contribute to them in terms of a wider movement that they hope will effect greater change in local, regional, and national communities. But, given the barrier-free nature of the Internet and online cyber communities, internationalism is also a part of this "wider movement" as well.

Therein lies some of the danger, too. We are all familiar with the recent revelations of Russian-financed agents purchasing advertisements whose sole purpose was to enflame partisans of the right and far-right in America. People later contributed to these in social media by forwarding, liking, or commenting on their Facebook pages. The ideas conveyed were emotional, propagandist, and distorted in terms of truthfulness. Nothing rational was proposed. That was the point, too: convey validation and self-aggrandizement through emotional appeals. As seen in the released advertisement in figure 2.1, run from July 16 to July 19, 2017, apparently more than 130,000 "people" liked this advertisement about national security, immigration, and borders (House Permanent Select Committee on Intelligence, 2018). Too bad it was Russian propaganda.

FIGURE 2.1
Screenshot of Russian-financed ad (ID# 1254) taken from Facebook from July 2017. *House Permanent Select Committee on Intelligence*

TARGETED ADS AS CONDITIONED RESPONSE

The source of such targeted ads goes far beyond the realm of Russian-funded political organizations. To some extent, beyond disclosing the existence of a product or service, all advertising is concerned with manipulation and conditioning. The persuasion of buying or using goods and services is what veers into the realm of manipulation and manipulative techniques, not unlike the techniques used in rhetoric and political persuasion.

Targeted ad technologies are now being used by Google, Amazon, and others in retail sales. You probably notice this after seeing adverts for items you recently looked at on Amazon or eBay. Some may even see ads related to e-mails they sent or received through Gmail. Such targeted ads can also create a sense of isolated bubbles and even artificial salience. Salience is quite interesting, though perhaps ineffective, as it seems based upon the idea that if you considered buying something yesterday, you'll be more likely to buy it if you see it again soon after—like today. Facebook, apparently, has at least *ninety-eight* data points it uses to track you and to target you for advertisements.

These targeted data points start from the obvious, such as name, location, age, gender, languages spoken, household, and so on. But they become increasingly person-specific, related to personal networks and personal lives, including anniversaries, relationship status (e.g., single, married, in a long-distance relationship), and stature within a family (e.g., a parent, grandparent, aunt, etc.). It expands into work lives, political affiliations, and class—especially whatever large-scale goods (like a car or refrigerator) you might recently have purchased. Finally, the remaining data points are very specific to the type of person they are targeting, especially things like the type of operating system you use, the type of online games you play, whether you use a credit card or a debit card, and so on. The level of detail about seemingly important personal matters that stretch into the realm of privacy and privacy law should be concerning to everyone.

Facebook can learn a lot about you, and when it partners with advertisers, third parties, and even bad actors (like Cambridge Analytica—to name but *one*), it can learn even more (Hindman, 2018). While each of these data points may be innocuous by itself (e.g., my anniversary date), in combination with the other items in the *aggregate*, it becomes easy to identify individuals' preferences, desires, or concerns. Our strengths as well as our weaknesses become readily apparent, and there's nothing to stop a bad actor that is selling some "good" as a front for really hoovering up your data to sell as its real means of making money. What happens to the data after that is even murkier, and the possibility that this data could be used as pressure points to make people do things becomes stronger (Dewey, 2016).

So how do these ads actually work? Whenever you go online—especially to a retail site but also to other sites such as Facebook, Yahoo!, or Google—the web browser you use sends information to a third-party ad network (these include doubleclick.net, Atlas Solutions, Baidu, etc.). The information is then stored in a "cookie," a small piece of written code that allows ad networks and websites to share information on what you view or buy. As shown in figure 2.2, when you enter another website in the same network, ads for the product you viewed somewhere else are sent to you based on the information drawn from that cookie. The ad network acts as a kind of intermediary, sending and gathering information about users back and forth from your computer to the network (Cameron, 2013).

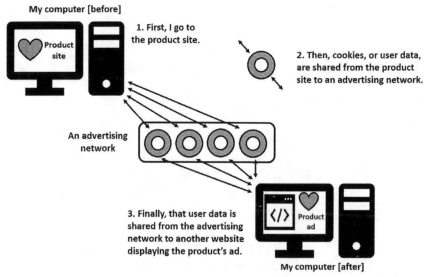

FIGURE 2.2
How targeted ads work. *Cameron (2013); redrawn by author*

These targeted ads run, however, on imperfect algorithms. We have all noticed this whenever incongruous things—perhaps an ad for one item we accidentally looked at by clicking on a random pop-up ad—start following you everywhere online, like newspapers, news feeds, and random blogs. In this case, the frequent appearance of this mistaken "interest" looks about as authentic as a pink lawn flamingo. The timing of these advertisements is often a little off, too. Many of us may have noticed automobile ads showing up for days and weeks *after* we've purchased a car. Just because it's recent, and even salient to our lives, doesn't mean we're going to buy *another* car anytime soon! I'm no Jay Leno. Or, in the case of many users who like to save time, we go online to Amazon or other shopping sites only when we're ready to buy. Afterward, receiving ads for the item you recently bought seems pretty useless.

In some cases, we also see that the incongruence of these ads can be unintentionally offensive, especially in the way they appear to be manipulating the fears and concerns of the perceived target audience (which is you, by the way). One example, shown in figure 2.3, advertises pick-pocket-free clothing for well-to-do travelers, as indicated by the image focusing on skin color (white), the suit (looks silk), and watch (looks expensive). Fine. The *New York Times* and its advertising affiliates at least know the demographics of their readers. The problem, however, is the combination of this ad with the stories suggested by the newspaper appearing directly above it. These stories, which are placed on the page by an algorithm, include topics such as hallucinogenic drugs, marijuana charges against blacks and Hispanics, and the flow of refu-

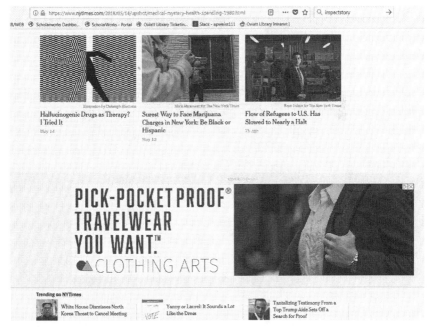

FIGURE 2.3
Screenshot from *New York Times* on May 16, 2018, at 9:40 a.m., PDT, on page with article about medical costs. *New York Times*

gees (legal or illegal) into the country. We could spend hours trying to pick apart what this says about the current state of the United States of America and typical readers of the *New York Times*, but that might not get us anywhere beyond the obvious tropes of fear, racism, and privilege. Interestingly, this advertisement showed up later the same day as I was reading an article by Jennifer Rubin of the *Washington Post* but in a slightly different form. As you can see in figure 2.4, the tag line "The CIA version of khakis" popped up while I was reading deeper about the Robert Mueller investigation into possible Trump campaign collusion with Russia during the summer of 2016. *You can't make this stuff up!* This clearly shows the unintended and even negative consequences of using an algorithm that by its very nature lacks an overall awareness of the wider culture and news events or, worse, is actually a reflection of how non-diverse and blinkered Silicon Valley really is. It is a mirror into the closed-off, even naïve creators of these algorithms.

Yet the point of these targeted ads, poorly wielded as they are, may not necessarily be complete accuracy or appropriateness. The point is to titillate and prod, to provoke and inspire. In other words, these "algorithms . . . nudge you to be social, based on your interests, behaviors and networks of friends. Without Facebook egging you on, you probably wouldn't be quite as social. Facebook is a major social lubricant of our time, often recommending friends to add to your circle and notifying you when a friend has said or done something potentially of interest" (Sundar et al., 2018). Though I would expand the concept of "interests" to include things such as fear, personal concerns, and pet peeves or annoyances, online media are essentially egging you on to "be more social" so that you'll ultimately purchase, and recommend purchasing, things with the greatest social lubricant of all: *your money*. And those issues of fear, racism, and privilege are no less lucrative for advertisers.

THE FUTURE OF THE SKINNERNET: 2 + 2 = 5, OR LESS IS MORE?

But what is the future of all this? Where are we going with the Internet as our main social driver? Is the *Skinnernet*, where all of our behaviors are modified and anticipated, a foregone conclusion? Are we doomed to accept that 2 + 2 will add up to Silicon Valley's predictive "5" when it comes to being controlled and conditioned by these tools? Now that most of us are aware of how and why we are being targeted, Facebook and other IT companies *out of financial necessity* have begun to alter their methods. No longer, they

Klondike Solitaire
Card game

Mahjongg Candy
Matching game

Word Wipe
Word game

Mahjongg
Dimensions
Arcade game

FIGURE 2.4
Screenshot from *Washington Post* on May 16, 2018, at 4:10 p.m., PDT, on page with article about the Trump Tower meeting with a Russian lawyer. Note the unintentional irony of the tagline "The CIA version of khakis" in the context of the ongoing Mueller investigation into espionage-like misdeeds. *Washington Post*

Opinions newsletter

Thought-provoking opinions and commentary, in your inbox daily.

E-mail address | **Add**

data we generate can be used not only against ourselves and our own wishes, but also that of third-party innocent bystanders who have no direct say in whether or not their information is taken and how it is shared.

REFERENCES

Cameron, D. (2013). How targeted advertising works. *Washington Post.* www .washingtonpost.com/apps/g/page/business/how-targeted-advertising-works/412/.

Dewey, C. (2016). 98 personal data points that Facebook uses to target ads to you. *Washington Post.* www.washingtonpost.com/news/the-intersect/ wp/2016/08/19/98-personal-data-points-that-facebook-uses-to-target-ads-to -you/?utm_term=.76a4487df581.

Hindman, M. (2018). How Cambridge Analytica's Facebook targeting model really worked—according to the person who built it. The Conversation. theconversation.com/how-cambridge-analyticas-facebook-targeting-model-really -worked-according-to-the-person-who-built-it-94078.

House Permanent Select Committee on Intelligence. (2018). Social media advertisements. United States House of Representatives. democrats-intelligence .house.gov/facebook-ads/social-media-advertisements.htm.

Philadelphia Museum of Art. (2018). *Exhibitions: Marcel Duchamp: Étant donnés.* https://www.philamuseum.org/exhibitions/324.html.

Sundar, S., Liu, B., DiRusso, C., and Krieger, M. (2018). Why it's so hard to #DeleteFacebook: Constant psychological boosts keep you hooked. The Conversation. theconversation.com/why-its-so-hard-to-deletefacebook-constant -psychological-boosts-keep-you-hooked-92976.

Tarnoff, B., and Weigel, M. (2018). Why Silicon Valley can't fix itself. *Guardian.* www.theguardian.com/news/2018/may/03/why-silicon-valley-cant-fix-itself-tech -humanism.

3

"Nudged"

Why Your Decisions May Not Be Your Own

DO WE MAKE OUR OWN DECISIONS?

All of us, I'm sure, have asked ourselves at some point in our lives where our decisions come from. Why, oh why, did I overpay for that scratchy old U2 record on eBay but not that other one on Amazon? (Or vice versa!) Why am I even buying vinyl at all? One day we decide on one thing, but then on another day we choose the complete opposite. Perhaps it's just a whim, and there's nothing deeper. But I suspect there's more to it. Certainly, some of this variability comes down to other factors such as social pressures and the application of technology, making it harder to decide sometimes whether our choices come from our own free will or if they are manufactured and predetermined. As we saw in the last chapter, the Internet and social media can push us into behaving in certain ways. Operant conditioning gives way to behaviors that are easily modified and manipulated by the main online movers and shakers. These include Internet providers, self-contained social media platforms like Facebook, search engines, independent websites of all types—including news sites (ranging from Yahoo! to the *Washington Post*)—and vendors like Amazon and eBay that bombard users with ads targeted to their specific data. Some of these targeted ads are used primarily to sell us something, but we can also be induced into exhibiting other types of behaviors as well.

Some call this "nudging," where decisions that on the surface seem to come directly from us may, ultimately, originate somewhere else. The decisions we make and the actions we take may have been encouraged in ways that we are unaware of consciously. And "nudging" may be the latest manifestation of this ongoing debate. Obviously, many questions come to mind. First, how is our ability to decide something impacted by technology? What role might "big data" practices, or the analysis of big data, play in our day-to-day decision-making? Specifically, what are the current methods (scientific or otherwise) behind the shaping of our behavior? What do we see and what do we ignore when we are being nudged? What happens when we are unaware of how our opinions and ideas are being shaped? All of these, of course, are good questions to consider—some are probably even unanswerable—as we move further along into the current Internet and surveillance age. This chapter will examine many of these unresolved questions while also looking at the science of manipulation, decision-making, and the growing practice of nudging.

THE "SCIENCE" AND "ART" OF NUDGING

The previous chapter focused on ways in which operant and behavioral conditioning encouraged people to actively engage in specific activities that they wanted to of their own volition, rewarding them with something pleasurable or punishing with something negative. To a certain extent, however, "nudging" incorporates much more subtle behavioral conditioning techniques implemented with indirect suggestion making (not that far from the old urban legend of "subliminal messaging"). This is accomplished by altering people's surroundings to trigger them into almost-subconsciously behaving in desired ways. Richard Thaler and Cass Sunstein, academics at Harvard, are the developers of the concept of nudging. They define a nudge in their groundbreaking work on "behavioral economics" as "any aspect of the choice architecture that alters people's behavior in a predictable way without forbidding any options or significantly changing their economic incentives" (Thaler and Sunstein, 2008). In simpler terms, people's options are set up for them, ostensibly to provide outlets for all possibilities but, in reality, to subtly promote a certain more-desirable choice above all others.

What is central to this concept is that the person's choices are *never limited by rules or banned outright through mandates or decrees*. Instead, behaviors are modified to the point that they appear less desirable to people, but without devising especially difficult or costly measures to implement them. Placing fruit at eye level in the supermarket would count as a nudge, for example, whereas banning the sale of soda or junk foods would not. In order for the choices to be decided in logical as well as predictable ways, the choice *architect*, essentially the designer of the way options are presented to people, must create a set of choices that align with how people actually think and behave but *without telling them what to do* (Thaler and Sunstein, 2008)! Therein lies the challenge.

Others have taken Thaler and Sunstein's research and refined the definition of nudging to make it a little more applicable to everyday life. One researcher, Pelle Hansen, sees it as "any attempt at influencing people's judgment, choice or behavior in a predictable way" (Hansen, 2016a). Hansen (2016b) continues, describing the act of nudging as something a little more specific: "Nudging is the systematic and evidence-based development and implementation of nudges in creating behavior change." Note how the emphasis is now on *evidence-based development* and implementation. We are, in this definition, being subtly manipulated into changing our behavior through the empirical evidence gathered about us (usually from data tracking). Specific behaviors can be changed by the use of nudging, but only effectively if people's behaviors are understood through tracking and the gathering of necessary evidence. In the age of big data analysis, this empirical evidence turns out to be *vast*.

Methods of Nudging

Tobias Mirsch and colleagues (2017) examined the research being done on behavioral economics and compiled a comprehensive list of the most frequently studied psychological effects. These include the following: framing, status quo bias, social norms, loss aversion, anchoring/adjustment, hyperbolic discounting, decoupling, priming, and the availability heuristic. We will look at each of these below.

1. Framing

In this technique, the presentation of potential decisions is controlled, allowing the decisions to be more predictable. A good example of this occurs with painting stripes on streets to give the perception of higher speed to drivers, encouraging many drivers to slow down.

2. Status Quo Bias

People, it has been noted, have a habit of keeping to the "status quo" of their lives, as the fear of changing something often looms larger in the mind than the benefit of starting something new, regardless of how beneficial it is. Some call this "inertia," colloquially. A good example of this resistance to change is found in retirement planning. People tend not to join retirement programs if they have to be proactive and enroll to start saving on their own. But if they are added to a program automatically, long-term participation rates spike and remain high, as people also generally do not quit these programs once they are in them.

3. Social Norms

This technique could easily be dubbed the "peer pressure" technique, or "file under obvious," where the unwritten rules and standards of a society are used to shape and guide a person's behavior. A current example includes campaigns to encourage people to wear seatbelts by claiming that nearly everyone wears them. This certainly works better, however, in monocultures like Japan, where social norms are clearly defined and widespread. It may be less effective in multicultural societies like the United States, where not all behave in similar ways and customs change from state to state, city to city, or even neighborhood to neighborhood (though it's still a good idea to wear your seatbelt).

4. Loss Aversion

This technique is based on the fact that negative things such as loss or personal disadvantage have a greater emotional impact on people than the positive things. The best example of this occurs in taxing "negative" products such as alcohol and tobacco to curtail their use; these are used in tandem with other strategies. For example, some governments apply "saint subsidies" to healthier foods for people in combination with so-called sin taxes. Another example is the display of "Only 2 left in stock (more on the way)" or other comments in your Amazon shopping cart, to get you to act more quickly and buy that thing already. In other words, people are often motivated to go out of their way to avoid what they see as penalties. In the Internet era, where people can see what others are doing at any time, FOMO, or the fear of missing out, is a strong motivator.

5. Anchoring/Adjustment

This technique looks at the tendency of people to latch on to certain information in the absence of other facts and who then adjust all their subsequent ideas or behaviors accordingly. This is most commonly noticeable when vendors show several price options for their products, especially where multiple versions of an item are available. Typically, prices are shown in sets of three, with the lowest and highest priced and then one in the middle. Your perception of cost is manipulated as you'll likely "anchor" yourself to that middle price, which *in reality* may be the most inflated of them all, and purchase if the middle price seems reasonable.

6. Hyperbolic Discounting

This operates on the realization that people act "inconsistently in terms of time." People tend to favor or over-value the present or near-present rather than a further-off future. This is also known as *salience*. You'll respond better to something when you are rewarded soon after doing it (usually something desirable like exercise, etc.) with vouchers, immediate cash-back incentives or coupons, and so on. The closeness in time to an event makes it seem more important to you; conversely, and here's the big problem, that feeling fades over time. So seize the day.

7. Decoupling

This situation occurs when the consequences or aftermath of an event are not seen as related or are diminished. The clearest example of this occurs when using credit cards. People purchase something but don't feel the immediate negative impact of owing money for it! Of course, that financial hangover arrives later with a bill in the mail. Yet even after that, the ill effects of owing money can be reduced by paying only a small amount of the amount due on the card. With the high interest rate, the debt owed on the card, however, can accumulate and snowball. Overcoming this behavior requires clearer disclosures or reminders of those impacts. If one were given a notice, for example, of one's balance owed on their credit card, or how much had been spent that week with the card, it would provide good feedback to help people—especially if they're on budgets.

8. Priming

This technique is probably the closest to outright manipulation, as it is applied before decisions are made in order to prompt a desired behavior. Eliciting intentions through well-placed questions such as "Whom do you plan to vote for?" nudges people to think about a final result that may bypass their more measured, "step-by-step" thought process, essentially skipping ahead of any of the doubts you might have had about whether you should vote. This technique might be useful in travel agencies. By having travel posters asking, "*Where* do you want to go?" this assumption bypasses any discussion of whether you actually want to go somewhere. Instead of the typical "*Do* you want to go somewhere?" it avoids the possibility of saying "no." In a library, this strategy could be adopted by having book titles displayed here-and-there asking, "What do you want to read *next*?" which bypasses the question of whether or not someone actually wants to read. This might help nudge patrons into more book checkouts.

9. Availability Heuristic

Recent and regularly presented "events are perceived as more likely than less present events." This is essentially the habit that people have of determining how likely it is that something will occur based on how easily they can recall it, *regardless of the actual chances of it happening*. This effect can be seen quite clearly in media campaigns regarding highly specific medical conditions, such as certain cancers, that may actually be quite rare among the population. In fact, as Dan Greller (2013) points out, "simply imagining a hypothetical scenario could increase an individual's perception of the likelihood of the event" (i.e., "if I can *imagine* it, it *must* be likely"). This can be used in a positive way to nudge people into certain "safer" behaviors, such as quitting smoking or drinking (or indeed implemented as warning labels on packs of cigarettes—or, as in the state of California, on bags of coffee). But it can also instill fear of a disease in people who are actually in good health or at low risk of contracting it. As we'll see later in the example of autism and vaccines, this might have larger negative consequences for the society if people stop giving vaccines to their children out of fear of a "regularly presented" disease, even if there's no connection.

EXAMPLES OF NUDGING/REAL-WORLD APPLICATION

Theory is one thing. But what about the real world? What about the practical applications of nudges? To answer this we really don't need to look very deeply. Examples abound all over the world, from the most industrialized, modern, and wealthy countries to the less-developed, poorer ones. Nudging can be employed across these disparate cultures and places in order to bring about specific behavioral changes in people.

Frequently cited as the most complex in the world, the Japanese train system can get a person just about anywhere in that whole region within minutes and hours, far faster than driving would allow. I lived in the greater Tokyo area for nearly a decade, and as a result, I am well-versed in traveling the subway and trains throughout the whole Kantō region. I traveled daily by train from my home in Saitama to areas as far-flung as Chiba and Ibaragi, all the way down to Yokohama and back, sometimes in a single day, starting at morning rush hour and ending at the evening crush. It was a job that would have been impossible in any other city in the world, save perhaps London or New York City.

During my years as a rider on Japan Railways and the Metro, I saw a lot of things and, really, the whole region through the window of a train. But one thing that always stood out was how orderly it was despite the daily shuttling and transferring of millions of people inside literal fast-moving tin cans. As an aside, at least 3.6 million pass through JR Shinjuku station a day and more than 13.5 billion rides are tallied per year among the whole of Japan. I never gave much thought beyond the crowds and the feeling of being "Packt Like Sardines in a Crushd Tin Box" (sorry, Radiohead). But, apparently, the way to keep 13.5 billion rides orderly over a year requires some important design and choice architectures. Enter nudge theory as applied to Japanese trains and Japanese society in general. There are clearly specific strategies and planning being undertaken to help it become this way (Richarz, 2018).

Mood Lighting

Riding a Japan Railways train every day packed in with everyone else, especially on a cold gray February morning, can be incredibly depressing. The Saikyō line from Omiya station to Akabane can seem especially bleak that time of year: neon-soaked, grimy concrete buildings punctuated by bare, sickly trees and half-hidden temples and shrines. Given the culture of overwork, the poor work-family balance, and a general lack of sleep, it is no wonder that Japan regularly ranks highest among industrialized nations in terms of yearly suicide rates. It's rare that you'll see someone just smiling and laughing on the train. Some of it is surely related to the stoic habits of Japanese society—one must *gaman-suru* (endure) while preserving your *tatamae* (your outward appearance and intentions)—but also from the sense of tiredness from lack of sufficient rest. Napping is almost de rigueur, much like the *sarariman* who wears his winter wool suit on October 1, out of obligation and expectations, even if it's still hot. To help alleviate some of these stressors, mood lights have been implemented at the tracks to improve general sense of well-being for stressed-out people. Given the high rate of suicides at Japanese train stations, these mood lights serve to lighten the load of burdened people. Furthermore, given how long people must commute daily, and the amount of time they might be waiting for their train to arrive, equipping stations with mood lights would certainly have direct impact on a maximum number of riders.

Train "Jingles"

Many arriving and departing trains have their own signature songs at stations. Some of the reason behind this is to improve people's moods upon the arrival and departure of the train. The songs are often jaunty and happy, rarely low-key or sad. These jingles serve multiple purposes. First, they let passengers know when trains are arriving or departing. This improves passenger safety. People rarely run into trains as doors are closing. Second, the jingles also appear to improve a person's general mind-set. Music has an impact on people, altering moods and impressions, but in this specific situation, it has the effect of calming riders and reducing their stress from the commute. People become so familiar with these individual jingles that they can tell the train line and the station by the musical notes alone.

Ultrasonic Deterrents

There are a lot of kids riding the trains in Japan, both with their schoolmates and by themselves. Yet they are also remarkably well-behaved, despite at times roaming around train stations together in large groups. Some of this is cultural, to be sure. But teenagers the world over are often the most likely to cause trouble compared to adults. So how do they prevent crowds of teenagers from causing problems or fighting with each other? One strategy employed by the train stations is to add sounds that bother and annoy only younger people. This has an effect on them, forcing many to suddenly feel uncomfortable in specific spots. This keeps them moving through stations and on to other places. Perhaps it's a bit cruel, but it seems to keep the stations orderly (Richarz, 2018).

Nudges in Other Countries

Japan is hardly the only place in the world to employ these types of nudges on their own people. Other parts of the world, including the United States, Great Britain, and even underdeveloped countries, have taken to adopting significant nudges in the name of improving people's behaviors. Some of these are more important and long-reaching than others, of course, but they all speak to the power that behavioral economics and insight can wield for beneficial societal goals.

Perhaps one of the most highly publicized examples of behavioral nudging is the least appetizing. Many are likely aware of the fly sticker pasted to the bottom of a urinal. While this is hardly a major public health issue, it does speak to how minor changes in overall user design can make significant changes in cleanliness and sanitation. In this case, the behavior is almost unconscious on the part of the person and mostly non-intrusive. Without telling men what to do, there was a reported 80 percent reduction in "spillage" resulting in an 8 percent reduction in cleaning costs (Ingraham, 2017). Given that many public facilities and transportation systems in the United States are cash-strapped, any reduction in costs should be seen as beneficial.

Taking the concept a step further, the government in Great Britain has devised a Behavioral Insights Team, also known as the "Nudge Unit," which aims to make significant changes in the daily behaviors of regular people. In a sense, behavioral insight becomes used as a policy tool, but with the difference being that many behavioral changes occur at the individual level instead of at the regional level. People change their behaviors without intentionally being asked to modify it to fit a top-down decree. The types of behavior addressed by the Nudge Unit include changing how people consume energy or how they might be inspired to become more socially conscientious (*Economist*, 2012). Their reports include such titles as *Behaviour Change and Energy Use*, which they devised in order to help "people to green their homes and be more energy efficient"; also, *Better Choices: Better Deals Consumers Powering Growth*, which outlines strategies to help people engage in sustainable economic and consumer behaviors. As David Halpern, head of the Behavioral Insights Team, outlines in his book *Inside the Nudge Unit*, their major insight is this: "If you want to encourage something, make it easy" (Halpern, 2015). The removal of barriers to complete something, he argues, makes the likelihood of doing it much higher.

Following the "make it easy" mantra, nudging has led to public health improvements within poor and third-world countries. Researchers found, for example, that providing poor mothers in low-income countries with a year's supply of chlorine during routine vaccinations at a doctor's office resulted in greater rates of using chlorine to sanitize their water later on. In the follow up, nearly 40 percent of these women still used chlorine to sanitize their drinking water, compared to 15 percent for those who were given a half-off discount to purchase chlorine themselves and to 20 percent of the households that were given just a single month supply. Furthermore, placing chlorine dispensers at water collection sites made the likelihood of households using sanitized water even more likely (Kremer et al., 2010). As Bauer describes it, the "dispensers provided a visual reminder when water was collected and made it easy to add the right dose. Along with promotion by community members, this approach increased chlorine use by 53%" (Bauer, 2016). These simple nudge strategies go a long way to preventing cholera and other water-borne diseases.

HOW THE INTERNET BECAME "CLICKBAIT," OR HOW WE ARE BEING NUDGED ONLINE

There are numerous examples of how people's behavior is being changed in the physical world in order to accomplish wider societal goals, or, as the case may be, narrower, self-interested goals. It's no different online, especially with the devices we use to log in online. As an academic on a college campus, I can't tell you how many times I've seen students bump into things or each other because they're staring down at their smart phones! A nuisance, yes, but sometimes fruitful in the case of online collaborations and improved teamwork. As Mirsch and colleagues mention, "Compared to physical contexts, digital environments provide several advantages for nudging: . . . [it] is easier, faster, and cheaper; moreover, the Internet provides specific functionalities, like user tracking, which allows personalization of nudges presented to users"

(2017). These technological advantages make nudging online even easier than in the physical world.

The most typical examples of online nudging involve shopping and targeted ads. As Aviv Revach, founder and CEO of Commerce Sciences Online, boasts, "We decipher the shopper's DNA." He continues in typical CEO fashion:

> Our algorithms can detect hesitant shoppers before they leave the store and automatically trigger the best relevant experience. This can include addressing their concerns (such as store safety, product question, price, etc.) or catalyzing motivation (by highlighting scarcity, authority, social proof, reducing choice to focus attention—i.e., "paradox of choice," emphasizing specific information to create a basis for a decision—i.e., "anchoring," achieving pre-commitment, etc.). (Quora, 2013)

The ads called up, then, are related to what they estimate is most salient to you: your most recent views on other websites (remember number six above, hyperbolic discounting?). Seeing the ads persist over time based on your shopping history is quite hard to get used to, but over time, many of us have stopped looking and have begun to tune them out.

Nudging takes other forms, too, beyond simple algorithmic ad tracking and includes feedback loops, monitoring and self-monitoring, and more. We've all seen, for example, the radar set up alongside the road that broadcasts back to us our current speed in real time as we drive past it. The psychology behind this is quite ingenious. A "feedback loop" is used to modify a person's behavior. In most of these instances, the driver has their speed relayed back to them on the radar's digital display. Instead of seeing this only on their dashboards, however, drivers' speeds are shared with everyone else on the road behind them. This causes many drivers to adjust their speeds in real time, even if there are no police patrol cars or speed traps in sight.

Similar approaches have been taken with online behaviors as well. Approaches to self-monitoring and feedback loops are evident in the plethora of online diet and exercise monitors. Self-monitoring allows algorithms to dispense advice based on the data you provide them. One good example of this is when Amazon provides the "shoppers also buy" label when you're looking at something; taking it a step further, some shopping websites try to push you into shopping by warning you that only a few items remain. Online discounts also help to spur shopping behavior, by providing member discounts but also discounts for immediate purchase (e.g., purchase now for a 10 percent discount, etc.).

Of course, the curious thing about monitoring is that when you're aware of it, you wind up changing your behavior to impress upon the observer whatever you want them to see. In other words, it's an act. This tendency, known as the Hawthorne Effect, was an early notorious wrench in the works of productivity studies of factory workers, contributing to the bias of the observer's study. It is quite possible, then, that we can game our own self-monitoring systems so that they will tell us exactly what we want to hear. The danger is that it contributes to a lack of understanding and awareness of alternate viewpoints. We might also, similarly, find ways to disable and avoid manipulative advertisements by rigging them to see only what we want them to see. I might, for example, purposely look at ads of cars even if I have no intention of buying one just to throw off the ad tracking.

PUSHBACK: THE FLAWS IN NUDGE THEORY

No theory, of course, is perfect, and nudging is no different. There have been some notable criticisms of the theory that remain cogent and important pushbacks to overly programmatic thinking. For some, it has been pointed out that if you have a hammer, everything looks like a nail. This can be detrimental to solving complex problems that often require multiple perspectives and imaginative responses. The practice of nudging can also be used negatively or counterproductively, resulting in the manipulation of people for questionable ends. Nudging requires a certain amount of trust that the leaders in charge are both benevolent and acting in society's best interests. But nudging, as we'll see, can easily bleed into techniques used to addict people or to coerce them into behaving poorly. Internet addiction is a dark, often underaddressed problem. Some nudges may become outright shoves in the direction of widespread, top-down social engineering.

The Real-Life Ineffectiveness of the Theory

One of the major criticisms of nudge theory is that it has been very ineffective for certain types of problems. In finance, for example, when it comes to retirement plans, or in social engineering designed to curtail the consumption of fast food, the "nudge is really a fudge" (Pasquale, 2015). The nudge-worthy solutions actually end up masking much greater societal issues that the nudge cannot fix. In the case of your 401(k), for example, the two great problems (and understated *risks*) of retirement savings are the inherent insecurity of the stock market and rising costs of health care. The instability of the stock market coupled with spiraling health care costs ultimately renders many retirement savings insufficient. The need to solve these two much larger systemic problems greatly outweighs the need for people to save their money in a stock-market-based solution. Furthermore, in the case of obesity in the United States, reducing the serving sizes of candy, soda, or other junk foods does not automatically improve health so long as people continue to consume them in *any* capacity. Carbohydrate cravings render serving sizes irrelevant as people will still have the physiological urge to overeat sugars and starches. Instead of one large bottle of soda, it's four smaller ones. Additionally, subsidies that greatly reduce the price of corn and sugar make it *significantly* cheaper and easier to purchase foods and drinks made with them rather than fresh fruits and vegetables. Focusing on the individual is ineffective in the face of these high-impact socially engineered policies or underdeveloped laissez-faire approaches (Pasquale, 2015).

Additionally, people object to the breezy description of nudging as "Libertarian Paternalism," on the grounds that it is both condescending and contradictory. The description strikes reasonable people as a clear example of Orwellian Newspeak, where the words in isolation are antithetical to each other, yet wind up creating a clever but confusing paradox that is, at bottom, meaningless. In this vein, a "libertarian," under the most commonly used definition of the word, would never force anyone to do anything, and certainly not through subtle and unspoken, manipulative means; while "paternalism" speaks to the power structure of men who know better than you do and should therefore make important decisions for you. It's like any other contradiction in terms—say "controlled chaos"—that when examined closely enough reminds us there's no truth in it.

Nudge, Grudge, and Sludge: Power Ruins a Good Thing

The main underlying assumption about nudging is that it is used for positive, socially beneficial purposes, ultimately and necessarily guided by the types of people who know better and act benevolently. Yet, here's where the theory can also go awry. It is well-known that people in positions of power often abuse it. Even if people think they are doing something beneficial for all, their actions still might result in a negative outcome. Some may just be spouting off lip-service in order to hold on to a position of power. Others may genuinely hope to create real change. But positive nudging or other social programs can be used to cover up unsavory, unethical, and non-beneficial behaviors and activities. Even the concept of paternalism assumes a kind of gender bias, making it seem like men have specific plans that would help all people, despite the fact that there are currently gender and race pay gaps within this society. The assumption, too, is that nudging can be used in a lot of situations even though the evidence suggests otherwise.

The most widely quoted statement from Richard Thaler and Cass Sunstein is that "if you want someone to do something, make it easier." But as one critic points out, "what if you want people to do the wrong thing? The answer: make *that* easy; or make the *right thing* difficult" (Harford, 2017). And, let's face it, making the right thing difficult can very easily depress participation in activities that may be socially beneficial yet difficult to perform. The most pernicious example of this is the recent spate of voter ID laws pushed by Republican lawmakers in the United States over the past twenty years (and the Jim Crow laws from the century prior). Similarly, the 2018 Supreme Court ruling *Husted v. Randolf Institute* ruled that an Ohio law allowing voter inactivity as justification to remove names from voter registration is constitutional. This allows registered voters to be removed from registries if they *fail* to vote in a previous or recent election and represents another nudge in the "wrong direction" by forcing voters to keep track of when they last voted and to repeat inconvenient red tape (Scotus Blog, 2018). Thaler himself calls this "*sludge*" theory: the implementation of confusing or restrictive rules to prevent or slow down actions.

Evidence of Thaler's "sludge" theory is also clearly seen in the website Dark Patterns Hall of Shame, a website that demonstrates the potentially black hat manipulative methods some IT companies employ to control user behaviors (darkpatterns.org/hall-of-shame). As seen in figure 3.1, people are being nudged online to forgo or to act indifferently to default privacy settings that appear in websites or web user agreements. The text in the very light shade, which concerns copyright and contact information, is nearly unreadable. Making intentions seem even murkier, the link to "unsubscribe" is not un-

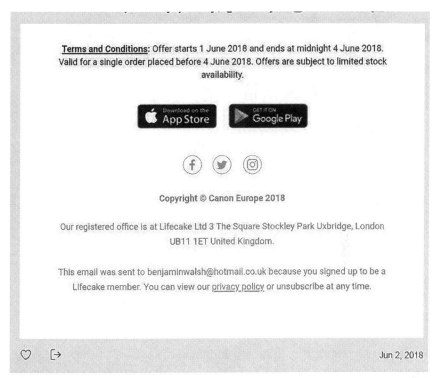

FIGURE 3.1
Screenshot for Lifecake, an app for photos and videos, showing the lighter inconspicuous text colors for important user information and a half-hidden unsubscribe link. *Dark Patterns Hall of Shame*

derscored like other hypertexts in the same message. This makes it even less likely that someone would go through the steps to drop the online newsletter unless they were sufficiently motivated.

Tim Harford, a writer for the *Financial Times*, takes Thaler's "sludge" idea a step further by calling the manipulation of online discourse—for example, via Twitter wars, "flame outs," memes that ridicule, fake news, and so on— "grudge" theory (Harford, 2017). Concrete evidence of the Russian government's attempt at "grudging" people in the United States, especially Donald Trump and #MAGA supporters, can be found on the website Hamilton 68 (see figure 1.2). This organization shows how the controversies of the day are deliberately magnified by Russian-linked Twitter accounts, serving to further ignite anger, dissension, and disbelief (Alliance for Securing Democracy, 2018). We will examine this in much greater detail in part III, "Information and Power."

A Brief Note on "Social Credit" Systems

It appears that social engineering through behavioral conditioning is poised to explode in the coming years. The Internet of Things (IoT), once it is linked with large-scale "social credit" programs, may move us from "nudge" theory to full-on "*shove*" theory. This shift has the potential to blur the boundaries between our own actions; our sense of free will; and the will of both corporations, which in the era of surveillance capitalism can find ways to keep you buying their stuff, and governments, which benignly or not-so-benignly wish to control their citizens' behavior (Coughlin, 2017). China's Social Credit System points the way to how this could be realistically implemented in other countries in the near-future (Kobie, 2019). The Social Credit System (SCS), started in 2014 and likely approaching nationwide implementation by 2020, is designed to rate the "trustworthiness" of a person within the context of Chinese society.

The system employs both carrots and sticks in encouraging and discouraging certain social behaviors. The end goal is to nudge people into becoming loyal Communist party members by making certain positive behaviors easier to do and more beneficial, while making negative behaviors personally detrimental. While this is merely in its infancy, the methods to engineer widespread assent while squashing dissent appears to have quite a lot of room for growth. Tied in with China's current facial recognition and crowd-control surveillance capabilities, the ability to maintain control through observation and subtle nudging becomes all-encompassing (Kobie, 2019). We will discuss the specifics and the wider implications of China's Social Credit System in greater detail later, especially in chapter 11.

The wide array of methods by which people can be manipulated into approved actions or suppressing their "subversive" thoughts should be sobering. There is really no reason to believe that such systems could not be implemented in England, Canada, the United States, Japan, or any other first-world industrialized countries. While it may seem unlikely now, mixing in these types of social credit systems with surveillance capitalist methods (i.e., incentivizing the tracking of personal information) may make it more palatable than just top-down, single-party political manipulations. But, one could argue, the results of severely curtailed personal freedoms through electronic means and nudging based on the surveillance of personal activities would be nearly identical.

Internet Addiction: The Itch You Can't Scratch, the Nudge You Can't Shrug

Many point to Internet addiction as a major factor that could fuel these social credit systems. We are being subtly nudged to stay online for as long as possible and even "numbed" to the deleterious effects of spending too much of our precious time alive in the fantasylands of cyberspace. The inability to stop playing Facebook's Farmville game seemed benign on the surface. Indeed, who hasn't gotten hooked on at least one video game in their lives? It's a great escapist outlet for millions. But below the surface, there were real-world consequences to being hooked on a game like this.

Yet, is addiction in users a real thing? Is it possibly just a scare tactic meant to curb people from spending all day in front of a screen or monitor? Although contradictory studies exist making it inconclusive that gaming is an addiction in the same way that heroin or hard drugs are, one researcher has found that "technology-related 'addictions' share some neural features with substance and gambling addictions" (Turel et al., 2014). The good news from their study, though, is that unlike drug addictions, which have long-lasting and even irreversible impacts on a body's physiology, people can restore their own homeostasis through cognitive behavioral therapy (Turel et al., 2014).

Yet even the short-term effects can be problematic. A report from the British government about Internet addictions suggests that overuse of the Internet and social media websites contributes to higher levels of depression in teenagers. The role of nudging and manipulative user design cannot be understated here. As we can see in figure 3.2, teens reported a significant level of negative impact on their sleeping patterns as well as feelings of depression and anxiety. Some reported loneliness. These can all be seen as somewhat physiological in origin. If teenagers were to get more sleep, they would likely feel a whole lot better, perhaps a little less anxiety-ridden or depressed from being rested. But one of the biggest impacts teens stated was FOMO, which seems more like a kind of social anxiety than a physical one. Teens felt that they were missing out on things more often when accessing social media, striking them with envy at the perceived happiness of others.

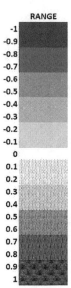

REPORTED IMPACT ON WELL-BEING (Negative to Positive)

Platform/Issue	Instragram	Snapchat	Facebook	Twitter
Sleep	-0.9	-1	-1.1	-0.8
Fear of Missing Out (FOMO)	-0.9	-1	-0.8	-0.5
Bullying	-0.6	-0.7	-0.8	-0.6
Body image	-0.9	-0.5	-0.6	-0.4
Anxiety	-0.6	-0.4	-0.5	-0.3
Depression	-0.4	-0.3	-0.4	-0.3
Loneliness	-0.2	-0.1	-0.1	-0.1
Access to health advice	0	-0.1	0.2	0.2
Real-world relationships	0.1	0.4	0.3	-0.1
Awareness of people's health	0.2	-0.1	0.7	0.3
Community building	0.5	0.3	0.7	0.6
Emotional support	0.5	0.5	0.5	0.3
Self-identity	0.7	0.6	0.5	0.6
Self-expression	0.5	0.8	0.7	0.6

FIGURE 3.2

Social media usage reported impact on well-being in teens and young adults in Great Britain. *Royal Society for Public Health (2017); redrawn by author*

One might see some of this FOMO as a result of "persuasive design." This can trap users into negative loops where they feel like they'll miss something if they are not "plugged in." All of this is designed to keep users on the sites. As Emily Waite (2018) acknowledges in *Wired*,

> It wasn't just Google that had perverse incentives; it was also Apple and Facebook, with their broad ecosystems of attention-grabbing apps. It was Snapchat, with its cleverly designed "streaks" to encourage teens to keep up their message volleys. It was every computer, and every phone. The tech companies of Silicon Valley referred to people as users, like a dealer talking about addicts.

The language of addiction should strike a cautionary note in all of us. Given the current opioid crisis in the United States that was exacerbated through the overprescription of *legal* painkiller medication, we are dealing with problems that developed entirely within the frameworks of laws and regulations. Problems hidden within systems go unnoticed until they become a public scourge. As Roger McNamee, advisor for the Center for Humane Technology, states, "The design of the phones is where the dark side starts, but not where it ends" (Waite, 2018). Something ubiquitous, largely beneficial to society, and legal, to boot, like a cell phone, benefits from its good reputation. But like legal painkillers, the most susceptible among us can fall victim to the underreported drawbacks of a generally beneficial thing or service. The reckoning came for the opioid manufacturers in 2019, but I wonder if the same will happen to the tech industry.

Ultimately, we will need to find ways to curtail or countermand the demands on our time that our mobile devices, Internet websites, and platforms are making. Countermeasures against the addictive and biased properties of these devices need to be developed. Furthermore, awareness of the addictive properties of social media, devices, and touch-screen technologies, as well as social credits and nudging itself, needs to be more widespread. Perhaps warnings need to be adopted; perhaps selling cell phones and Internet devices to children needs to be better regulated.

It seems unlikely that Silicon Valley will find a way to police itself, however. Given the revelations about Facebook's deal to share its information with the Chinese company Huawei, among others, which came in the weeks *after* Zuckerberg testified in Congress, it seems unlikely Facebook and other IT companies will allow congressional regulations to kill their golden goose (LaForgia and Dance, 2018). As Zeynep Tufekci notes in her excellent book *Twitter and Tear Gas*, "The networked public sphere is not a flat, open space with no barriers and no structures. Sometimes, the gatekeepers of the networked public sphere are even more centralized and . . . even more powerful than those of the mass media" (Tufekci, 2017, p. 162). We are living in a dangerous time. Facebook and other social media networks clearly have had opportunities to share our data without compunction; their consolidation of their own power and their ability to make machines that perpetuate this may harm us all even if it is not *technically* illegal to do so.

The Grand Bit-con

On a final note, given the many documented negatives that come from the overuse of computers, mobile devices (smart phones), and social media, can we find ways to nudge ourselves *off* these things? What strategies can we take to improve our lives through a kind of counter-nudging to the nudging of these devices? These are serious questions that we will need to address as the Internet moves primarily from PCs and mobile cell phone devices to the

Internet of Things. When our refrigerator knows more about us than we do ourselves, we may be in trouble! When we are unable to function without referring to our digital avatars or our digital devices, we will also be in trouble! It's not far off. Perhaps user design can find ways to countermand the addictive qualities of online use. Perhaps meters and other types of self-monitoring devices can wean us off overusing the Internet. If not, we run the risk of "a Grand Bit-con," unaware that what we think is beneficial is *actually* harming us.

REFERENCES

Alliance for Securing Democracy. (2018). Tracking Putin's propaganda push . . . to America. Hamilton 68. dashboard.securingdemocracy.org/.

Bauer, R. (2016). A nudge in the right direction: How behavioral economics could make your life easier: 11 ways nudge theory works in the real world. World Economic Forum. www.weforum.org/agenda/2016/08/a-nudge-in-the-right -direction-how-behavioral-economics-could-make-your-life-easier/.

Coughlin, J. (2017). The "Internet of Things" will take nudge theory too far. *Big Think*. bigthink.com/disruptive-demographics/the-Internet-of-things-big-data -when-a-nudge-becomes-a-noodge.

Economist. (2012). Nudge nudge, think think. www.economist.com/node/21551032.

Greller, D. (2013). "If I can imagine it, it must be likely"—The availability heuristic. Invisible Laws Blog. www.dangreller.com/if-i-can-imagine-it-it-must-be-likely -the-availability-heurisitic/.

Halpern, D. (2015). *Inside the nudge unit: How small changes can make a big difference*. London: Virgin Digital.

Hansen, P. (2016a). What is nudging? *Behavioral Policy*. behavioralpolicy.org/what -is-nudging/

———. (2016b). The definition of nudge and libertarian paternalism—Does the hand fit the glove? *The European Journal of Risk Regulation, 7*(1), 155–74. Available at SSRN: ssrn.com/abstract=2652958.

Harford, T. (2017). Nudging can also be used for dark purposes. FT.Com. Retrieved from libproxy.csun.edu/login?url=https://search.proquest.com/docview/19748894 97?accountid=7285.

Ingraham, C. (2017). What's a urinal fly, and what does it have to with winning a Nobel Prize? *Washington Post*. www.washingtonpost.com/news/wonk/wp/2017/10/09/whats-a-urinal-fly-and-what-does-it-have-to-with-winning-a-nobel-prize/?utm_term=.bf7f6cbf22c0.

Kobie, N.. (2019). The odd reality of life under China's all-seeing credit score system. *Wired*. www.wired.co.uk/article/china-social-credit.

Kremer, M., Ahuja, A., and Peterson-Zwane, A. (2010). Providing safe water: Evidence from randomized evaluations. Harvard Environmental Economics Program. heep.hks.harvard.edu/files/heep/files/dp23_kremer-ahuja-petersonzwane.pdf.

LaForgia, M., and Dance, G. (2018). Facebook gave data access to Chinese firm flagged by U.S. intelligence. *New York Times*. www.nytimes.com/2018/06/05/technology/facebook-device-partnerships-china.html.

Mirsch, T., Lehrer, C., and Jung, R. (2017). Digital nudging: Altering user behavior in digital environments. Thirteenthth International Conference on Wirtschaftsinformatik, February 12–15, St. Gallen, Switzerland.

Pasquale, F. (2015). Why "nudges" hardly help. *Atlantic*. www.theatlantic.com/business/archive/2015/12/nudges-effectiveness/418749/.

Quora. (2013). What are some examples of the real-world use of behavioral economics? Quora. www.quora.com/What-are-some-examples-of-the-real-world-use-of-behavioral-economics-Im-looking-for-examples-where-the-insights-of-behavioral-economics-were-used-to-great-effect-in-the-real-world.

Richarz, A. (2018). The amazing psychology of Japanese train stations. City Lab. www.citylab.com/transportation/2018/05/the-amazing-psychology-of-japanese-train-stations/560822/.

Royal Society for Public Health. (2017). #StatusofMind. www.rsph.org.uk/our-work/campaigns/status-of-mind.html.

Scotus Blog. (2018). *Husted v. A. Philip Randolph Institute*. www.scotusblog.com/case-files/cases/husted-v-philip-randolph-institute/.

Thaler, R., and Sunstein, C. (2008). *Nudge: Improving decisions about health, wealth and happiness*. New Haven, CT: Yale University Press.

Tufekci, Z. (2017). *Twitter and tear gas: The power and fragility of networked protest*. New Haven, CT: Yale University Press.

Turel, O., He, Q., Xue, G., Xiao, L., and Bechara, A. (2014). Examination of neural systems sub-serving Facebook "addiction." *Psychological Reports.* 115. 10.2466/18 .PR0.115c31z8. www.researchgate.net/publication/269414387_Examination _of_neural_systems_sub-serving_facebook_addiction?enrichId=rgreq -968196853b4cdd5a59f4565a73590944-XXX&enrichSource=Y292ZXJQYW dlOzI2OTQxNDM4NztBUzo0MjQ1NDI5MjY1Nzc2NjdAMTQ3ODIzMDMyO TI0Ng.

Waite, E. (2018). Google and the rise of "digital well-being." *Wired.* www.wired .com/story/google-and-the-rise-of-digital-wellbeing/.

4

Surveillance Capitalism and the "New Economy"

A warfare state thus naturally militates into a surveillance state.

—*J. B. Foster and R. W. McChesney*

A "GRAND BARGAIN" OR A "GRAND CON"?

In the last chapter, we looked at how we can be subtly pushed to act or make decisions without full awareness of the outside influences shaping them. This chapter, however, looks beyond the growing trend of "nudging" and into the wider sphere of social and economic activities. We will begin to consider what wider forces exist beyond the digital platforms that have spurred the Internet to grow and develop at a massive, global scale.

On the surface, all seems fine. We are generally able to use the Internet safely and derive a huge amount of satisfaction in using it. This ranges from our personal relationships and our individual information needs and curiosities to our shopping and consumption desires. Yet this new information economy has become dominated by the methods and tools of "big data," which tracks and predicts people's behaviors through the analysis of the vast amounts of digital information they generate.

Defending the Internet as an engine of free-market innovation, Omar Ben Shahar, a typical example of what one might call a "big data apologist," sees these new methods of big data information collection and analysis as a "grand bargain," or in his words, "free services in return for personal information"

(Ben Shahar, 2016). Sounds perfectly reasonable, doesn't it? It's a simple one-for-one trade of equal services for equal and appropriate amounts of personal information. Ben Shahar and many like him argue that this exchange benefits consumers through the increase of innovations and services provided. Any issues of privacy are generally ignored by the customers themselves. So, if *we* don't care, he seems to be arguing, then there shouldn't be any problem! The customer knows best. He even goes so far as to assert that "there is no market failure in the Big Data sector and no proven need for protective regulation," eventually concluding that "consumers are happy to use their privacy as the *New Money*, and they are getting good value for it" (Ben Shahar, 2016).

But is this a reasonable bargain? Is this a fair and equitable exchange of services for something like privacy? Is this even a sensible argument that holds up under the merits? Ben Shahar's reasoning, of course, is *extremely* debatable. A lot of sticking points come up regarding this so-called bargain. Who, for example, controls the data that gets collected? Is this really an equal partnership between the data collector and the user? What privacy will remain once we've lost it to third parties? Can we get it back if we ever change our minds? Do we even know who these third parties *are*?

Aside from Ben Shahar's ignorance on the matter that the NSA and FBI's data collection is, somehow, on a much smaller scale than "big data" (spoiler alert: it *isn't*), we really shouldn't expect a writer in *Forbes* magazine, or any other pro–Wall Street magazine for that matter, to provide a clear analysis of capitalism's structural flaws or have an understanding that IT companies like Google or Facebook *do not function on the same social contract as past corporations*. The fact of the matter is that these companies exist at "hyperscale," far beyond anything seen before, perhaps signaling a new model of capitalism (Zuboff, 2015). So unless these questions can be clearly addressed and answered, one must conclude that the "Grand Bargain" could easily by altered into a "Grand *Con*," capable of distorting the private lives of everyone online—which essentially means anyone and everyone trying to live a normal life "on the grid."

Several economists and academics have started to reassess the initially underexamined assumptions that people like Ben Shahar, Google's chief economist Hal Varian, and many others have asserted about "big data" and its capacity to be altered into monetized data-revenue streams. While many still see IT companies in rosy terms of their novel innovations and naïve transparency—and many may still believe that Google actually follows its famous "Don't be evil" slogan—others are starting to view the IT world with a far more cold and critical eye than in the past two decades.

John Foster and Robert McChesney, in a 2014 article appearing in the *Monthly Review*, coined the term "surveillance capitalism" to help frame the discussion away from the *technophilia* of the modern big-business world. They trace the development of the Internet and its tracking capabilities from origins in the United States' postwar militarization. In their minds, the U.S. government developed a clear policy of what they define as "Keynesian militarism." They describe how, in the aftermath of World War II, consumer demand was *manufactured* by fear and corporate innovation intertwined with military research and development.

John Maynard Keynes is perhaps the most influential economist of the twentieth century, a founder of modern macroeconomic theory. Keynesian economics proposes that government policy can guide a free market–based economy in times of trouble. Indeed, fearing a regression to the economic malaise of the 1930s, the aim of the U.S. government in the immediate postwar period was to avoid a recession at all costs. Along with government interventions to spur the U.S. economy, the marketing sector was envisioned as a key driver in this demand-driven economy. Already by the 1950s, marketing firms operated as highly organized systems to track customers and employ sophisticated psychological manipulation. Indeed, "by 1962," Foster and McChesney report, "56.2 percent of the sales of the electronics industry in the United States were going to the military and the closely allied civilian space industry" (2014). In other words, surveillance was just one small step removed from the American electronics market. The Defense Advanced Research Projects Agency's (DARPA) nascent communications network (the aptly named DARPANET) ultimately evolved into the Internet itself. It was created to help "develop technologies of digital surveillance in close alliance with the NSA, along with military drone technology" (ibid.).

This close-knit collaboration between sales and marketing, an emphasis on economic growth, and the simultaneous development of surveillance technology have formed the basis of our current modern economic model. The documents released by Edward Snowden from the NSA's Prism program in 2013 show just how pervasive and tightly interweaved the surveillance state has become with the business sector, with nearly 70 percent of all Internet traffic in 2009, commercial and private, passing through the NSA's servers (Green-wald, 2014). In terms of current technologies and surveillance capabilities, a decade represents a lifetime of rapid change. We have clearly moved from a military-industrial complex to a military-*digital* complex. Some have even dubbed this tight interplay between commercial and government entities the "government-corporate surveillance complex" (Edwards, 2014).

Shoshana Zuboff, a professor and researcher in economics at Harvard Business School, elaborates upon the concept of surveillance capitalism a little further. Less focused on the application and historical roots of military surveillance, she examines the conceptual underpinnings of capitalism itself and the impact that digital technologies and data tracking can have on our economics and social structures. She describes the current age as developing "a new logic of accumulation" (Zuboff, 2015, p. 75). Where the previous system of capitalism accumulated wealth through reciprocal relationships that depended upon individuals as both a source of employees but also customers, IT companies are now distancing themselves from these long-standing "structural reciprocities" (p. 80) and mutually beneficial arrangements. In simpler terms, these companies are extracting data and information from people and their behaviors (both their employees and their customers) while minimizing the social responsibility of their actions. IT companies currently avoid meaningful oversight of both government regulations and watchdog organizations, maximizing profit margins cynically based on the number of "eyeballs" on the content rather than the content itself.

In fact, the more divisive or controversial the content, the more profitable it becomes as more and more people view it and comment on it (either in support or outrage), further eroding the historical mutually beneficial arrangements that provided social stability. By feeding on ongoing viral controversies, companies like Google, Twitter, and Facebook have been able to develop rapidly, outstripping the abilities of governments and regulations to keep their power from growing too quickly and for abuses to be left unresolved. As long as shareholders are happy, the integrity or the social impact of the data collection and information sharing remains secondary, if not completely ignored. Apple's unprecedented trillion-dollar valuation is but one more example of this growth of capital that outstrips societal concerns about privacy, data usage, sustainability, and technological invasiveness.

The importance of this loss of mutually beneficial, socially conscientious relationships between companies and societies should not be downplayed. Corporate accountability in the United States has been on the wane for decades as companies move offshore or become multinational and multi-jurisdictional. The description of the corporation as a "psychopathic" person has clear roots in the outrageously poor decision by the U.S. Supreme Court to designate corporations as people. This incredibly quick hyperscaling has further eroded the social fabric of all countries at an unprecedented pace, stretching already asymmetrical power relationships beyond their breaking points. If we converge the two applications of surveillance capitalism, both as an outgrowth of the military-industrial complex and as a new type of corporate entity operating at powerful and *unassailable* size, we begin to see the incredibly pathological trends in future organizations and the eventual move toward a pervasive surveillance-capitalist dystopia.

INFORMATION BROKERS IN THE "NEW ECONOMY"

Much has been made of the large multinational corporations or the near-monopolies of Google, Facebook, and the like, but there are other important actors in this "New Economy" that are just as influential but far more nebulous. One of these central actors is the information broker, an entity or person who trades in data, purchasing and aggregating it from multiple sources to sell to others. They tend to operate behind the scenes, but their impact on our lives is as powerful as the largest IT companies. There are at least 121 data brokers operating in the United States, probably more, but they operate in the shadows and with little oversight. In 2019, Vermont became the first state to attempt a regulation of data brokers (Vermont General Assembly, H.764, Act 171, legislature.vermont.gov/bill/status/2018/H.764), but the law still doesn't provide much information to consumers about these data brokers. We don't know, for example, whose data is collected in a broker's database or to whom they sell it. We can't access our own data in their databases or directly appeal to these brokers to opt out of data collection (Melendez and Pasternack, 2019).

So, given the secrecy and the lack of recourse most of us have, who exactly, then, *are* these data brokers? What are the implications of their actions on human privacy, free societies, and democratic institutions themselves?

Let's look a little more closely.

Figure 4.1 shows the complexity of the data tracking and profiling landscape of the online world, ranging the full gamut of online activities from media and publishing (e.g., Disney, Viacom, etc.), telecoms (AT&T, mobile carriers, etc.), IT platforms (Google, Facebook, Amazon, etc.), finance (lending, credit, collection agencies, etc.), public sector (utilities, law enforcement, etc.), and retail (brands, travel, etc.). Each of the brokers also focuses on specific types of data, ranging from customer management (e.g., Acxiom, MailChimp), to advertising technologies (Adobe, Neustar, ad networks), to business IT (FICO scores, Palantir, etc.), to risk data (Equifax, Lexis Nexis), and finally marketing data (Acxiom, etc.). The diversity and amount of data being collected on every one of us is astounding! Many of these companies also overlap various types of data collection, making it more difficult to discern just exactly what is collected, by whom, and for what purpose.

Indeed, one of the largest data brokers in the United States is Acxiom (you can find it straddling both the "customer management" and "marketing

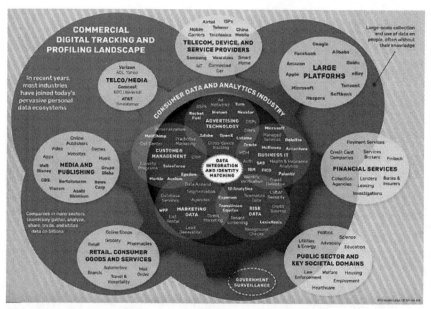

FIGURE 4.1
Visualization of the commercial digital tracking and profiling landscape of data brokers. *Wolfie (2017)*

data" segments in figure 4.1). It is a name that most people have probably never heard, but it's certainly hiding in plain sight. If you do a Google search, its site comes up at the top, with clear information about it from its website and a side box from Google. It says: "We solve critical use cases"; "Transform marketing"; and "People are the heart of what we do." Even the blurb from Google with its stock prices listed describes it as a "database marketing company." Seems harmless enough. More balanced and factual sources such as Wikipedia appear next, providing more history about the company and some aspects of a controversy it was involved with. But none of this really tells us what's going on.

Acxiom claims to have files on 10 percent of the world's population with 23,000 computer servers processing in more than *50 trillion* data transactions each year. It apparently keeps an average of 1,500 data points on more than *200 million Americans*, which is 62 percent of the population. Likely most of you reading this book have some sort of digital trail they are tracking. These "digital dossiers," as they have named them, follow us around in a combination of both online and offline digital data revealing information about our life choices, our class, our spending, where we live, and so on. As brokers, though, they don't necessarily work with the data itself. Instead they sell it to their own clients, packaging the content in such a way as to maximize profit, while tantalizing them with richer and richer "leads" for selling. The more granular the information, they argue, the better the portrait of the potential customer base a sales team might reach. As Foster and McChesney note, customers for Acxiom "include twelve of the top fifteen credit-card issuing companies; seven of the top ten retail banks; five of the top ten insurance companies; six of the top ten brokerage firms; eight of the top ten media/telecommunication companies; seven of the top ten retailers; eleven of the top fourteen global automakers; and three of the top ten pharmaceutical firms. Its clients include about half of the largest one-hundred corporations in the United States" (Foster and McChesney, 2014).

To educate their potential customers, Acxiom provides ample sales information. The problem with this is that it downplays concerns over personal privacy and legality while overemphasizing (or cherry picking) their results and personal feedback. One egregious example of this appears on their website in an advert for a webinar entitled "Data Privacy: What the Consumer Really Thinks." Marketed to their corporate clients, this webinar apparently intends to prove that online customers are "A-OK" with giving up their privacy. In fact, they argue, along similar lines as Ben Shahar above, that online users actually *expect* to lose some privacy! Users are really "data pragmatists," they proclaim, who rationally and consciously choose to exchange their privacy for whatever small goods and services companies will provide them (Acxiom, 2018).

But nothing could be further from the truth, as we have seen in multiple critiques of big data, privacy law, and the current events happening all around us in the realm of cybersecurity. Breaches occur quite often. Election hacking is still a problem for the United States. "Pragmatism," if that's really what it truly is, has nothing to do with this. This state of affairs is especially concerning since a consumer's choice to be pragmatic with their data—which in my mind means that they have the power to *choose* for themselves personally beneficial outcomes—often winds up *not being a choice at all*, given the hard-to-read, boilerplate-language website user agreements we are confronted with.

Indeed, the problem with surveillance becomes even worse when confronted with the fact that Acxiom has worked closely with the FBI, the Pentagon, and the U.S. Department of Homeland Security. Foster and McChesney note that in 2001, "Acxiom appointed General Wesley Clark, the former NATO Supreme Allied Commander in Europe in the Kosovo War and a future U.S. presidential candidate, to [Acxiom's] board of directors. The company paid Clark over $800,000 as a lobbyist, primarily in relation to the Department of Defense and Homeland Security. Through Clark, Acxiom began working with Poindexter's DARPA-based TIA, helping set up the technological systems for total surveillance of the U.S. and global population" (Foster and McChesney, 2014). Additionally, Acxiom also worked with the airline JetBlue to use public and private traveler records in a purported defense against terrorist attacks. This is probably just the tip of the iceberg in terms of how data is being brokered and "hoovered." All of this points to clear connections between the country's largest data broker and the U.S. national security apparatus.

Of course, we shouldn't just pick on Acxiom. There are many other companies of varying sizes, each within their own spheres of influence, that deal in the buying and selling of personal information. Data brokers in the United States include Experian, the credit score company; Epsilon, a "global marketing company" that turns "data into personalized customer experiences—driving growth for some of the most well-known brands worldwide" (Epsilon, 2018); CoreLogic, provider of "consumer, financial and property data"; Datalogix, yet another consumer data collection company; inome, which owns the background check service "Intelius"; and Recorded Future, which focuses on "real-time threat intelligence." Others include Choicepoint, owned by the data/publishing giant Elsevier, which also owns the well-known (at least in library and law circles) Lexis/Nexis databases, and the notorious Cambridge Analytica, which claims it has psychological profiles of 220 million U.S. citizens based on 5,000 separate data sets.

Though the amount of data collected on people by Cambridge Analytica may not be eye-opening by itself, especially in comparison to Experian, Epsilon, or Intelius, their use of the data for specific political purposes regarding the 2016 presidential election surely is. What these excessively large numbers tell us is that the scale of the data that is being brokered across all these disciplines and industries is far beyond normal comprehension. Furthermore, data is being used far beyond the stated, nominal intentions. We are essentially drowning in data.

But not only that. We are also increasingly defined *by* that collected data and therefore defined by the *trackers themselves*. In nearly all aspects of our lives, we are tracked to the point that all mysteries about us, all wants we have or desires that spur us, can potentially be anticipated. In the case of a background check, for example, we have no say in how our past actions, accumulated debts (whether intentional or not), and personal proclivities come to be portrayed by third parties increasingly dependent upon selling your information to satisfy their shareholders.

It is clear, then, that stronger regulation needs to be enacted. Vermont's legislation was certainly a step in the right direction. But given just how much information is collected by these more than 120 unregulated businesses, the law is clearly too narrow in scope and too weak in implementation to have a widespread impact on our daily lives.

LIFE IN A DIGITAL FISHBOWL: THE CONVERGENCE OF CONSUMER CONSUMPTION AND THE SURVEILLANCE STATE

Here's another important question: what happens when all of our needs *are* anticipated within these system-defined criteria? As we saw in the previous

chapter on nudging, we are not always aware of how outside forces are pushing us to act in specific "desirable" ways. Many of our wants can be com-
pelled by system designs and algorithms. Consumption may be impelled by
the periodic—even unwanted—analyses of our states of being. We may be,
therefore, on the cusp of a society that is so overly tracked and nudged that
needs are both anticipated and spurred on by such algorithms. Zuboff sees
this as a logical result of the asymmetrical power relationships between data-
gathering corporations and the societies they purportedly both rely on and
serve. The rule of law, she argues, is being superseded by this new approach.
In this "rule by algorithm," where our consumption behaviors are determined
by formulae using the raw data generated from our various mobile and wired
devices and online behaviors, it will be hard to tell where our desires end and
our observers' wants begin. The result is that behavioral compliance becomes
the best way to ensure that profits continue for the select few companies that
control our data. "Big Other," as Zuboff calls it, is watching you.

These visions of an all-encompassing tracking of all lifestyle choices for the
sake of convenience and profit are not that far off. The Internet of Things is
right around the corner, promising to flood us all in an even larger deluge of
data streams stemming from our various household hardware and appliances.
It will make our current life seem quaint and the amount of data we now
generate almost like a creek in comparison. And the wolves are circling. Even
major economic magazines like *Forbes*, for example, are getting into the act,
asking their readers, who are presumably the captains of industry or at least
the middle-managers of industry, the enticing question: "When will cities
begin to monetize their residents' data?" (Leetaru, 2018). Yes. When, *indeed*?

Of course, the public's imagination for these "smart" cities is fueled in part
by science fiction and its application in real-world scenarios, in much the
same way Elon Musk seems to think he is living out a sci-fi fantasy with his
rocket ships to the Red Planet and Tesla's Roadsters shot into space. Google,
which always wants to out-dream even the wildest dreamer, is proposing its
first "Google City," which they describe as "the world's first neighborhood
built from the Internet up" (Scola, 2018). Of course, what we must not forget
is that along with a new neighborhood being built, our own old-fashioned
privacy may also be *eliminated* "from the Internet up." It's certainly a beautiful, even utopian, idea. But, realistically, this may be a stretch. Our societ-

ies are built upon physical, legal, and sociological frameworks that have taken hundreds if not thousands of years to develop. Cities take centuries to reach maturity, and their infrastructures require constant maintenance and renewal. Google, with its tendency to throw money at problems without necessarily thinking through the best strategies or considering the long-term consequences, might not be able to "disrupt" the city as quickly as it thinks it can. Look no further than how well Google Books replaced physical libraries, and you'll understand why I'm skeptical.

But what about something truly revolutionary? It's always difficult to prognosticate—and it's so easy to get it wrong (anyone except me remember DAT tapes?)—but some emerging technological trends are rising that point the way toward what once seemed unimaginable. While a city "built from the Internet up" may be a bit of a Silicon Valley pipe dream, a city based on a mixture of transformative technologies incorporating online digital information, wired physical surveillance and tracking devices, new concepts of financial and social transactions, and an unbreakable provenance may be right around the corner—for better or worse.

We need look no further than the development of Decenturion, an out-of-nowhere organization that is looking to establish a mysterious IT-based crypto-society. The organization touts itself as "the first fully decentralized autonomous state in which economy, governance and communications are built on a *blockchain*" (Decenturion, 2018). While it certainly sounds impressive, how this is accomplished isn't entirely clear.

Blockchain, which is a relatively new technology, forms the basis of most cryptocurrencies such as Bitcoin, Litecoin, Zcash, Dogecoin, and the like. The currencies are designed to work as an exchange medium using cryptography to secure transactions, to control creation and distribution (i.e., digital issuing of the coin), and to verify transfers among its stakeholders. Blockchain, as the basis of this exchange, functions as a ledger in digital form that allows users to track any and all changes made to it. As a result, the ledger provides a simulated digital provenance for the information to prevent unwarranted copying, reduce fraud, and eliminate theft. Blockchain is touted as an unhackable system; as a result, it forms the necessary sense of trust essential to financial and social transactions.

Based on this, I assume a person's "citizenship" identification in Decenturion would be recorded within the base blockchain ledger, allowing the "state" to keep track of all the digitally recorded actions of a particular citizen. It wouldn't matter where they lived, then, or what language they spoke, so long as they were part of the registry. It's certainly an interesting concept that moves beyond current geo-political boundaries and social contracts. But several immediate questions about this mysterious group come to mind. First, who can join? How much would it cost? What benefits are there to joining? Are there drawbacks? Is it even legitimate?

Of course, the use of blockchain can be extended beyond cryptocurrency uses (and the Decenturion experiment) and is moving into the control of digital media. The problem with digital copies of media, such as audio recordings or photographic images, is that they can be easily replicated, copied infinitely and redistributed, or altered and repurposed. However, if digital media were bound by blockchain ledger rules, a digital provenance could be established, allowing for provable ownership of something typically seen as ethereal in its binary nature. This might prove useful in the fight against fake news, especially deep fake videos. We would be able to see any manipulations made to the originals in telltale signs in the blockchain ledger.

On the downside, though, one can imagine the problems that would arise with the technological omnipresence of the blockchain's registry combined with a social credit system and the use of an overarching surveillance system. If this happens, as it seems China is intent on doing, we are not far from a kind of "digital dystopia" where we are all bound by ironclad and unhackable digital contracts in the form of blockchain code (Pandey, 2018). The result would be a decentralized, omnipotent, and unassailable tracker of every aspect of one's life. And these so-called smart societies, not dissimilar to the utopian drive propelling Decenturion and Google City, are being proposed in nascent forms across the world based on more granular versions of "the cloud," called fog, or mist computing. Dubai and other cities in the Middle East with deep pockets from oil reserves have been proposing such smart cities that track their inhabitants and are designed to anticipate their needs.

A BREAKDOWN OF THE LIBERAL WORLD ORDER AND CONSTRUCTING THE SURVEILLANCE STATE

We are awash in the datalization of the world, stemming from capitalist systems that run on an internal tension between artificially created scarcity and the inherent abundance of digital information. Ultimately, the problem in the United States stems not so much from the coercion of governments or the force of military juntas and totalitarian states forcing their wills upon us with their violence. We have, instead, willingly bought into the loss of privacy and the erosion of our rights in exchange for some minimal benefits online (Haselby, 2018). We have come to accept, perhaps like the proverbial boiling frog, a slow-warming but steadily growing discomfort, which we are fooling ourselves into believing will not get much worse. It just can't get worse, can it?

With other paradigms of governance based on blockchain, AI surveillance, or social credit, as well as authoritarianism itself, it is no foregone conclusion that capitalism will prevail. Surveillance capitalism in particular seems to take the worst aspects of worker exploitation and unequal class power structures while also overthrowing long-established conservative policies, norms, and societal structures. In most ways, it's a Faustian bargain. For short-term, even minimal, gains, we wind up having our freedoms eroded and our privacy lost. And even if we are able to resist their seductive charms or if the ideas are proven to be to too good to be true, the powers that seem to be pushing and the temptations for people to sell out their brethren seem to be too great.

In the cautionary tale of Theranos and Elizabeth Holmes, we see in the failure and fraud of one company exactly what we are up against. There are whole industries willing to sell parts of us, no matter how small or large or essential, out to their investors. Mining data from our own blood tests seemed incredibly attractive to many investors, even snookering some very famous people (Heffernan, 2018). Elizabeth Holmes's company failed in this instance and was punished for her deceptions. But the germ of the idea still remains: wearable or embedded technology monitoring health and physiological reactions and conditions at all times is the future.

This all-encompassing health monitoring may be helpful to a select few people with chronic health conditions. But where is the oversight? Where are the limits to this? Does the company providing this monitoring service get a free pass to sell our data? Does it get to sell things to us when it sees, for example, that our blood sugar has decreased or blood pressure has increased? We can't rely entirely on the oversight or the goodwill of a company's board of directors to expose the truth, either. It is easy to speculate that for all the data Theranos has collected on users regarding blood samples, it likely still exists on servers or hard drives somewhere. And, as we have seen among various Internet-shamed casualties in the media who said or wrote something regrettable or vile years ago, the information doesn't just die because we've forgotten about it. It is conceivable that out of the ashes of one Theranos there will rise another company just like it under a new name bent on dominating the market for the data they can extract from our bodies.

The next logical step may be the diminishment of these concentrations of power in the name of stability and security. One hesitates to rely on slippery slope logic to make the case for eroding rights and diminished privacy, but sometimes the canary in the coalmine is an accurate predictor of someone's impending fate. Depends on the canary, of course. Depends on what's killed the canary, too. But woe to us when social media, Google, and the other giants in the tech world begin to surveil our own banking and other financial records, as Facebook recently proposed (Glaser et al., 2018). It is clear that the world is changing in ways we cannot even imagine and moving at lightning speed. The clearest evidence of this is in the new ways that people are conceiving of organizing not only economic systems but also social systems through emerging technologies, as in Decenturion's example. While it is obvious that our current systems and methods of industrialization are unsustainable, especially in light of current climate change and the reduced capacity for our planet to absorb and reduce the amount of CO_2 in our atmosphere, nothing viable currently exists to replace them.

Yet, as with all new technologies, their promise seems to outshine the problems associated with them. We constantly fall into the same traps, technology after technology. As with all new digital technologies, the initial benefit seems to be a little too blinding, forcing us to not see the surveillance and tracking capabilities that further encroach upon our lives. Blockchain, for example, which ironically was used to help create cryptocurrencies to hide one's identity when exchanging money, can now be used to further track and create unbreakable identification schemes of economic activity through its ever-tracking ledger technology. Decenturion seems to be able to accomplish the same thing for its "citizens": buy into its system of digital currency and online activity and you can benefit from its cadre of co-citizens living wherever they choose—a world without borders that could only work if everyone were clearly both anonymized in terms of physical whereabouts and national "identity," yet fully tracked within the confines of Decenturion's digital systems. It may work as an independent society for some time, but like many digital technologies, it can be replicated and reapplied somewhere else once the code is shared and reworked. It is unclear to me if this will be a benefit to people or a horrible mistake. I am unsure if we are replacing a flawed but relatively free system of living for one that eliminates freedom entirely.

REFERENCES

Acxiom. (2018). On-demand webinar: Data privacy: What the consumer really thinks. Acxiom LLC. marketing.acxiom.com/US-WBNR-DMADataPrivacy -LP-Ondemand.html?&utm_source=twitter&utm_medium=social&utm _campaign=edu-dma-webinar.

Ben Shahar, O. (2016). Privacy is the new money, thanks to big data. *Forbes.* www .forbes.com/sites/omribenshahar/2016/04/01/privacy-is-the-new-money-thanks -to-big-data/#255fccda3fa2.

Decenturion. (2018). decenturion.su.

Edwards, B. (2014). *The rise of the American corporate security state: Six reasons to be afraid.* San Francisco: Berrett-Koehler.

Epsilon. (2018). The industry's most advanced data-driven marketing. Epsilon. us.epsilon.com/.

Foster, J. B., and McChesney, R. W. (2014). Surveillance capitalism: Monopoly-finance capital, the military-industrial complex, and the digital age. *Monthly Review.* monthlyreview.org/2014/07/01/surveillance-capitalism/.

Glazer, E., Seetharaman, D., and Andriotis, A. (2018). Facebook to banks: Give us your data, we'll give you our users. *Wall Street Journal.* www.wsj.com/articles/ facebook-to-banks-give-us-your-data-well-give-you-our-users-1533564049.

Greenwald, G. (2014). *No place to hide: Edward Snowden, the NSA, and the U.S. surveillance state.* New York: Metropolitan Books/Henry Holt.

Haselby, H. (2018). Orwell knew: We willingly buy the screens that are used against us. *Aeon.* aeon.co/ideas/orwell-knew-we-willingly-buy-the-screens-that-are-used -against-us.

Heffernan, V. (2018). Elizabeth Holmes' downfall has been explained deeply—by men. *Wired.* www.wired.com/story/elizabeth-holmes-downfall-has-been -explained-deeplyby-men/.

Karlin, M. (2014). Six reasons to be afraid of the private sector/government security state (interview with Beatrice Edwards). Truthout. May 16. truthout.org/articles/ six-reasons-to-be-afraid-of-the-private-sector-government-security-state/.

Leetaru, K. (2018). When will cities begin to monetize their residents' data? *Forbes.* www.forbes.com/sites/kalevleetaru/2018/07/19/when-will-cities-begin-to-monetize-their-residents-data/#4b86fbce4661.

Melendez, S., and Pasternack, A. (2019). The data brokers quietly buying and selling your personal information. *Fast Company.* www.fastcompany.com/90310803/here-are-the-data-brokers-quietly-buying-and-selling-your-personal-information.

Pandey, E. (2018). How U.S. tech powers China's surveillance state. Axios. www.axios.com/china-us-technology-surveillance-state-5672b822-fdde-45f9-ac77-e7b5574e9351.html.

Scola, N. (2018). Google is building a city of the future in Toronto. Would anyone want to live there? *Politico.* www.politico.com/magazine/story/2018/06/29/google-city-technology-toronto-canada-218841.

Wolfie, C. (2017). *Corporate surveillance in everyday life: How companies collect, combine, analyze, trade, and use personal data on billions.* Vienna, Austria: Cracked Labs.

Zuboff, S. (2015). Big Other: Surveillance capitalism and the prospects of an information civilization. *Journal of Information Technology, 30,* 75–89. doi: 10.1057/jit.2015.5.

II

DRINKING DIRECTLY FROM A FIRE HOSE: THE IMPACT OF INFORMATION GLUT, CONSPIRACY THEORIES, AND INTERNET BALKANIZATION

5

Information Overload and How to Combat It

Where is the Life we have lost in living?
Where is the wisdom we have lost in knowledge?
Where is the knowledge we have lost in information?

—*T. S. Eliot, "Choruses from 'The Rock'"*

TOO MUCH OF A GOOD THING

There are times when I'm online and I find myself going in a loop: from one website, let's say it's the *Washington Post*; to the next, Yahoo!; to yet another, *Axios*; and back again. Around and around. In almost every way this is really dumb. I just checked the site a few hours or even a few minutes ago but find myself mindlessly and needlessly going back. Some of this is just the force of habit and unexamined nudging. I see an article, get a rush of interest at seeing another article, and then get caught cycling back to the original article. Why, it occurs to me from time to time, when I have literally *billions* of possible topics and webpages online to go to, do I haunt the same few sites? Why do I find it so hard to go out of my way to view something completely random? The answer obviously escapes me since I keep doing it. But it happens in any number of situations: buying wine, choosing music, looking for a book in a large bookstore, or browsing my Netflix feed. Perhaps we can chalk it up to the impact of modern life and our society of automated overabundance and planned scarcity. First-world problems, I guess.

But why is this tendency to freeze in the face of so much information such a universal thing, if it's primarily a "first-world problem"? And is it really so modern? In some ways, we are drawn to repetition and are hardwired to enjoy things we have done many times over. If, for example, you have a large collection of music, whether it be digital or vinyl or compact disc (or even 8-track tapes), you will likely repeat and return to the same few albums or songs within your collection more than any others (Spiegel, 2014). In fact, it's been determined in research studies that "90 percent of the music we listen to is music we've heard before" (Margulis, 2014). Perhaps it's a limitation of the human mind, but when confronted with innumerable choices and wide vistas of free content, we tend to go with what we have chosen in the past. In the case of music, there's something about the repetitiveness of it that comforts as it entertains.

This tendency to narrow down our own choices is not limited to music or those websites we frequent. There are other examples that may speak to other problems related to too many choices. Confronted with a huge selection of red wines, each with a different terroir and grape varietal, I find myself unable to choose one and, instead, buy the one I bought the last few times. Sometimes it's just too difficult to decide with so many variables. I curse our modern abundance, but I probably shouldn't. It is an issue facing anyone with a large number of options. In extreme cases, too many options paralyze us into not making any choices at all! When faced with a large bookshelf of books or a thousand channels on cable, we forgo choosing anything. We back off and maybe leave the bookstore or settle with staring at the channel guide. Or we procrastinate, delaying the difficult choice, putting off that essay we need to write for class (or that chapter due to my editor). But I digress. When we run up against these limitations of the mind and psychology, we could be said to be suffering, in part, from *information overload*, an old problem that seems to chronically affect humans across all eras and all civilizations.

A (CONCISE) HISTORY OF INFORMATION OVERLOAD

In this modern age of big data and incessant information bombardment, it might come as a big surprise that people have complained for centuries, even millennia, about too much information. It is nothing new, as Roman philosopher and orator Seneca reminds us: *Distringent librorum multitude* ("The abundance of books is distraction"). The bible has a little to say on the matter too: "Of making many books there is no end; and much study is a weariness of the flesh" (Ecclesiastes 12:12). Additionally, every technological advance in history related to writing and publishing has, in some way, been perceived as impacting our capacity to handle information for the worse.

People, it seems, like to complain about new stuff.

In Ancient Greece, for example, Plato lamented the development of the written word as the destroyer of people's memories, which were prodigious at the time as a result of "memory palace" techniques widely in practice. The Roman Codex took the parchment scroll into a more portable and storable format, allowing for the development of larger personal libraries, which became a fad among the wealthy—even if they didn't know how to read. Seneca's admonition about too many books couldn't stem the tide of upper-crust fashions, apparently. The printing press from the fifteenth and sixteenth centuries seemed to provide new sources of information anxiety to the people of that time, even as it improved the speed and scope of how ideas and information were shared. Some of that complaining may be out of a frustrated desire to collect it all. The desire for a worldwide encyclopedic—or *encircled* knowledge, in other words—is a long one, stemming back, again, to at least the Greeks and Romans.

It seems, too, that as long as information has been gathered and collected, either in comprehensive libraries such as Alexandria's or in localized monasteries, people have struggled to find effective means of managing information (Blair, 2010, p. 14). These methods of trying to corral information include writing itself (either as hieroglyphs or as alphabets and cuneiform) and using it to compile lists. Copious note-taking and the development of concordances and bibliographies further helped to summarize or identify important works. People also accumulated texts and began organizing them by subjects, book titles, or author names. Limiting the quantity of books out there through so-called weeding or developing a "canon" of the best and most important texts has helped people to manage the growth of information. Finally, people ensured information could be more efficiently shared by compiling "digests" and abridgments of important works or creating anthologies, which date as far back as the Ancient Greeks and literally means a "collection of flowers."

While this historical print perspective is important to reflect upon for its impact on current collection development practices in our physical libraries, digital media and technology compounds the problem of information overload. The examples above speak primarily about printed materials designed to last centuries but which often did not. Print media was often held only by the very rich. Distribution channels were incredibly fragile. Canonization and anthologizing were (and are still) also subject to the political forces and power structures that shape their development, often marginalizing the less powerful.

We are now, however, working with an entirely new beast when it comes to information technology. Digital media proliferates through copies independent of the resources that created them. As long as electricity is available to power it, digital information can be replicated, changed, shared, and remade until the limits of the system have been met. It is not quite infinite, but it is close enough sometimes for practical purposes. As a result, the ability to stockpile information quickly grows beyond our modest capacities to govern it by brain power alone.

It is also more difficult for people to accurately ascertain the overall quality of digital media. While books and CDs are often judged by the quality of their containers' physical characteristics (the aphorism is not always right!), digital media are much harder to evaluate in terms of their own physical properties. The pulp dime-store novels of the 1930s and 1940s have literally been ignored because of the cheap materials that went into making them. Sometimes the cheapness of the container acts as a stand-in for the cheapness of what's inside. In this light, the Internet is a game-changer when it comes to democratizing information, while it is also contributing to our own cognitive overloads. When everything is stripped of its container, it gets harder to separate the wheat from the chaff.

Such anxieties have a way of seeming new and unique, especially when they are associated and intertwined with emerging technologies. But they are, in fact, deep-seated human behaviors responding to very similar situations.

STATES OF CONFUSION: SYMPTOMS AND CAUSES OF INFORMATION OVERLOAD

So what is information overload and how do we identify it? The term itself has come to mean a lot of different things to different researchers over the years. One definition sees information overload as how much information people can incorporate into their "decision-making process" before their ability to make an accurate decision starts to decline (Eppler and Mengis, 2004).

At some point, in other words, we lose our ability to make an effective decision. The key is figuring out how and when this happens. As demonstrated in figure 5.1, our accuracy in making a rational decision starts to decline at a certain point. For these researchers, information overload is really a matter of measuring a person's ability to make rational decisions against a theoretical peak or optimal set of conditions. But this actual limit may be hard to find, and so it may not be easy to determine when or how someone might actually be experiencing information overload.

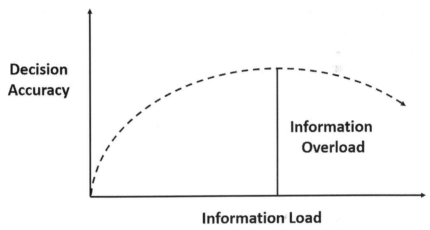

FIGURE 5.1
Graph showing accuracy in making decisions declines when the amount of information a person needs to process increases too much. *Eppler and Mengis (2004); redrawn by author*

Another way of looking at information overload is concerned less with that characteristic curving decline and looks more at a person's innate abilities. When the amount of information goes beyond our ability to process it, we are said to be overloaded (Eppler and Mengis, 2004). This is somewhat similar to the previous theory, since it still assumes there is a decline from "optimal" conditions. But the main difference is that the theory focuses much more on our own natural mental limitations than on the amount of information a person may have encountered, or even the types of decisions that have to be made. People, it is argued, reach this state of stress and confusion when they are pressed up against their mental limits. It really points out that people are not always the most rational individuals who make clear-cut decisions. We are subject to irrationality and physical interference (such as pain or joy or depression) and, as a result, prevented from consistently processing information rationally.

Going a step further, some see information overload in terms of mental and physical capacity only, as if our attentions or mental fitness were like buckets that reached their limit when too much information fills them up (Eppler and Mengis, 2004). Of course, information is not necessarily a thing with physical properties to begin with. How, for example, does one measure an amount of information as a countable thing? How much would fill up our own personal mental buckets? Twenty words? Five sentences? This book chapter? Thinking about it in this way, it seems a little ridiculous.

Energy levels also play a role. Overload happens, in some theories, when you try to add and process information beyond your available physical energy. When you surpass your physical and mental energy, information overload is said to have occurred. This means that it could happen to any person at any time, even within the same day (say, after a large lunch or after a sleepless night), depending on the level of energy you have at that moment. But the problem is that, as useful as this metaphor or image may be to visualize information overload, the truth is that a switch does not merely get flipped once an unseen limit or boundary is surpassed. We are all creatures bound to our physical rhythms, and our intellect falls and rises based on these.

As a result of these inconclusive results or unpredictable variables, some have turned to the role of time limits and pressure in information overload. We've all experienced from time to time at work or in our personal lives the trouble of making a decisive decision when rushed or hurried. Having to meet deadlines, especially those imposed upon you by someone else, can impact your sense of information overload. The less time you're given to complete something, the more acute the sensations of information overload can seem. You could envision this as the intersection of demands for processing information for the task and the time available to complete it sufficiently. The other concepts mentioned above focus on the internal workings (and personal limitations) of a person, but they also fail to acknowledge that external conditions contribute to this feeling of anxiety and stress.

Yet there's also the problem of the nature and type of information you're handling. It's believed that simple tasks and generic information (i.e., emotionally neutral subjects) will contribute far less to a person's feeling of information overload than information that's emotionally charged. Deep and complex information may be far more difficult for people to process, and as a result, people might be more likely to experience information overload with such "heavy" information. Overload is caused not merely by the *quantity* of information, cognitive and physical limitations, or even external pressures such as deadlines and time limits, but *also* by the type and nature of the information itself. Some are triggered by past traumatic experiences that others might find neutral (Eppler and Mengis, 2004). As we'll see in chapter 11, online moderators suffer trauma and even show symptoms of PTSD from the amount and nature of the extreme things they see and read online. In the end, external benchmarks and measurements cannot entirely explain all the variations people have in their capacities to process information. Sometimes it boils down to personal subjective experiences. Our personal state of being as well as our sensitivity to triggers has just as much an effect on us as anything else.

Ultimately, information overload is the result of a combination of important factors. There may be physical measurable limits reached or more subjective causes to the problem of information overload. Some limits are personal and context-specific. Other limits are the result of the amount of data encountered, measurable quantities of information, or the cause of specific time constraints and deadlines. Sometimes it's the type of information, and sometimes it's the person triggered by the information. Sometimes it's the time of day or the level of physical energy we have. No matter, it is still important to find out what our limitations are and how the new technology we're exposed to impacts it. How we can cope and alleviate these problems can be devised once we isolate the causes. The fact that we see so many causes reveals that we can now devise multiple approaches to improving our lives.

PROPOSED SOLUTIONS AND COPING STRATEGIES

So how *do* we improve our lives? How do we find a way to cope with the deluge of information that we constantly encounter? How do we find ways to cope with the various causes of information overload? What can we do to alleviate the external causes of information overload while also addressing the internal ones? This section will address a few solutions and coping strategies.

One thing we can do is to actively organize the information we find. On the bright side, this is often done by us habitually—even unconsciously at times.

Think about your house: envision where you keep your keys, your jackets, or your record collection. Keeping them in one general spot—one locus—is an important aspect of information management. At work, if you keep things in piles or in folders, you are employing information management techniques. If you keep your books arranged on a shelf, you are working in information management. You are keeping the forces of information overload at bay by keeping your world, and your mind, ordered. Libraries, of course, over the millennia have done this on a much larger scale, acting as protections against a rising tide of information. They keep entropy at bay, in a sense, as they organize life and information with their rational categorization and clustering of ideas. Libraries have solved specific information management problems and allow users to find things a little more easily, helping to alleviate many of the problems we associate with information overload. They help users find their way through the glut of information.

But when the amount of information goes beyond what a person or even a large organization can reasonably read through, as is happening now, we are in trouble. To alleviate problems of information overload, or "infobesity" as they call it, some people are advocating severe reductions in the amount of information a person encounters at any one time (Bawden and Robinson, 2009). They see information glut as similar to fast food: full of empty calories and light on substance. So, instead of managing and collecting all possible information through a scheme or plan to keep it, people should instead learn to minimize their sources of information.

This approach is known as "satisficing." In essence, a person decides to read no more beyond their initial need for information. *Just enough is good enough* in this strategy. A wider approach is ignored in favor of a narrower analysis or truncated summarizations. As you can imagine, this leads to some extreme situations where people choose to ignore pretty much everything outside their field of interest. Call it the curse of overspecialization. If too many books are published a year, the argument goes, it's better to just ignore them all (Good, 2017). This is not entirely uncommon when professors become experts in their fields. We end up having to ignore other specialists in different fields just to stay up to date in our own!

Interestingly, some scholars are using digital information technology to work around the problem of having too much to read. One scholar in the humanities, for example, started to examine eighteenth- and nineteenth-century British literature texts by mining the digitized book corpus. The scholar avoids reading full texts personally and instead relies on an algorithm to present snippets of information, terms or phrases, that he can later sort through. It's an extreme position to take, but one that has its roots in information overload. The scholar has abandoned reading altogether—one of the major skills of a humanities scholar, by the way—and now sifts through data looking for patterns.

Not all advocate taking up such an extreme position, however. In fact, along the lines of the "slow food" movement, people are starting to suggest doing the opposite: "slow reading." These practitioners advocate quality over quantity and extended time to understand a single text over speed reading through numerous texts. It is not much different than the memorization techniques taken by orators like Cicero, Isocrates, Demosthenes, and others, who advocated memorizing and internalizing a few foundational texts. There is no substitute for the quality of the read, in other words. At bottom is the realization that not everything can, nor should, be read. Selectivity and discerning taste becomes an essential tool. One can conceivably slow it down and learn more about a subject this way than through skimming and cherry-picking across a wide surface.

The most important ally, however, in the fight against information overload appears to be education itself, and the learning of *how* to learn. The need for "meta-literacy," or "information literacy," in which people are aware of *how* and *why* they learn, becomes essential. It can be argued that the various concepts of cognitive overload, information overload, and information anxiety should fall under the wider concept of meta-literacy. If meta-cognition, cognition, and self-reflection are pillars of information literacy, it follows that anything impacting a user's ability to accomplish these things should be addressed as well. The pathology of information overload seems to have a therapeutic solution in awareness of how one learns.

Information literacy can also help to point out our own personal blind spots. Left unaddressed, information overload can have a negative effect on a person's ability to learn, make decisions, or seek out new things. At the heart of information overload is a kind of discomfort, a feeling of unease, brought on by uncertainty and ambiguity. People are often confronted with multiple viewpoints or radical interpretations of the same set of facts. This causes some painful dissonance, especially if that information is emotionally or politically charged. Information literacy and an awareness of meta-literacy could help alleviate information overload in people as it alleviates cognitive anxieties and the feelings of cognitive dissonance.

Withdrawal from new information makes the tendency even worse. People will often discount the views that make them uncomfortable, even if the counterargument is based on irrefutable evidence. This leads to even further extreme views. Making things more difficult, too, is the fact that learning how to tolerate ambiguity is not so easily done. Some researchers have found that despite being highly educated and well-trained in their fields, engineers have been more likely to adopt radical ideologies (Farrell, 2015). So, it is not merely that learning factual, discipline-specific information can help one avoid this information pathology among people. Instead, a balanced education focusing on meta-literacy skills provides the necessary tools for incorporating and balancing alternative viewpoints and learning how to better tolerate ambiguity.

MEMORY PALACES AND DIGITAL DETOX: STRENGTHENING YOUR MEMORY, REDUCING STRESS

It has been suggested in numerous reports that our constant exposure to mobile devices and information technologies, convenient as it is, ultimately diminishes our capacity to remember things. On one hand, it's a helpful crutch to get through some of the daily tasks we have to navigate in this hyperconnected world. We no longer need to remember phone numbers by heart since they are stored right there in our cell phones. We no longer need to even remember our wallets as long as we have our phone to pay with electronic cell-phone bank transfers or debits. But the unnoticed downsides to this immediate convenience may be especially negative in the long run. The Greek philosopher Plato believed that our reliance on written language would diminish our capacity for memory, which he felt was the highest form of mental exercise. Readers who skimmed through a text without memorizing it, Plato argued, would never reach a deep understanding of the text, unlike those who had taken the time to memorize it. He may have been onto something. If we are unable to remember much of anything factual, and significantly addled as a result of our weakened memory, it may be that we are more prone to information overload. New technologies have essentially made the memory map unnecessary for all of us while exacerbating our cognitive overload.

But perhaps all is not lost. We can always resume the memorization techniques of the ancients. In past eras, creating a "memory map" or "memory palace" was seen as the best method for keeping your life and your information managed. (As an aside, our word *topic* is derived from the Ancient Greek word *topos*, which was the "place" in our mental map where we would keep a concept or information we wanted to remember.) Look on Amazon and you'll find any number of self-help book titles (e.g., *Moonwalking with Einstein*; *The Memory Book: The Classic Guide to Improving Your Memory at Work, at School, and at Play*; and more) that will point the way to improving your memorization techniques, including how to build your own memory palace. The human mind is uniquely fashioned for remembering places and direction.

Try it yourself. (Go ahead, I'll wait.) Close your eyes and visualize your house. What rooms do you have? What is in them? Even if it's sketchy at first, over time and with practice, you'll be able to remember quite a lot about your house through this very simple exercise. It requires, however, that you abandon your memory crutches and trust your mind to show you what you already know. You also may find yourself strangely calmer and refreshed from this exercise, too.

After years of screen dependency, some people are returning to these older methods of information organization, aided in part by unplugging and undergoing a "digital detox." The concept is fairly simple: remove or reduce the amount of time you spend in front of a screen performing daily Internet-specific tasks or habits. The lack of distraction can work wonders, especially as smart phones and mobile devices have been "linked to reduced social interaction, inadequate sleep, poor real-world navigation, and depression" (Molloy, 2019). Reducing that overabundance of screen time proves to be beneficial to personal mood, improved sleeping habits, and, of course, a better memory. Though it is unclear if it's merely the change of scenery or environment that helps, it is obvious that spending too much time tied to a screen, focused on continuous external stimuli, will have some wearing effect on the mind's attention. If anything, at least remove the phone from your bedroom so you're not tempted to use it in the middle of the night. Perhaps the better rest will help keep your mind fresh and might stave off the fatigue that also contributes to cognitive decline and overload.

Information overload continues to play a large part in many of the information pathologies we experience in our daily lives. For many of us, trapped in our own sound bubbles and echo chambers, it is comforting to cut off the ideas that bother us. We prefer to avoid the feelings of anxiety and ambiguity that arise from cognitive dissonance. As a result, satisficing can play both a positive and a negative role in our lives. If we constantly shut out alternative views, we may lose touch with the way things really are. On the other hand, we just cannot read or encounter everything. It requires a balanced and pragmatic approach. It requires an understanding of one's limitations—which is perhaps the hardest thing to ever know—and an attempt at meta-literacy or metacognition. Solving the problem may be as simple as identifying the symptoms of information and cognitive overload and finding ways to alleviate them, especially by reducing our screen time and, by extension, improving our memories.

REFERENCES

Bawden, D., and Robinson, L. (2009). The dark side of information: Overload, anxiety and other paradoxes and pathologies. *Journal of Information Science, 35*(2), 180–91.

Blair, A. (2010). *Too much to know: Managing scholarly information before the modern age.* New Haven, CT: Yale University Press.

Eppler, M., and Mengis, J. (2004). The concept of information overload: A review of literature from organization science, accounting, marketing, MIS, and related disciplines. *The Information Society, 20*(5), 325–44.

Farrell, H. (2015). This is the group that's surprisingly prone to violent extremism. *Washington Post.* www.washingtonpost.com/news/monkey-cage/wp/2015/11/17/this-is-the-group-thats-surprisingly-prone-to-violent-extremism/?utm_term=.061a2799ff87.

Good, A. (2017). The rising tide of aliteracy. The Walrus. thewalrus.ca/the-rising-tide-of-educated-aliteracy/.

Margulis, E. (2014). *On repeat: How music plays the mind.* New York: Oxford University Press.

Molloy, F. (2019). Smartphones are making us stupid—and may be a "gateway drug." The Lighthouse. lighthouse.mq.edu.au/article/august-2019/smartphones -are-making-us-stupid-and-may-be-a-gateway-drug.

Spiegel, A. (2014). Play it again and again. NPR. www.npr.org/sections/health -shots/2014/04/07/300178813/play-it-again-and-again-sam.

6

Conspiracy, Belief, and the Compromising of Research

We see vividly—painfully—how technology can harm rather than help. Platforms and algorithms that promised to improve our lives can actually magnify our worst human tendencies.

—*Tim "Apple" Cook (CEO, Apple)*

WHAT'S A CONSPIRACY THEORY?

What's a conspiracy theory? We hear the term all the time, but what does it actually *mean*? We hear about absurd ideas borne out of ignorance, partial truths, willful blindness, or more. Most of the time we dismiss these things as "crackpot" theories, the delusions of guys in tinfoil hats, or just bizarre untested and untestable ideas from untrained minds. We are often mildly amused or incredulous at the titillating headlines in the *National Enquirer* at the supermarket cashier. *Who would believe such stuff?* we ask. *It's got to be a joke.* Yet one thing is certain: it sure sells papers.

The idea of a conspiracy theory is based on a form of radical skepticism, where our basic conception of a shared reality is questioned at its most fundamental levels. The most famous example of this concept is Rene Descartes's thought experiment about "the evil demon" that exists to fool us into believing a complete illusion of the external world. In modern versions, this demon is reimagined as a person reduced to "a brain in a vat." The implication of this, regardless of which version you consider, is that if you cannot be sure that you are *not* a brain in a vat, then you cannot rule out the possibility that *all* of your beliefs about the external world are false (Hickey, n.d.). The *Matrix* film trilogy gives us the cinematic version of this type of radical skepticism, where humanity is deceived in mind while the body is enslaved by evil machines for a malicious purpose.

As far-fetched as this sci-fi story is, the kernel of truth is this: the uncertainty we face when considering whether reality exists is enough to push people over the edge so much that they begin to *systematically* and *habitually* doubt their own senses and discount the evidence of a testable reality. In simpler terms, doubt about the reliability of our senses creeps in, and we begin to distrust everything. Much of the psychological impetus for these conspiracy theories, and radical skepticism in general, is the mistrust of power and feelings of losing control—whether it's over one's body, one's senses, one's government, or one's self-knowledge. In thrall to a nightmare vision of powerlessness at its most simple and compelling, we envision not only ourselves as having no control but that this sense of autonomy we take for granted is an illusion. More worrying is that the conspiracy becomes a debasement of the basic purpose of information itself, which is *to inform*, and turns any fact or concept into just another form of manipulation. The rabbit hole never ends.

The phenomenon of radical skepticism bleeds into everyday life. We notice the fevered paranoia of the fringe, in their mish-mash of right- and left-wing theories of conspiracy and complete madness: flat earthers; JFK riddles wrapped in mysteries, inside enigmas; faked moon landings; chemtrails in the sky; "Paul is dead" Beatles speculation; Roswell aliens; false flags; crisis actors; spies; fake news; alternative facts; lizard people/reptilians; doppelgängers and evil twins; you name it. Apparently, and very depressingly, at least twelve million people hold the belief that "lizard people control politics" (Bump, 2013). These paranoid fantasies often come out of nowhere to completely consume susceptible people. These fantasies appear, in some ways, to be an attempt to explicate those feelings of powerlessness that people sense in their lives. The five-week period in 2018 from the end of September to the end of October—which saw us witness the Kavanaugh confirmation madness, the increased attacks on the media ("CNN Sucks," "dishonest media," and other slogans), the #MAGAbomber, and the murder of eleven Jews in a synagogue in Pittsburgh—clearly illuminates the problem of losing the touchstones of truth and a reliable, confirmable grasp on reality.

FABRICATION AND FALLACY: THE TOOLS OF CONSPIRACY
AND BRAINWASHING

One of the easiest methods of fooling people is by subverting the truth from within well-established channels for communicating factual information. This occurs in the realm, especially, of scientific research and the misuse of rhetorical tools meant to persuade, but also in the debasement of journalism and its credentials. Let's start with a telling and contemporary example of how conspiracy theories are born. The Brett Kavanaugh Supreme Court nomination hearings is a good example of how conspiracy and compromised and specious methods of "evidence gathering" can enter into the public forum and be used in ways to convince others of absolutely outrageous things. Dr. Ford's accusation of sexual assault by Brett Kavanaugh in the early 1980s was like a heat-seeking missile that brought out a partisan anger I have not seen in ages—or at least since the last news cycle. Some of that madness stems from the utter bombshell nature of the revelations and their timing. Some of it is a symptom of the hyperpartisan, "politics-as-sports-fandom" nature of life in the United States in the early twenty-first century, not unlike the "Blues" and "Greens" chariot-racing fans from the early Byzantine Empire centuries ago. Everything old is new again.

Some of this current madness stems from the rearing of uncomfortable truths that many in middle age had forgotten. In my own case, it brought me back to my own public high school days during the late 1980s, where house parties, drinking and drug use, and lax parental oversight were pretty commonly bragged about among peers (but never admitted to authority figures).

No matter where on the political spectrum you fall or whom you actually choose to believe in this matter, Dr. Ford's accusation succeeded in bringing out some of the most egregious and ham-fisted defenses I have ever seen, including this whopper from Ed Whelan, who was at the time of the incident president of the Ethics and Public Policy Center and a Kavanaugh confirmation adviser. On Thursday, September 20, 2018, Whelan took to Twitter "with screenshots from Google Maps, scans of old yearbooks and floor plans ripped from Zillow.com (among other *not-at-all-absurd* pieces of 'evidence') ... [and] tracked down a potential location for the attack that Ford alleges. He then publicly identified another Georgetown Prep classmate of Kavanaugh's as Ford's possible attacker, though Whelan is careful to say he has 'no idea what, if anything, did or did not happen in that bedroom at the top of the stairs' or whether any sexual assault even took place" (Emba, 2018).

Sadly, the absurd and willful obfuscation of the accuser's story is far from the worst thing about this. We were also observers of the birthing of a conspiracy theory *in real time*. As Whelan lays out what he sees as a "logical" defense of Kavanaugh, we see his bad-faith argumentation become clear: using specious logic, guilt by association, and circumstantial evidence, this so-called lawyer fabricates a counterargument against a possible sexual-abuse survivor. He even *fingers another potential suspect*, which opens him up to litigation and liability. Talk about malpractice. And this person is supposed to be a leader for a center on *ethics*! Making things even worse for those who want to know what was said and when, the man subsequently deleted his tweets. Researching this only one day later, I had to rely on the *secondary* reporting of a blogger on Mashable, an Internet platform and media company of notoriously uneven quality, in order to get the screenshots of the Twitter feed to find out what Whelan actually wrote (Sung, 2018). See figure 6.1 for these tweets.

This inability for people (including journalists, historians, and even the mildly curious) to gather evidence contributes to the general problem of

FIGURE 6.1
Screenshot of a deleted Twitter stream from Ed Whelan, president of the Ethics and Public Policy Center, from September 20, 2018, asserting an unfounded and misdirecting conspiracy theory that suggests another person assaulted Dr. Christine Ford. Deleted soon after posting. *Twitter*

combating all conspiracy theories. When there is no recourse to evidence, we are at a complete disadvantage to fabulists of any persuasion or political slant. They can spout out anything, delete it, and then reappear (or not) with it later. This is the true tragedy of Twitter and the online world. They are contributing directly to the breakdown of logic, verifiable information, and credibility by allowing the deletion of these false statements and not providing a stable context for *anything*. For all is malleable, even information, and the truth bends to *truthy*.

And this is how conspiracy theories are born: they wither in the light of truth and stable contexts but grow in darkness and behind obscured factoids. When deletion and redaction are allowed in the public record, as with Ed Whelan's tweets, we lose the chain of evidence that allows us to discredit these false accusations. And false accusations, like rumors, have a life of their own.

Muddying the waters to obscure what really happened has real-world consequences. Less than a month later, Cesar Sayoc sent out a dozen pipe bombs targeting Democratic Party officials and well-known media figures, such as Robert DeNiro and CNN News. The man, who was captured on tape attending a Trump rally in February 2017, was allegedly spurred on by the anti-truth rhetoric spouted by the president of the United States. The pipe bombs were meant to frighten and intimidate those believing an opposing view—an act of domestic terrorism, in other words. Thankfully no one was injured or killed and the man was remanded into custody. But the subsequent weekend following the terrorist threats from Sayoc brought us the murder of eleven innocent people in a synagogue as a result of the paranoid fantasies of a white supremacist and anti-Semite in Pittsburgh.

It becomes clear after witnessing these events unfold in real time over a period of weeks that there is a downside to the belief in faulty information. When people are not held in account for their malicious beliefs, it harms those around them. This is not an academic, theoretical position, either. It is a realization that the freedom to believe whatever you like must be tempered with the responsibility to not harm others. The stakes are incredibly high.

ERROR AND FAKERY IN RESEARCH

Another issue that impacts our ability to tell truth from fabrication is the development of junk science, falsified research, and the rise of "predatory" publishers. One of the most notable frauds in recent years that still seems to endure was the study led by Andrew Wakefield that linked the rising rates of autism in children to measles vaccinations. No study in recent history appears to have contributed more to the confusion and persistent misinformation about vaccinating children than this study. Indeed, the survey from Public Policy Polling in 2013 showed that more than *sixty-two million people* in the United States still continue to believe that vaccines are linked to autism (Bump, 2013). It does not seem to matter that the study was debunked and discredited. The researcher himself admits to using compromised evidence, while simultaneously harboring an extreme conflict of interest. This is troubling. Autism by itself is troubling and fraught with emotion for families, but to give false hope to parents where there is none and then to expose other children unnecessarily to the risk of disease is even worse.

Fakery in research is not an isolated phenomenon. Indeed, this is but the tip of the iceberg. Research conducted into the number of retractions and corrections made in the top research journals found that there were more in the top-tier journals than the lower tiers. Think about that: more errors were found in the top journals than in the so-called second-rate ones. It seems counterintuitive that higher-ranked journals should have more errors. But Björn Brembs (2018), in an explosive paper on error in academic journals, asserts that

> data from several lines of evidence suggest that the methodological quality of scientific experiments does not increase with increasing rank of the journal. On the contrary, an accumulating body of evidence suggests the inverse: methodological quality and, consequently, reliability of published research works in several fields may be decreasing with increasing journal rank.

The most prestigious journals also account for the largest amounts of retractions (Fang and Casadevall, 2011), and most of these retractions stem from publishing fraudulent statements or mistaken results (Fang et al., 2012).

Why is this? One recent example may help to illuminate why this happens. Kohei Yamamizu of Kyoto University's Center for iPS Cell Research and Application (CiRA) publicly admitted to falsifying eleven of the twelve figures he had published in his research article for the journal *Stem Cell Reports*. Why would he risk his reputation and that of the university to publish a paper? Yamamizu claims he merely wanted "to make the paper look better"

(Murai, 2018). But that combination of perfectionism and self-doubt is only one part of the equation. The competitive nature of the short work term Yamamizu was engaged in as a post-doc (i.e., *temporary*) researcher contributed to the high-stakes pressure to perform that comes with academia. In order to continue working for the university, Yamamizu felt an immense pressure to ensure that his paper was accepted by the leading journal in his field. This might have extended his time at CiRA, where 90 percent of the scientists are on short-term contracts, or could have provided him with an opportunity to work elsewhere on a permanent basis. If he was not retained or hired elsewhere, his career would have been effectively over. As it stands now, it's over anyway.

Yet other universities in Japan have also seen other scandals related to research institutes as well. For example, at Tokyo University, Japan's top-ranked university and one of the top research institutions in the world, "fabrications and falsifications of data and images were detected in five papers supervised and coauthored by two researchers at its Institute of Molecular and Cellular Biosciences" (Murai, 2018).

But let's not pick on only Japan. Institutions worldwide have dealt with the problem of fraudulent and misapplied data in research. Indeed, error has been found in a significant number of journals. But honest errors are generally more easily and quickly spotted. *Fraudulent* error, which is purposely applied misstatements of fact, however, takes more time to identify and correct. Yet, even upon identifying errors, retractions and corrections are relatively rare. Only about 10 percent of errors spotted in a survey of articles were eventually corrected (Linton, 2013).

Furthermore, the overall hypercompetitive nature of academia generally prevents meaningful changes from taking hold. As in Yamamizu's case above, the pressure to show positive results in research is crushing. It is not enough, for example, that your research shows a "null hypothesis" (i.e., that results were inconclusive). In some disciplines, despite all the time, effort, and funding it took to complete the research, it is better *not* to publish at all if your hypothesis is proven to be inconclusive. The pressure for positive results is so great that people will go to extreme lengths to stretch and contort their results—"torture the data," as my colleague at California State University, Northridge Abe Rutchick says—until the data fits the hypothesis. "Hacking" *p-values* is one common technique to bring out statistical significance in the data. In other words, numbers can be misused to manipulate conclusions. Sometimes it's a minor tweak with little consequence, a little white lie, so to speak, to help foster or preserve a career. Sometimes it fuels conspiracy theorists like anti-vaxxers.

Some researchers have also resorted to using purposefully vague or hedging language to get results past peer reviewers. One study suggests that there are identifiable characteristics of fraudulent research found in authors' writing styles. Researchers might use more jargon or confusing linguistic constructions in a fraudulent paper than one that is aboveboard, for example (Carey, 2015; Markowitz and Hancock, 2015). This "obfuscation index" of identifiable fraud strategies suggests that there is a clear problem in the academic publishing world. Solving these problems will require clear reform in the way that research is conducted, published, and tested for accuracy. Reform in this area of academic publishing is also stymied by the rise of the predatory journal, which accepts payment for publication and usually rejects no one. Peer review may or may not be offered. Universal acceptance, however, is guaranteed.

Ironically, the prestige gained by their past notable publications may end up being a liability in the long term for the high-tier academic journals. Part of the increase in errors noticed may be that there are more readers of these articles and therefore more people testing the validity of the results. Some of the rise in noticed errors may also be because getting tenure or securing prime positions in academia are dependent upon appearing in these journals. As a result, people may be more likely to throw caution to the wind and fudge results for short-term gain. In the long, drawn-out process of academic publishing, which can sometimes require years to publish a single article, it's better to retract or amend later than to never get accepted at all.

Finally, there is the ongoing problem of private companies impacting how scientific results are reported. Many of us are familiar with the dubious science that came out during the 1950s and 1960s about the "benefits" of cigarette smoking. So-called Big Tobacco underwent a systematic misinformation campaign to discredit the science behind the ill health effects noticed in tobacco users. Their own false reportage and junk science delayed the eventual release of the truth about the true damage that cigarettes were wreaking on smokers, as well as those around them. It was only after "smoking gun" evidence was found that the tobacco companies admitted just how widespread their misinformation campaign really was.

In a contemporary example that sinks to the level of the tobacco companies, gun manufacturers in alliance with the National Rifle Association have
applied political pressure on the U.S. federal government by pushing for bans
on federal funding for gun-related research (see, for example, 1996's Dickey
Amendment, which states, "none of the funds made available for injury prevention and control at the Centers for Disease Control and Prevention [CDC]
may be used to advocate or promote gun control"). The suppression of data
and fact goes a long way to hide the truths that people should have access
to. It would work wonders for American gun control policy if research were
actually funded by the U.S. federal government. Instead, we are beholden to
special interests that prefer to speak of conspiracies, such as "false flags," "crisis actors," and hoaxes (like with Sandy Hook), or fantasy solutions that rely
on arming teachers or a "good guy with a gun" whenever the reality of gun
violence rises again. Thoughts and prayers become a deflection from the reality that *hard data* on gun violence and the impact that gun control provides
is being suppressed for purely ideological reasons.

But these problems point to something of even greater danger than denial:
the misuse, misapplication, and manipulation of data itself on a massive scale.
The *Chronicle of Higher Education* points out, in an excellent analysis of how
private companies are still interfering with academic research, that social
media companies like Facebook have come to control the "data about human
behavior" (Parry, 2018). It is not so far-fetched to imagine that companies,
especially those with something to lose if negative information is released,
will try to suppress, modify, or alter data to fit their own conceptions for their
own benefit. The results shared in academic research may be ultimately suppressed, or worse, skewed toward misinformation, if we cede control of the
data about ourselves as well as the means of sharing and protecting it. As with
Big Tobacco in the 1950s, or the gun manufacturers right now, when research
is manipulated or curtailed, we lose the ability to make informed and data-
driven decisions to shape reasonable public policy.

THE DATA EXPLOSION AND ITS IMPACT ON RESEARCH METHODS

Big Data Grows Too Big to Fail

Some of the problems we are facing in terms of information pathologies
are not merely psychological or the result of deep-seated flaws brought
about by external pressures or internal radical skepticism. Some of the

problems of fakery in research and the spread of misinformation and conspiracy theories are exacerbated by the technological advances that have changed the way information is gathered and examined. It is no secret that we are living in an era characterized by the vast amount of information we have willingly created about ourselves and the amount of information that is observed—both overtly and covertly—by any number of third parties, be they governmental, public, or private. Almost anything connected to the Internet can gather data on us, including our smart phones and computers, wearable devices (e.g., Fitbit, etc.), household appliances, and even our children's toys. All of these have mechanisms capable of gathering data on us, including our locations, speech patterns, opinions and ideas, and general living habits. It all adds up to a massive stream of information, capable of being mined and analyzed, bought and sold, interpreted and re-interpreted for monetary gain or political advantage.

But what impact does the use of large data sets, or "big data" analysis, have on the ways in which science is conducted or new knowledge is generated? What happens to the scientific method when the data set grows beyond a single person's ability to parse it? How does it alter the ways in which scientists conduct their experimentation? Reproducibility in research, for example, has become a recent big issue, as some reports have suggested that a large number of experiments, especially in psychology and the social sciences, are not replicable. But how did we get into this situation? Let's examine how incorporating "big data" changes the way that scientists conduct their research.

The scientific method has been practiced over the centuries by building testable hypotheses. Experiments will either confirm a hypothesis to be true or prove it to be false. Correlations, which show links between observed events, are one of the things scientists look for, but they are not the most important thing. Instead, researchers have been mostly interested in finding out "the underlying truths" connecting events and conditions. A model helps us to identify the variables, draw out *useful* correlations, and see the connections. With a model we essentially connect disparate data sets together. But this long-standing method in science is steadily being altered by the amounts of massive data collected, separate from models and independent of hypothesizing. Indeed, where correlation was considered tangential to the model—one step in the longer process of drawing out connections—it is now being seen as *sufficient by itself* to understand complex systems and variables. As Chris Anderson (2008), editor for *Wired*, argues, "We can analyze the data without hypotheses about what it might show. We can throw the numbers into the biggest computing clusters the world has ever seen and let statistical algorithms find patterns where science cannot."

But what is lost when this method is pushed aside? Once again we have to reconsider the importance of models in science. For as we all should know, correlation does not equate causation. If we want to know the origins for something observed in nature, relying entirely on correlation can easily lead us astray. The "Redskins Rule" is a good example of how correlations can be misleading. People noticed between the years 1940 and 2000 that whenever the Washington, D.C., NFL football team won the final home game of the season prior to an election year, the party of the incumbent president retained the presidency, and when the team lost, the opposition party won. While interesting, and a representative example of a correlation, this is also explained entirely as coincidence. There is no way that the outcome of the football game directly impacted the results of an election months away. Similarly, relying on correlation too much in research may lead one toward some similarly ridiculous conclusions.

The reliance on big data may also lead to problems of reproducibility in research. One of the characteristics of a successful hypothesis is that it can be reproduced by others under the same conditions. Without this ability to test and retest, we are unable to verify if something is true or is false. As eminent philosopher of science Karl Popper has said, an untestable hypothesis is an assertion of faith and "does not speak about reality" (Popper, 1959). As a result, attempting to replicate a study is essential to the scientific method. Without it, it is not science. However, the Center for Open Science (COS) has shown that only 36 percent of replicated studies in psychology research resulted in statistically significant findings, a serious decline from the 97 percent in the original studies they drew from (Open Science Collaboration, 2015). With such a large drop in the replication of the original results, it is becoming clear that research methods and results need to be more clearly examined. Unfortunately, the deluge of data that reviewers must sift through, the dropping of hypotheses and modeling, and the impossibility of replication all point to a growing crisis in research.

On the Perils of Dataism (or, When You're a Hammer, Everything Looks Like a Nail)

There is also a danger of being seduced by current ways of thinking that are considered to be "paradigmatic." Right now, many scientific disciplines rely heavily on the methods outlined above: that big data (and massive amounts of information) will yield the best results as long as appropriate algorithms are generated. Artificial intelligence provides the promise of this type of power to parse the hidden meaning within sets of numbers or massive corpuses of digital texts. But the danger in this approach is that one starts seeing *everything* in terms of data.

Yuval Noah Harari, author of the highly influential and widely popular book *Homo Deus: A Brief History of Tomorrow*, seems to have fallen into this trap. As well-known as it is, overall, it is a disappointing book full of egregious errors and mischaracterizations, especially with respect to the relationship between data and information, which he seems to see as a simple hierarchical structure. Data, in his conception of it, leads to information, which leads to knowledge, and finally wisdom. Such hierarchical models are somewhat useful as a rule of thumb, but the relationship between these various states of being is far more complex (and problematic) than this model would suggest. The conclusions he draws from this very flawed model are suspect at best. For example, Harari sees future world civilizations devising new "data" religions that rely on an algorithm to give meaning to people. "Just as free-market capitalists believe in the invisible hand of the market," he writes, "so Dataists believe in the invisible hand of the data flow" (Harari, 2017, p. 391). Fair enough. Someone might be convinced that everything stems from how data flows from one thing to another. People have been convinced of far stranger things. It may not be a testable theory, and not scientific in the Popperian sense, but it is certainly a nice image.

He continues, however,

> As the global data-processing system becomes all-knowing and all-powerful, so connecting to the system becomes the source of all meaning. . . . You are part of something much bigger than yourself. . . . Data religion now says that your every word and action is part of the great data flow, that the algorithms are constantly watching you and that they care about everything you do and feel. Most people like this very much. (Harari, 2017, p. 391)

This is so far-fetched that it borders on the ridiculous. Most fundamen-talist sects—whether Christian, Buddhist, Islamic, or other—are in essence anti-technological movements that seek a way back to pre-technological times, when life was assumed to be simpler. A religion based on data and surveillance (called "Dataism" by Harari) would only serve to exacerbate these conflicts, especially as the system becomes "all knowing and all power-ful." One can imagine "information terrorists" or "data iconoclasts" finding ways to destroy the tools of the "Dataist" infidels. Harari's assumptions are far too simplistic to come true, especially as it ignores the way humans actu-ally behave.

He also seems unaware that data itself is not really a *thing*. It exists "with-out an essence of its own" (Borgman, 2015), only within the context of its ascribed purpose, easily changed and manipulated to meet the current needs of its users. Data is also in some ways an assumption about the world, a result of a philosophy that believes we can understand the world through gather-ing evidence. But, as we all know, so much escapes the purview of the data collector; sometimes the tool gathering the data is attuned to only a small scope, missing the remainder of the environment around it. Sometimes to gain anything useful from data, we have to cherry-pick what best serves our purposes while ignoring the rest. And, let's face it, if you have *faith*, you have no need for data anyway.

The lesson to take from Harari's viewpoint about "Dataism" is not the concept itself. Anyone can believe what he or she wants to. It is more a cau-tionary tale about how someone has succumbed to the seduction that digital information and data will somehow solve all our problems, while failing to look at the negative truths that necessarily come with it.

A Word on Self-Delusion

Now, I suppose, is as good a time as any to talk about self-delusion. What happens when otherwise intelligent and reasonable people become convinced that their own wild theories are the truth? What if I happen to become con-vinced suddenly that the moon landing really was faked and that all the evi-dence was fabricated? What if they are true believers and not merely trying to trick someone?

As mentioned above, once an idea becomes untestable and lies outside es-tablished methods and processes for examining it, it ceases to be scientific. It has happened a lot in history: as people have strived to make gold from base elements, find the "original" Noah's Ark in archaeology, confirm and prove the historical existence of certain biblical figures, justify a flat earth, and so on. We need to be reminded that once we stop looking at the evidence, and consistently checking and cross-checking it, we cease to be scientific. We cease to be rational interlocutors of nature. Instead, we cross the line of the cutting edge of new ideas and transgress into factual dead ends, unverifiable nonsense, and intellectual culs-de-sac. As Veronique Greenwood writes about her own grandfather, Francis Perey, whose scientific theories in physics were seen as the workings of a deluded mind, "There's a fine line between being a maverick scientist and being a little bit lost" (Greenwood, 2018). And the tragic nature of this is not that a promising career or a bright light is led astray. No. The tragedy is ours because we are all capable of this type of self-delusion. It takes strength, education, and near-constant vigilance to maintain our clearest sight.

RECLAIMING THE INFOSPHERE WITH DAYLIGHT, VETTING, AND PROVENANCE

The philosopher Luciano Floridi identifies this overall phenomenon of error and misinformation in research and in the online world as the polluting of the *infosphere*. He describes the infosphere as a kind of information commons used to "rebuild trust through credibility, transparency and accountability— and a high degree of patience, coordination and determination" (Floridi, 2016). He believes people are susceptible to fakery and falseness because they appeal to preconceived ideas and vanities. Our frailty is all too human. He also argues that we have lived in a post-truth era for at least the past four hundred years, since printing became widespread. Considering how pervasive these problems are, and how negatively they impact our quality of life, it becomes imperative that we develop some solutions.

The COS has made great efforts to alleviate these problems. Their approach is to conduct meta-analyses of large-scale results appearing in scholarly literature. They provide a framework for exploring various science and social science disciplines, including the Reproducibility Project: Psychology (RP:P), the Reproducibility Project: Cancer Biology (RP:CB), Collaborative Replications and Education Project (CREP) and Crowdsourcing a Dataset, and the Many Labs project. The goal of these various projects is to attempt to replicate the results of well-known scientific research. In the cancer biology project, for example, they aim to learn "more about predictors of reproducibility, common obstacles to conducting replications, and how the current scientific incentive structure affects research practices by estimating the rate of reproducibility in a sample of published cancer biology literature" (COS, 2018). In other words, they are attempting to find out what prevents research from being reproducible, including how external pressures (e.g., "publish or perish") or internal biases (e.g., untested paradigms or mistaken assumptions) affect the results.

The COS is also investigating another method of improving how data is used and reused in research by using social media to examine data sets. They call this "crowdsourced data set analysis." It is described as "a method of data analysis in which multiple independent analysts investigate the same research question on the same data set in whatever manner they consider to be best" (ibid.). The purpose of this is to establish "a protocol for independent simultaneous analysis of a single dataset by multiple teams, and resolution of the variation in analytic strategies and effect estimates among them" (ibid.). The purpose of these and other methods in verifying scientific research is to improve our digital information commons (our infosphere) and to refine what we mutually agree to be true.

Blockchain is another recent technological advance that attempts to provide provenance for digital information and data. There is generally no consensus on a common digital history (CB Insights, 2018). We are finding that online everything is malleable. Contexts shift in perpetual cycles. Trust and truth become malleable and subtly subverted. Blockchain, however, allows users to track over time any alterations and additions made to its digital "ledger." More importantly, this technology allows "untrusted parties to reach consensus on a common digital history," something completely missing in our online discourse right now. The application of this technology is most widely seen in cryptocurrencies and the use of digital identifications to help track financial transactions. It is also proposed as a solution for a universal ID that is capable of being used beyond borders. It would be of help, for example, for the children of refugees to help keep track of them and to prevent their kidnapping.

The problem with blockchain, however, is that it can also compromise privacy and anonymity. These are exploitable by bad actors looking to control through digital means and the asymmetrical power structures inherent to surveillance capitalism. Yet blockchain, along with crowdsourcing, might also provide a clear provenance for the data sets used in scientific research. This external verification would help to improve the ways in which the data are analyzed while also providing documented evidence of how the researcher used the data.

So where do we go from here? It is clear that we need better methods and technologies that provide a fixed context and clear provenance for digital information and objects. As blockchain can contribute to a shared digital history, we may need to rely on ever more sophisticated methods of tracing our digital histories, our bread-crumb e-bits, if you will. That would help to solve some of the problems we are facing with falseness in research and the proliferation of fake news. But these won't change some of the fundamental flaws in humanity, especially the tendency to accept rumors and conspiracy theories. There is a clear need for a sense of moral and ethical responsibility when it comes to our beliefs. William Kingdon Clifford writes in "The Ethics of Belief" from 1877 that "it is wrong always, everywhere, and for anyone, to believe anything upon insufficient evidence," which "is no longer hyperbole but a technical reality" (Uribe, 2018). This may have seemed an unnecessary thing to point out twenty years ago, or even seemed a bit too extreme, but the need for ethical responsibility may need to be codified as part of a new twenty-first-century digital-age imperative.

Perhaps we were not meant to understand everything. Try as we might, the grand unified theory of everything may always lay tantalizingly out of our reach, looming above us like the stars in the night sky: visible but ultimately unreachable beyond our own computer and technologically mediated devices. The most insidious of these pathologies of thinking, the radical skepticisms we see in the worst conspiracy theories, require the most individualized attentions and may have the least possible universal solutions. It is up to individuals, instead, to become aware of their limitations and realize that faith and fact can be easily mixed up.

REFERENCES

Anderson, C. (2008). The end of theory: The data deluge makes the scientific method obsolete. *Wired*. www.wired.com/2008/06/pb-theory/.

Borgman, C. (2015). *Big Data, little data, no data: Scholarship in the networked world*. Cambridge, MA: MIT Press.

Brembs, B. (2018). Prestigious science journals struggle to reach even average reliability. *Frontiers in Human Neuroscience, 12*, 37. doi.org/10.3389/fnhum.2018.00037.

Bump, P. (2013). 12 million Americans believe lizard people run our country. *The Atlantic*. www.theatlantic.com/national/archive/2013/04/12-million-americans -believe-lizard-people-run-our-country/316706/.

Carey, B. (2015). Stanford researchers uncover patterns in how scientists lie about their data. Stanford News. news.stanford.edu/2015/11/16/fraud-science -papers-111615/.

CB Insights. (2018). What is blockchain technology? CB Insights Research. www .cbinsights.com/research/what-is-blockchain-technology/.

Center for Open Science. (2018). Research. cos.io/our-services/research/.

Emba, C. (2018). Enough with the doppelganger theory. *Washington Post*. www .washingtonpost.com/blogs/post-partisan/wp/2018/09/21/republicans-enough -already-its-time-to-slow-down-on-kavanaugh/?utm_term=.cb993344e146.

Fang, F. C., and Casadevall, A. (2011). Retracted science and the retraction index. *Infection and Immunity 79*, 3855–59. 10.1128/IAI.05661-11.

Fang, F. C., Steen, R. G., and Casadevall A. (2012). Misconduct accounts for the majority of retracted scientific publications. *Proceedings of the National Academy of Sciences of the United States of America 109*, 17028–33. 10.1073/pnas.1212247109.

Floridi, L. (2016). Fake news and a 400-year-old problem: We need to resolve the "post-truth" crisis. *Guardian*. www.theguardian.com/technology/2016/nov/29/fake-news-echo-chamber-ethics-infosphere-Internet-digital.

Greenwood, V. (2018). Science is full of mavericks like my grandfather. But was his physics theory right? *Atlantic*. www.theatlantic.com/science/archive/2018/11/science-full-mavericks-like-my-grandfather-was-his-physics -theory-right/574573/.

Harari, Y. N. (2017). *Homo deus: A brief history of tomorrow*. New York: HarperCollins.

Hickey, L. (n.d.). The brain in a vat argument. Internet Encyclopedia of Philosophy. www.iep.utm.edu/brainvat/.

Linton, J. (2013). All journals need to correct errors. *Nature, 504*, 33. www.nature .com/articles/504033d.

Markowitz, D., and Hancock, J. (2015). Linguistic obfuscation in fraudulent science. *Journal of Language and Social Psychology, 35*(4), 435–45.

Murai, S. (2018). Unstable work seen as a factor as Kyoto University admits iPS researcher falsified data in paper. *Japan Times.* www.japantimes.co.jp/ news/2018/01/23/national/science-health/kyoto-university-says-researcher-ips -institute-falsified-data-formed-foundation-paper/#.W66sb_knbDA.

Open Science Collaboration. (2015). Estimating the reproducibility of psychological science. *Science, 349*(6251), aac4716. doi: 10.1126/science.aac4716. osf.io/ezcuj/ wiki/home/?_ga=2.171171241.867980999.1541804292-1739785169.1540940296.

Parry, M. (2018). The Chronicle interview: Private companies are destabilizing academic research. How will scholars respond? *Chronicle of Higher Education.* www.chronicle.com/article/Private-Companies-Are/244927?cid=at&utm _source=at&utm_medium=en&elqTrackId=3429af8ce9dd4a319db9cb543 ebe7212&elq=7d1c366dd9014d448e97f53e1cd39419&elqaid=21218&elqat=1&elq CampaignId=10098.

Popper, K. (1959). *The logic of scientific discovery.* London: Routledge.

Sung, M. (2018). Man tries to use Zillow to prove Kavanaugh's innocence and ends up owning himself with screenshots. Mashable. mashable.com/article/ed-whelan -uses-zillow-kavanaugh-innocence-conspiracy-theory/#o8JPtt93zaqY.

Uribe, F. (2018). Believing without evidence is always morally wrong. *Aeon.* aeon .co/ideas/believing-without-evidence-is-always-morally-wrong.

7

"Whose Culture Is It, Anyway?"

Ownership of Culture in a Digitized World in Danger of Fragmenting

[The Internet is] completely laissez-faire, with no really effective engines for choosing or searching and everybody being much more interested in the economic and material aspects of it than some of the aesthetic and ethical and moral and political questions attached to it.

—*David Foster Wallace (Lago and Wallace, 2018)*

A "MASSIVE" PROBLEM

It is impossible to overstate the impact that the Google Books digitization project had on people in the early 2000s. When the project was initially announced, there were literal outcries against it from libraries, cultural institutions, publishers, authors, readers, and more, who felt blindsided by the sudden announcement of the digitization project. Google's approach didn't help things either. They pushed ahead with their ambition to digitize "all the books" and include them in a digital library for the whole world, to replace what they saw as the library's fusty, old-fashioned card catalog. This completely ignored the fact that many libraries had *already* moved on to digital library collections (with e-journals and digitized student theses) at least ten years before this announcement and that libraries had begun dropping card catalogs *as early as the 1960s* in favor of electronic ones. But this was *new* and it was *Google*—which had rarely made any mistakes on its way to the top of the Internet search world—so everyone took them (and their suddenly deep pockets) very seriously.

Looking back on it all now, it's funny that we ever really took them *that* seriously. Despite the number of books scanned (now about 30 million), this still represents less than a quarter of the estimated 130 million books that have ever been published. When you look at the quality of the scans, you'll find that they are sorely substandard. Access any digitized book at random and you'll likely find significant amounts of poorly scanned pages. When you look at the metadata (i.e., the information about the book itself), you'll find errors in the publishing information, the book title, the author's name, the dates of publication, and so on. When you try to find books in a series (say, for example, the Loeb Classical Library's fifty-one volumes), it's difficult to know if you've found all of them. When you try to search for texts in the digital library, you are left with the sneaking suspicion that titles have been missed, that different editions of the same title are unaccounted for, and that errors have been left unfixed. Additionally, you'll find that most of the texts are visible only in partial view, with only a select few pages available for readers, or they are completely inaccessible.

In light of their initial ambitions, the Google Books project can really only be seen as a complete failure. It has replaced *nothing*, and similar or related book-scanning projects have surpassed them in terms of sustainability and relevance. The HathiTrust project gathered the works of the university library partners in the Google scanning project and set about doing things differently: with transparency; due diligence in copyright clearance; the support of libraries, librarians, and information managers; and the use of established *library* best practices. The Internet Archive, another platform for open digital web content, also provides public domain books from the Google Books project and works with various communities and stakeholders to establish best practices for sharing all types of digitalized media, ranging from Grateful Dead concert bootlegs to video game emulators to independent music labels' records.

One of the more interesting aspects of Google's "Massive Digital Library" (Weiss, 2014), beyond the size of the collection they created, is the fluctuating conceptualization of *ownership* and *control* of digital content. Aside from the public domain materials that are by law open to all for use and reuse, Google has essentially staked a claim over the digital corpus it has created. It allows users to search through its index but not to browse or look through specific texts deemed to be under copyright control. Adding to the frustration for those outside of Google, getting at the details of the project over the years has been difficult. Many of the digitization partners, especially some of the academic partners (including Keio University in Japan), were required to sign non-disclosure agreements. As a result, any details about their book selection processes, their digitization techniques and best practices, or even the locations of their digitization labs remain *unconfirmed* (Weiss, 2014).

Prior to the resolution of the lawsuit via the Second Circuit Court of Appeals judge Denny Chin's ruling in 2015 (*The Authors Guild, Inc., v. Google, Inc.*), Google had arranged a settlement in 2008 with libraries and other institutions and authors to provide access to these books for a licensing fee. The Google Book Search Settlement Agreement was ultimately rejected three years later in 2011, and Google was forced to endure the trial to its end. Notably, Judge Chin wrote that it was "incongruous with the purpose of the copyright laws to place the onus on copyright owners to come forward to protect their rights when Google copied their works without first seeking their permission" (Chin, 2011). This prevented the company from essentially claiming a right to financial compensation through licensing of the digital corpus for the copyrighted works of millions of others, while also completely avoiding liability through settled agreement with the Authors Guild.

The case continued for another four years. Ironically, Google was able to prevail, despite the settlement rejection, as it was seen in the judge's later ruling to have provided a "transformation" of the original print materials into something new, with at least *some* public benefit. The defense of their project also hinged on the concept of using the data in a "non-consumptive" manner. What this means is that the texts can be searched and analyzed computationally in a way that is *not the same as a person reading a text*. As seen in the results of the Google Ngram viewer in figure 7.1, digitized texts are "mined" to extract data and evidence (in this case the frequency of words), rather than made available for traditional reading for information, scholarship, pleasure, or other purposes. The main difference appears to be the shift in perspective about the meaning of the texts as aggregated digital evidence (i.e., data) parsed by mechanical means. It is a novel distinction, to be sure, but one that unfortunately serves to *dehumanize* the original purpose of literature.

The problem now (and similar to Judge Chin's reasoning in the settlement rejection) is the limited access that *real* people have to this digitized corpus. Google controls access to the digitized texts, allowing researchers to

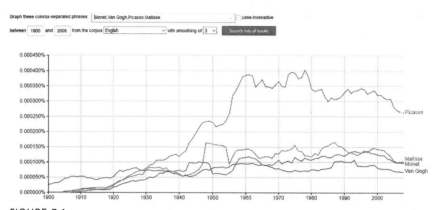

FIGURE 7.1
Who owns a book's data? Google controls access to author works for non-consumptive uses, as shown in Ngram Viewer screenshot above. *Google*

search through the dataset upon request but not to have much control over individual copyrighted content. Google also controls, in a sense, the reasons and motivations for why people would want to access the information found in those texts. People often browse and read at random beyond directed and research-oriented text mining. There really aren't a lot of people who will be willing to download the massive files of the Google Books Dataset (GDS) (2.9 terabytes, or 2,970 gigabytes, of data) or know how to parse the texts using appropriate algorithms once they have them. Even the provider of this set through Michigan State University admits the "dataset is not meant to be used as a source for reading material, but rather as a linguistic set for text mining or other 'non-consumptive' research" (MSU Libraries, 2018). Unfortunately, for most people, non-consumptive use equals no use at all.

But it also raises a set of truly difficult questions. Who really gets to control our culture when it becomes digital? And why? Is it Google or the authors (or their publishers) that get to take control? What allows Google to stake a claim over millions of works created by others over several thousand years? These questions will undoubtedly remain contentious and unresolved until new models and paradigms change how we view Silicon Valley and other IT disrupters.

The digital world and the new paradigms of information sharing have so altered the previous conceptions of who owns a culture that it is unclear anymore who should be the beneficiaries. This chapter will explore many of the issues raised by these new digital power structures and cultures.

DIGITAL CULTURES: THE NEW PARADIGMS FOR INFORMATION SHARING AND OWNERSHIP

Copyright and the Rise of Intellectual Property

The printing press has been called one of the greatest innovations in human history, accounting for the quickest possible dissemination of information for nearly four centuries from 1440 to 1840, until the development of reliable electronic communication media. We are still under the influence of the print world, even as its dominance is finally starting to wane as digital media rises. We live, to be sure, in a print-digital hybrid world, having not entirely abandoned paper and analog formats while also diving headfirst into digital ones. Yet some parts of our society have been slower to adapt to the changes brought about by electronic media than others.

Copyright law is one such area. Copyright law developed out of the early impacts of the printing press, where medieval guilds strived to maintain control over the works they created, preserve their power structures, and maintain influence within their societies. Even as authors and creators have been told that they are the beneficiaries of the law, over the centuries it has been seen that copyright law primarily protects publishers at the expense of creators. Profit in the publishing world depends upon the scarcity they create and subsequently regulate. Longer and longer copyright terms, as they have developed over the past two hundred years in the United States (and other countries, too), stretch that regulation far beyond its usefulness.

However, now that electronic media dominate how we publish things, we need to look at things in a different way. Digital online media operate on the same principle as the Xerox machine but taken to massive scale. As author and futurist Kevin Kelly (2016) suggests, "The Internet is the world's largest copy machine. If something can be copied and it touches the Internet, it will be copied." He clarifies this thought further in his book *The Inevitable*, "This machine copies every action, every character, every thought we make while we ride upon it" (Kelly, 2016b, p. 61). As such, the Internet stretches the original boundaries of copyright law and tests both its viability and its durability. To post *anything* online is to essentially agree to copies being made of it in order to share and transfer the data from user to user. On a small private network, this act of copying something in digits to send to another person probably doesn't violate the heart of copyright; on a massive scale involving millions or even billions of people, however, copyright regulations are dwarfed by the sharing of digital information across multiple platforms, networks, and systems. This ability to share anything, anywhere, at any time threatens the regulatory abilities of the media companies that control most of the copyrighted works. The music industry's heavy-handed penalization of regular people during the early 2000s at the height of the Napster file-sharing and downloading mania demonstrates this militant regulatory role that media companies can play.

We also cannot rule out, on the larger scale, the privatized interests that control digital media via proprietary software, hardware, and networks. Our devices now come with a specific political viewpoint built into them, which skews toward the neoliberal ideas of laissez-faire economics as mediated through devices designed to spur economic growth and shareholder satisfaction. If nearly all aspects of a society can be "imbued with the logic of the marketplace," as Trevor Owens (2018) describes it in his excellent book on digital preservation, digital media with its screen-mediated and profit-driven mantras are hardly transparent and neutral players. Companies control the devices, the content that can be displayed on these devices, and the avenues of access to them.

The free-market paradigm dominates American thinking to the point of *cant* and *propaganda*, which serves to ignore or downplay the flaws that exist in this perspective. The irony of the "marketplace of ideas" is that if the market determines what succeeds and what fails, as well as the prices of specific goods based on the consumers' demand for them, then a successful writer, artist, or musician will have to simultaneously balance both widespread celebrity with manufactured scarcity via stringent copyright enforcement.

It's contradictory at best and schizophrenic at its worst. Artists have to be both carrot and stick, exhibitionist and ascetic, simultaneously spurring demand for their works based on their notoriety, while also setting up barriers (and the justifications) to consume them. The art is tantalizingly put out there for the consumer to see, but it is also kept just out of reach, accessible for the right price to purchase and, ideally, *repurchase* in new and improved formats—rarely given freely to anyone, unless there is a catch.

The convoluted story of the "Happy Birthday to You" song is one example of stifling culture for the sake of profit. This one song, which was cribbed from a previous song published in 1893 ("Good Morning to All"), was litigated for decades by its publisher Warner/Chappell music, before it was finally proven in 2016 that it should have been in the public domain all along. But this was not before the publishers ruthlessly enforced their "rights" for nearly eighty years and charged commercial users of the song fees—including times when it was sung at children's birthday parties in restaurants or in Hollywood films. Ultimately, the song generated nearly $2 million per year for the publisher from its licensing fees. Some businesses created their own birthday songs just to avoid the fees (Reuters, 2016).

To add to the troubles that this cultural gatekeeping poses, in one of the more controversial legal decisions in the history of the United States, the Supreme Court ruled in *Citizens United v. Federal Election Commission*, 558 U.S. 310 (2010) that corporations have the same rights to free expression as a real human being. Anything can be corporatized, in this reasoning, and anything can be reduced to market forces, including the concept of "person." Generally speaking, the law discourages psychopathic power-grabbing in people, but in the form of a "corporation," it is seen as both profitable *and* justifiable. It is therefore not a longshot for corporations to begin asserting that, as "people," they should also have the right to access and control our culture at-large. The Google Books project shows this power-grabbing ambition on a grand scale: digitize *all* the books; disrupt the library, publisher, and author in one fell swoop; control all the books they possibly can through limited digital access; commodify the culture through advertising revenues while also forcing the books to be used in proscribed non-human but specifically Google-friendly ways. What Google and Facebook and the others in the "FANG gang" are doing is essentially claiming culture as a *corporate* right, not a personal, individual, or even collective right of living, breathing citizens.

Culture is, in this conception, the lowest-hanging fruit that is ripe for the taking and appropriate for monetizing and exists merely for the sake of marketing it to other corporations or selling back to people as "data"—in other words: *digital opportunism*. We should be very careful about how this will impact future generations. As future generations rely more and more on screen-mediated technologies, the bulk of our culture will be filtered and repurposed through them. Assumptions of transparency and neutrality in technology will be challenged as this comes to light. We will likely find that what we assumed to be transparent and neutral technologies are in reality opaque, created and supported by ulterior motives beyond our control to resist.

Copyright is just one aspect of the forces at play. There are other ways to regulate and control creative works as well, including patents, the development of proprietary data, and the rise of licensing agreements. This is given the catch-all description of "intellectual property." Yet this term is somewhat confusing to the average person. Samir Chopra, professor of philosophy at Brooklyn College of the City University of New York, argues that the "ubiquitous use of [the term] 'intellectual property' began in the digital era of production, reproduction and distribution of cultural and technical artifacts. As a new political economy appeared, so did a new commercial and legal rhetoric. 'Intellectual property', a central term in that new discourse, is a culturally damaging and easily weaponized notion." He continues, "'Intellectual property' covers a lot of ground" but, he asks, "What kind of property is this? And why do we refer to such a menagerie with one inclusive term?" (Chopra, 2018).

In his mind, the term, unlike specific terms like copyright or patents, grossly misstates the relationship that power and law have on creative and intellectual works—to our detriment, as well. The technology of digitization only makes the ubiquity of intellectual property even worse, chilling creativity for fear of litigation or just merely stepping on someone else's toes. Combined with new concepts of corporate "personhood" and the nearly unassailable ascendency of free-market laissez-faire economic worldviews, "intellectual property," as it is practiced and defined through an increasingly screen-mediated world, may entangle us all in its far-reaching morass—especially at a time when the Internet of Things is starting to track everything we do.

The Decline of the Commons and the Corporatization of Culture

As more items become copied and shared online, other aspects of our societies have started to decline, especially the information commons and the freely shareable and modifiable culture that we take for granted. Paul Heald's research, in one telling example, has shown that books still under nominal copyright restrictions between the 1920s and 1990s, a roughly seventy-year period of time, are *less likely* to be reprinted by publishers than books falling in the public domain (Heald, 2013). Recently published books from the 2000s and 2010s are still new enough to be findable, but if one wants to find a copy of an out-of-print text from the 1970s, you may be out of luck. These texts may be abandoned by the authors or their estates, meaning no one exists to claim them anymore. This is highly likely in the case of obscure books from the 1920s and 1930s as most authors would be at least 120 to 130 years old by now. The authors or their relatives may be unknown or unfindable. The publishing houses that held the copyrights may also be defunct and their former owners unreachable. But despite these realities, publishers are nevertheless unwilling to risk reprinting these works, even if they still contain relevance or value and some demand for them persists. Some publishers purposely sit on titles they own and wait for an interest to develop at a later date, like some in the film industry will sometimes option a film script to prevent a rival from making it.

The hole in our culture is also starting to contribute to "information deserts" that have a wider impact than just those directly affected areas. The large number of books available only in older, first editions places an undue burden on libraries or other memory organizations to keep such books available, even if fewer users are interested in them. As with anything that has suddenly become scarce, prices rise and prevent future users from reasonably acquiring them. The loss of bookstores selling used or even new books in local neighborhoods has declined in the age of Amazon. Not every neighborhood in the United States even has equal access to these overburdened libraries or small bookstores, and neither does every state in the union value or want to provide the funds for essential public services from government agencies.

In some cases, we fall back into the trap of monetized services. It is not far-fetched to imagine an Internet—seen as a utility until the recent net-neutrality repeal—that requires toll access to everything. Get ready for a literal nickel-and-dime, toll-road, pay-to-play Internet experience, where everything is available for a price, regardless of the legal permissions and broad rights provided in the U.S. Law Code's fair use provisions (17 U.S. Code § 107). Digital rights management (DRM) restrictions applied to music CDs in the early 2000s, for example, or the mistaken removal of videos from YouTube provide good cautionary tales about how software solutions and algorithms easily impede a person's right to use copyrighted content *fairly*.

This is not merely a technological issue, either. It is a constitutional issue and a legal *right* for people to have access to their own culture for the purpose of changing and improving it. First of all, fair use provides a lot of leeway for personal and transformational uses of copyrighted materials. Algorithms and software restrictions—which are designed specifically by corporations to fulfil their own specific goals—do not interpret the subtleties of copyright law very well. Perhaps they are designed in some cases to gloss over those subtleties. Second, the original purpose of copyright law was "to promote the Progress of Science and useful Arts, by securing *for limited Times* [italics mine] to Authors and Inventors the exclusive Right to their respective Writings and Discoveries" (United States Copyright Office, 2018). This concept of progress—and *not*, you'll note, profit—was considered so important to the founders of our country that it was *written into the constitution.* The key consideration here is that the amount of time for controlling the visual arts, written works, and scientific discoveries is *limited* and not meant to last forever.

In fact, as seen in figure 7.2, when the Constitution was first written in the late eighteenth century, the copyright term was only fourteen years with an additional fourteen years possible with registration—no more than twenty-eight years total. Now, it is no less than seventy-five years (life of author plus seventy-five years) but often closer to 120–150 overall, depending on the author's longevity. Imagine if we had to contend with copyrighted works from the time of the Civil War! No Ken Burns film, that's for sure. But that is the extent of the restriction (and confusion) that coming generations will have to work through. It helps no one—except Disney or similar content owners, perhaps—and it certainly doesn't promote progress in the arts or sciences.

Finally, the issue of excessively long copyright in order to protect works from piracy belies the fact that most works still under copyright lose their marketability due to lack of interest in them after a certain amount of time. The exceptions, such as the Beatles, Stephen King, Mickey Mouse, *Star Wars*, and the like, prove the point that most copyrighted works are forgotten after a period of time and are *rarely* revived once forgotten. For every *Moby Dick* or similar work ahead of its time rescued from the dustbin of history, there are thousands of forgotten works left inaccessible because of extended copyright terms. Heald's research demonstrates this decline in available texts in the physical print book world. But while the correlations he found between copyright status and being out of print is one thing, providing clear and predictable models of this effect is quite another.

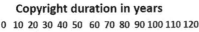

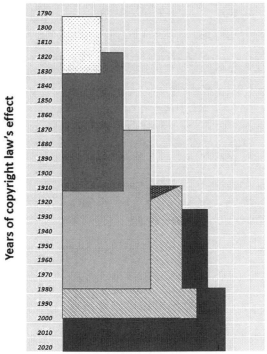

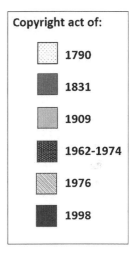

FIGURE 7.2
The growing length of copyright terms, starting at twenty-eight years in 1792; it now often exceeds one hundred years, when factoring in the life of an author plus seventy-five years, or 120 years for so-called corporate authors. *Wikipedia; redrawn by author*

Cristian Candia and his research partners have taken a step toward more clearly illuminating this issue. Their research paper, "The Universal Decay of Collective Memory and Attention," shows a mathematical model and quantified prediction for the forgetting and abandoning of artistic works within a society (Candia et al., 2018). These researchers argue that the attention paid to the arts in our culture fades over a specific and *universally predictable* period of time. In their study, they found that biographies published online about sports stars, for example, retained the longest period of attention in our society—approximately twenty to thirty years—but they gradually faded out after this period; popular music, on the other hand, seems to have the short-est period of attention—approximately five to six years (Candia et al., 2018). How quickly we forget! It is sobering.

Of course, you'll have noticed that this is a *very short period of time* in com-parison to the potentially 100 to 150 years of a typical copyright term. This raises the main question, then of why—if it is clearly fated for 99.9 percent of these works to be forgotten after a few years, or decades at most—do we persist in foisting excessively long copyright terms upon them? Aside from the obvious exceptions that might still make money for the rights owners and their heirs after a hundred years (looking at you, Bob Dylan; you, too, Mickey Mouse), the remainder of these works ought to be freed at some point much earlier than their full copyright terms. To do otherwise and insist upon keep-ing these works frozen in the law long past their relevancy ultimately contra-dicts the original intention of copyright law itself.

We must begin to ask ourselves not only what the problem of restricting content to ourselves will result in, but also what is the overall impact on a society that has its information restricted? What are the negative effects of restricting information about our own culture from ourselves? What hap-pens when a premium must be paid to access better quality information? The answer is obvious: we are ultimately stifling our own progress and killing the golden goose at the same time.

Internet Islands, Censorship, and Fragmentation: The Balkanization of the Web

The problems facing our culture are not just restricted to the notable flaws in copyright law. Other forces are at work that curtail the free flow of infor-mation online, resulting in information islands or deserts, where people are limited in the amounts of factual, non-politicized or non-partisan informa-tion they can access.

It certainly may come as no surprise to many informed readers that the World Wide Web is starting to show cracks in its unified front. The Internet started off as a relatively small, highly specialized communication network (DARPA) fueled by the utopian dream of information sharing and relative openness among its end users. As it grew, individual users, whether by pure innocent design or by wanting to believe the best that they'd been told about the Internet, focused on the individual benefits that openness and interper-sonal communications could provide. Those still exist, of course.

These important but improbable visions came to notable fruition in the Middle East during the so-called Arab Spring of 2010–2012. It has since that high mark of non-violent revolutionary zeal turned swiftly darker, more violent, and increasingly dystopian (Tufekci, 2017). Some of the countries of the Arab Spring experienced non-violent overthrow of their autocratic governments, such as Egypt and Tunisia, and stepped somewhat toward democratic leadership (though Tunisia is the sole remaining democracy); others such as Yemen and Syria fell into chaos and civil war. To curtail these violent events, quite a few governments resorted to Internet blackouts and censorship. Aside from the ongoing surveillance, spying, and hacking dangers that have become ubiquitous in online life, there is also the closing off of both minds *and* borders. The Internet in various regions of the world is rapidly becoming a fiefdom of warring factions, some political, some spiritual, some governmental, and some economical. The Internet is sadly, in a word, on the road to fragmenting.

Internet Fragmentation: An Overview, a report by the World Economic Forum, examines three potential factors for Internet breakup, including technical, governmental, and commercial fragmentation. In technical fragmentation, the basic infrastructure of the Internet breaks down in terms of interoperability and the overall exchange of data and information from a purely technical and infrastructural point of view. Governmental fragmentation, on the other hand, occurs when policy and actions from governing bodies prevent people from using the Internet for specific political purposes. Finally, commercial fragmentation occurs from business practices that constrain users from creating, distributing, or accessing information resources (Drake et al., 2016). Each of these methods of fragmentation represents a real threat to the Internet as a worldwide network and erodes the promise of digitally generated equitable relations between countries. These threats stem not only from the technological issues of networking the whole world in varying economic and geographical locales but also from government policy and international corporate practices. Indeed, the governmental and business fragmentation that we are beginning to see take hold in the web can occur simultaneously and in concert with each other.

One of the clearest examples of this working together to sequester the Internet along political borders and party policy is China's attempt at creating its own online network. Control of the citizenry seems to be the goal, and they have taken some extreme steps to close off the Internet to their countrymen, even as they use it to attack the West. Additionally, Google had apparently been *working in secret* and coordinating with the Chinese government to develop a new search engine that meets the protectionist needs of the Chinese Communist party. By creating its own version of the web—in a sense, one that predetermines and filters what citizens can and cannot view—China is setting up a parallel information highway of highly constrained bounds and electronic guardrails. Google has crossed into the realm of every other self-serving corporation. This is merely the latest in a long line of curious power-grabbing developments from that company.

To their credit, some of the Google employees working on these projects have come out against them. In an unusual approach, employees working on a project wrote an open letter to encourage Google to cancel their work on "Project Dragonfly," as it is known internally (Salinas and D'Onfro, 2018).

Their letter states:

> Dragonfly would . . . enable censorship and government-directed disinformation, and destabilize the ground truth on which popular deliberation and dissent rely. Given the Chinese government's reported suppression of dissident voices, such controls would likely be used to silence marginalized people, and favor information that promotes government interests. (ibid.)

Censorship is really but one more aspect of social control. It determines who can and cannot participate in the culture or determines the boundaries that those in a culture cannot transgress. Such pathological intentions with regard to free and open information make it an especially pernicious way of abusing power and marginalizing people whose viewpoints are seen as antithetical, heretical, or merely on the wrong side of power. As the Google employees state in their open letter, the company should "commit to transparency, clear communication, and real accountability" (ibid.). These are the values of a democratic society. Liberal democracies have the strength of their ideas as an advantage over closed and repressive societies. It is a shame that Google—and the other FANG companies for that matter—have made a calculated business decision to abandon them. Whose culture, *indeed*?

The Internet can function as a great tool for liberal democracies, provided that they can avoid the pitfalls of the neoliberal "market forces" that attempt to privatize information while also avoiding the traps of rising nationalism. Unfortunately, the fragmenting of the Internet will only make this type of nationalistic control and ideological censorship even more powerful, while also weakening the free societies in the world, as it essentially allows the foxes free rein in the henhouse. As the philosopher and political thinker Simone Weil suggests, democracies that devolve into warring factions unable to compromise cannot protect themselves against the rise of a political party whose sole aim is to destroy that democracy. The same may hold for the open web: certain factions exist and work within a free Internet seeking to undermine and destroy it.

A Note on Art in the Age of Mechanical Reproduction

Finally, problems with online culture and the battle for control over it are further exacerbated by the nature of digital media itself, which exists, at the bottom of it all, as copies of copies (of copies!), replicated repeatedly. There are some negative implications stemming from this fact. Walter Benjamin in his seminal 1936 work on communication theory, "The Work of Art in the Age of Its Technological Reproducibility," has suggested that the technologies that allow for facsimile reproductions of works destroy the original cultural artifact's uniqueness. He writes that "even the most perfect reproduction of a work of art is lacking in one element: its presence in time and space, its unique existence at the place where it happens to be" (Benjamin, 2008). The problem is that originality and uniqueness become harder to enforce the more widely something is copied and distributed. On the Internet, originality and uniqueness are subsumed by mass-scale copying and sharing. Digital objects are made unique only by their potential to be remixed or "mashed-up." Yet the irony of the mash-up, like a viral meme, is in its own susceptibility to become further subsumed by more mass-scale copies and dependent upon the digital platforms for ubiquitous sharing. It's a digital meat grinder for original content, mass producing new meat for the same grinder, ad infinitum.

Going back to Google Books and any of the other massive digital libraries, we should consider what other impacts they have on us besides their constant access or their artificial restrictions. What impact does the loss of an item's uniqueness have on our culture? On the positive side, we are able to see digital facsimile copies of rare Vatican manuscripts, for example, or old books that would be too fragile to touch with human hands. But what does the knowledge that we are looking at one of potentially billions of digitalized (and *datalyzed*) copies do to the uniqueness of those manuscripts? What does it do to the uniqueness of our culture?

Again, we turn to Benjamin: "That which withers in the age of mechanical reproduction" he writes, "is the *aura* of the work of art." Now aura is admittedly a rather unclear term here. What he likely means is that aura is an artifact's originality, its uniqueness in time and space, its location within a culture, and the esteem it carries in the hearts and minds of the people viewing it. He continues, "That withering [of aura] *kills our connection to tradition*, to the ineffable magic of the original, and—in short—to the entire history of how humans once related to art" (Benjamin, 2008). Losing that one-on-one connection to art means we also lose a connection to not only the truth of something but also the wisdom it was meant to impart.

This loss of connection and, I would argue, this lost context and provenance is profound. It leads, as noted previously in chapter 6 and later in chapter 9, to the information pathologies of hoaxes and conspiracy theories, fake news and misinformation, and the overall distrust of information you don't already know.

Additionally, with apologies to Oscar Wilde, one might argue that a culture that knows the price of everything knows the value of nothing. We have lost some of the *non-monetary* values that these unique objects carry within our cultures. We have lost the ability to see and interact with these cultural objects without a price tag attached to them, bound, as they are, by the abstruse moniker of *intellectual* property and mediated through patented screen technologies. They may be shared, or they may be locked behind paywalls or rendered inaccessible to those on the wrong side of the digital divide, but they have also lost their essences, their *auras*, their unique values to inspire and define the best aspects of any given culture. As one of my former professors in Byzantine art history and iconography once asserted, images were once priceless. They were objects to be revered. Now they are as common as dirt.

FUTURE DIRECTIONS IN DIGITAL CULTURES

So where do we go from here? What can the digital world offer us if its model of cultural and content ownership is so protean and the promise of people working together sours from mistrust and breakup? Ownership through the controlling of copyright has reached a bit of an impasse. It works for the largest corporations, the content publishers and broadcasters, but not always very well for the creators, who tend to litigate on their own with much less financial backing to do so or sometimes prefer not to protect their work as rigidly. Despite all this, there are a few bright spots and potential solutions to these ongoing problems.

Unfreezing the Public Domain

The public domain remains a vital part of an open and free information commons. In 2019, the public domain, after being frozen in place for roughly twenty years since the Copyright Term Extension Act (aka the Sonny Bono Copyright Act, aka the Mickey Mouse Protection Act) was passed in 1998, will finally begin to add new works. As Lila Bailey at the Internet Archive—one of our greatest online digital public libraries—reports, "Tens of thousands of books, films, visual art, sheet music, and plays published in 1923 will be free of intellectual property restrictions, and anyone can use them for any purpose at all" (Bailey, 2018). Each year after this, provided no changes occur to the current copyright law, works from subsequent years will begin to be released. In 2020, works from 1924 will be released; in 2021, works from 1925 will be released; and so on. New works from the past will finally begin to pass again into the public domain, allowing others to find and share them, reuse and rehash them. What we've missed in the two decades since the public domain froze is the ability to use past models for new things. We are roughly twenty years behind pre-1998 levels of public domain access. Had the law remained unchanged in 1998, we would currently be starting to access items from the 1940s.

The importance of this unfreezing cannot be overstated. As Bailey explains further, "The public domain is our shared cultural heritage, a near limitless trove of creativity that's been reused, remixed, and reimagined over centuries to create new works of art and science. The public domain forms the building blocks of culture because these works are not restricted by copyright law." A stronger public domain will absolutely help with the development of a more robust creative commons. People need to be able to see and use their own culture. They need to have the agency within their culture to decide what is of value and what is not. If they have limited or no access to it, judgment about the merits of our past cultural achievements cannot be made. Cultures are created by both our own acts of selective judgment and our desires to enact change. A broader, deeper, and more robust public domain will surely facilitate this.

Shared Cultures and Shared Power Structures: Rejecting the Digital Divide

There are models that exist that can help us to share power structures and provide equal access to cultural touchstones. These shared cultures can find a way to reject the abuses of power that some of the legal framework has institutionalized. When we ask, "Who gets to 'own' this culture?" rather than allow those holding all the cards to control access to content, we need more radical and shared visions of content and culture. We need new concepts of ownership beyond just copyright and beyond the rights management (especially DRM) that comes with copyrighted content. A newer, more holistic approach to the use and reuse of materials needs to be developed.

Some, for example, see the appropriation of cultural artifacts, especially in the digitization and online sharing of traditional designs or literatures, as an act of colonialism. Disney's use, for example, of the Maori tattoos and other cultural artifacts in their film *Moana* shows how copyright can trample upon the ancient cultures of another traditionally marginalized group of people. Under current U.S. law, Disney can claim copyright infringement on their characters should anyone copy them or use them in "unauthorized" ways, even though these are themselves based upon millennia-old images. The power structure favors the corporation and its deeper pockets, not the indigenous tribes of the South Pacific and New Zealand. Scholars and intellectuals have pushed back against these tactics by adopting so-called decolonial strategies that call for the protection of indigenous authors, racialized communities, and minority authors or creators who work outside of the United States.

Additionally, those who live in poor communities, as well as those marginalized by the dominant culture, begin to suffer from a digital divide as well. As Martin Hilbert (2018) and his fellow researchers suggest, the digital divide is here to stay. However, he suggests that we can also employ multiple strategies to make sure that digital content remains accessible and usable. We can ensure through the development of e-Democracy initiatives (see more details in chapters 12 and 13) that personal ownership and community agency can be preserved for real people and their cohorts, not just for corporations; that online life need not be subjected at all times in all aspects to market forces; that the freedom to create and recreate remains strong so that cultures may flourish; and, finally, that the holes in our culture can be filled and refilled as needed.

Fighting Fire with Fire: Algorithms, Content Analysis, Fair Use, and Open Access

Aside from copyright policy and sociological countermeasures, we can also look to technological solutions to our problems. One of the best features of the HathiTrust digital books collection is its ongoing copyright clearance program. The organization employs volunteers from across the country to delve into the copyright status of the millions of digitized books in their online collection. Books that are determined to be in the public domain after a rigorous analysis are then released to the general public. This can happen if the work was never properly registered for copyright in the first place or was never re-registered when required. Assumptions about the copyright status of published works are often incorrect, but it takes time to verify them. Fortunately, the HathiTrust project is a concrete way to open up copyrighted works while also avoiding litigation from unexpected rights owners.

But what if there were other approaches to determining a work's value? Candia's research into the fading of cultural works found that the act of forgetting occurred within a predictable range of time. If the act of remembering or forgetting cultural artifacts can be quantified, perhaps we could create an algorithm, or at least a set of best practices or protocols, to help determine how much an artifact has, in fact, been forgotten. This algorithm or protocol might help us to better determine the cultural value of an item and assess the risks of reusing that work or opening it up to everyone as part of our shared cultural heritage. If works are completely forgotten, why should we persist in preserving the barriers denying access? The open access movement, which advocates for the opening of price and admission barriers to scientific and social research, has come to be seen as another answer to this problem. By providing openly accessible journals in health and science, for example, people in poorer countries are able to utilize life-saving information or adopt societal-improving innovations more easily.

It is clear, though, that regardless of how it is accomplished, there does need to be a new approach to how content is managed and shared in the digital realm. Ownership remains a slippery concept when digital objects can be copied ad infinitum, with or without the permission of others. Western individualism values the efforts of the single person above his or her community, but that viewpoint is at odds with cultural groups and even among families, which keenly feel the ties that bind them. These differences will remain in tension with each other long after the problems of the Internet are solved. As we'll see in part III, addressing these discrepancies in the relationships of people will become essential as information and power are intertwined for both good and ill.

REFERENCES

Bailey, L. (2018). Join us for a grand re-opening of the public domain. Internet Archive Blog. blog.archive.org/2018/12/05/join-us-for-a-grand-re-opening-of-the-public-domain-january-25-2019/.

Benjamin, W. (2008). *The work of art in the age of its technological reproducibility, and other writings on media*. Cambridge, MA: Belknap Press of Harvard University Press.

Candia, C., Jara-Figueroa, C., Rodriguez-Sickert, C., Barabási, A., and Hidalgo, C. (2018). The universal decay of collective memory and attention. *Nature: Human Behaviour*. doi.org/10.1038/s41562-018-0474-5.

Chin, D. (2011). *The Authors Guild, Inc., vs. Google, Inc.* (05 CIV 8136). United States District Court Southern District of New York.

Chopra, S. (2018). The idea of intellectual property is nonsensical and pernicious. *Aeon*. aeon.co/essays/the-idea-of-intellectual-property-is-nonsensical-and-pernicious.

Drake, W., Cerf, V., and Kleinwächter, W. (2016). Internet fragmentation: An overview. World Economic Forum. www.weforum.org/reports/Internet-fragmentation-an-overview.

Heald, P. (2013). How copyright keeps works disappeared. Illinois Program in Law, Behavior and Social Science Paper No. LBSS14-07; Illinois Public Law Research Paper No. 13-54. dx.doi.org/10.2139/ssrn.2290181.

Hilbert, M. (2018). E-democracy. MartinHilbert.net. www.martinhilbert.net/category/research/e-democracy/.

Kelly, K. (2016a). The Internet is a giant copy machine. Tweet. Kevin Kelly Twitter Page. twitter.com/kevin2kelly/status/724327067865612289.

———. (2016b). *The inevitable: Understanding the 12 technological forces that will shape our future*. New York: Penguin.

Lago, D., and Wallace, D. F. (2018). A brand new interview with David Foster Wallace. *Electric Literature*. electricliterature.com/a-brand-new-interview-with-david-foster-wallace-71c03223294b.

Michigan State University Libraries. (2018). Data description: Google Books dataset. Michigan State University. lib.msu.edu/gds/.

Owens, T. (2018). *The theory and craft of digital preservation*. Baltimore, MD: Johns Hopkins University Press.

Reuters. (2016). U.S. judge rules copyright for "Happy Birthday to You" invalid. *NBC News*. www.nbcnews.com/business/business-news/u-s-judge-rules-copyright-happy-birthday-you-invalid-n514766.

Salinas, S., and D'Onfro, J. (2018). Google employees: We no longer believe the company places values over profits. *CNBC*. www.cnbc.com/2018/11/27/read-google-employees-open-letter-protesting-project-dragonfly.html.

Tufekci, Z. 2017. *Twitter and tear gas: The power and fragility of networked protest*. New Haven, CT: Yale University Press.

United States Copyright Office. (2018). Copyright law of the United States. Title 17. www.copyright.gov/title17/.

Weiss, A. (2014). *Examining Massive Digital Libraries: A LITA guide*. Chicago: Neal-Schuman Publishers.

III

INFORMATION
AND POWER

8

The Online Surveillance State

Those who would give up essential Liberty, to purchase a little temporary Safety, deserve neither Liberty nor Safety.

—*Benjamin Franklin*

Nothing that is vast enters into the life of mortals without a curse.

—*Sophocles*

THE LOOMING WORLD OF DIGITAL TRACKING AND SURVEILLANCE

It is the age-old conundrum: freedom or safety? We all know what Benjamin Franklin had to say on the matter, but in a complex, post-industrial democratic society like ours, what needs more emphasis? We certainly have the freedom to do as we please, but do we have the breathing space to exist safely without destructive forces compromising it? In previous chapters, we touched upon the outsized impact of the Internet upon our lives, including not only the culture at large, but also upon our thinking, our communication styles, and our general economic activity. The vastness of this reach comes with the double-edge sword of tracking our behaviors and activities. Shoshana Zuboff (2015) argues that the new model of capitalism we are currently faced with is a curse, in the words of Sophocles, destined to overtake us all. Along the same lines, murky quasi-capitalist corporations and outright authoritarian regimes have employed the Internet to the same ends of tracking users' economic as well as political behaviors, representing a severe threat to open and free networks (Griffiths, 2019; Taylor, 2019).

Yet even open networks, benign as they seem to be on the surface of things, have their downsides. As George Dyson (2019) writes, "The search engine is no longer a model of human knowledge, it *is* human knowledge. What began as a mapping of human meaning now defines human meaning, and has begun to control, rather than simply catalog or index, human thought." Numbers and the machines that manipulate them rule the world, he says. The problem is that there appears now to be little oversight over who controls the machines. The line between human control and machine control is getting blurrier with each advancement in artificial intelligence.

It is clear that we are going to need to devise ways to ensure that democracies can be sustained and nurtured in cyberspace, even as some of the platforms themselves can undermine the concept of freedom and liberty itself. Furthermore, this encroachment upon personal liberty has now gone beyond merely observing how people use the Internet for economic activity or personal communication. It extends into surveilling how people behave and observing what they actually think or intend to do. It is in this vein that surveillance, an age-old technique among governments and ruling coalitions, becomes the dominant force and leitmotif within our online and digital cultures—especially if George Dyson is correct that the search engine and Internet in general are the embodiments of human knowledge and thus capable of controlling human thought.

A HISTORY OF SURVEILLANCE

The origins of spying are long and complex. Technology has been used hand-in-hand with spying and military intelligence as long as warfare has been conducted, with references to it appearing in Sun Tzu's *Art of War*; in ancient Egypt, Rome, and Greece; in feudal Japan; and more. The earliest real-world application of Galileo's telescope, for example, was its use as a spyglass to keep track of incoming ships to the city of Venice (Ferris, 1989). Since its expense was so prohibitive, and astronomy had very little relevance to daily life, one way to ensure that telescopes could be available for their intended purpose was through exploiting the real-world concern and demand for "security." That urge to find things out about our neighbors, to keep tabs on them in case they try something nefarious, may be hardwired, related to personal and group safety as well as to securing an advantage over enemies or rivals.

What concerns us most now, however, is not the long and tortuous history of spying, but instead the construction of the modern surveillance state, equipped with information and telecommunications technology. What we want to examine in particular is how the surveillance state in its recent history has come to adopt digital information technologies to spur its growth.

East Germany: "The Most Surveilled State in History"

Reginald Whitaker (1999) in his book *The End of Privacy: How Total Surveillance Is Becoming a Reality* calls the twentieth century "the century of Intelligence." Although spying has been around as long as humanity itself, it is mainly in the twentieth century, he argues, that spying became an "organized bureaucratic activity," concerned with the systematic acquisition and sorting of information (ibid.). The most well-known example of this bureaucratic approach to spying is Communist East Germany from the immediate postwar period until the fall of the Berlin Wall in 1989. Whitaker traces the development of the East German Stasi as a combination of Nazi Germany's "Gestapo and [Soviet Union's pre-KGB] Cheka . . . with a surveillance apparatus that penetrated every nook and cranny of civil society, turning friends into informers against friends, even spouses against spouses" (ibid.). The Stasi attained an incredible ratio of one official surveillance agent for every two hundred citizens. Some estimates, however, when factoring in part-time and unofficial informers, calculate an agent for every 6.5 people (Koehler, 1999). It is no wonder that East Germany is often considered the most surveilled state in history (Rosenberg, 2007), especially as the West (including West Germany, the United States, England, etc.) simultaneously engaged in counterespionage activities against their counterparts in East Germany.

By the fall of the Berlin Wall and the reunification of Germany, however, surveillance had undergone significant changes. By that point, it utilized more electronic video and audio recording devices than traditional cloak-and-dagger approaches. But these new devices were nevertheless rooted in analog technology: audio tapes, traditional film, and, of course, voluminous paper files and transcripts. After the collapse of East Germany, as Stasi agents shredded, burned, and destroyed as much as they could, 600 million scraps of paper were still recovered, and despite being scrambled by ripping and shredding, much of the information contained in them could eventually be retained (Rosenberg, 2007).

Despite the exhaustive collection activities the Stasi undertook, the materials thankfully remained bound to their analog materials, limiting the extent to which that information could be shared. Unfortunately, technology has advanced significantly since the end of the Cold War. Digital technologies have evolved to the point that what seemed impossible a few decades ago, such as facial recognition and artificial intelligence (AI) algorithmic decision-making, is now becoming widely implemented. Worse, conversations that used to disappear once they were over can be recorded, stored, accessed, and shared across digital platforms worldwide. Digital technology has the power now to eliminate the "ephemeral" from our daily lives. Things that used to be forgotten and lost to time might now persist eternally among the undying ones and zeroes.

Surveillance in the United States

The rise of organized surveillance activities in the United States mirrors other countries in terms of adopting new information technologies and the growing encroachment of surveillance activities on daily life. It all starts with the Federal Bureau of Investigation's founding in the late nineteenth century and continues with the agencies established around World War II. As a result of the Cold War, the National Security Agency, the Central Intelligence Agency, and the FBI all began or ramped up surveillance activities in the 1950s and 1960s and have not ceased since then. Since the September 11, 2001, terrorist attacks, more leeway has been granted to the intelligence community to fight its war on terror.

Yet the United States has over the decades also fought to keep surveillance at bay, even as issues in national security have become ever more prominent. The Church Committee, or known in formal parlance as *The Senate Select Committee to Study Governmental Operations with Respect to Intelligence Activities (1975–1976),* was one of several key investigations in the mid-1970s, following the Watergate Hearings, the release of the Rockefeller Report (aka the United States President's Commission on CIA Activities within the United States), and the investigations of the Pike Committee (aka United States House Permanent Select Committee on Intelligence) into the abuses of surveillance and covert operations undertaken by secretive intelligence organizations.

The Church Commission examined the state of the surveillance community and found clear abuses at the hands of the United States' intelligence-gathering organizations, including the FBI, CIA, and NSA (U.S. Congress, 1976). It especially found fault with the minimal oversight and their general lack of regard for the rule of law. In a telling quotation from the Hoover Commission Report from 1954, the report states: "There are no rules in such a game. Hitherto accepted norms of human conduct do not apply. If the U.S. is to survive, long-standing American concepts of 'fair play' must be reconsidered" (ibid.). The Church report pinpointed the main issue that remains unresolved today (and may even be more relevant than ever before): how do we reconcile acting in secrecy while also attempting to maintain an open *constitutional* democracy?

The impact of the Church Committee has been long-standing. One of the main pieces of legislation to stem from the Church Committee was the Foreign Intelligence Surveillance Act of 1978 (FISA). This legislation outlined clear limitations for the intelligence community, including electronic surveillance activities, physical searching, pen registers (i.e., number tracing), and access to business records. However, the immediate aftermath of the terrorist attacks on September 11, 2001, brought about swift "Church bashing" (Miller, 2008) and a call to abolish or weaken FISA. In response to this, the most comprehensive loosening of FISA occurred weeks after the September 11 terrorist attack with the USA PATRIOT Act of 2001, an acronym for Uniting and Strengthening America by Providing Appropriate Tools Required to Intercept and Obstruct Terrorism Act of 2001. Described as legislation "to deter and punish terrorist acts in the United States and around the world, to enhance law enforcement investigatory tools, and for other purposes" (U.S. Congress, 2001), the USA PATRIOT Act covered various aspects of national security, including domestic security, surveillance, anti-money-laundering initiatives, border security, and information sharing.

Title II of the act, however, is the more controversial part of the law. It established the government's ability to surveil both non-citizens and citizens alike. Wiretapping permissions were subsequently expanded to allow government access to personal e-mail accounts and websites. Warrants were given broader permission to include cell phone voicemail accounts. Later amendments to the act in 2007 expanded the limits initially imposed upon espionage activities and provided even more room for interpretation for intelligence organizations to spy on a greatly expanding number of people.

Edward Snowden and the Revealing of Post-9/11 NSA Spying Programs

The NSA's spying program has only grown in scope over the years since 9/11. The numbers calculated by researchers and journalists from various sources, including the notorious WikiLeaks, are staggering. Referencing the Snowden files, Glenn Greenwald quotes an NSA insider stating that the "collection [of information] is outpacing our ability to ingest, process and store to the 'norms' to which we have become accustomed" (Greenwald, 2014). They are so inundated with the data surveilled from users of electronic media and devices that the technology used to process and interpret it cannot keep up.

One of the ways government agencies have been able to justify the scope of these programs to the public is by drawing out the difference between *content* and *metadata*. In their reasoning, the edge between these two concepts is where the bright line of surveillance exists. Content is the meat of the information—the potential evidence itself—but much of it is often off-limits to law enforcement agencies without warrants. However, *metadata*, which is described as merely the external descriptions *about* the content, is treated differently. This "data about the data" exists in the form of caller names, phone numbers, geographical positions, lengths of phone calls, timestamps on when calls were made, and so on. The NSA argues that the scope of their program is irrelevant since they are not gathering the content, just the *description*, of the calls.

But the problem with the NSA's surface justification for this is that metadata can very often act as "a proxy for content" (Greenwald, 2014). Seemingly innocuous details such as the length of a conversation or the time of a phone call can indicate much about person's state of mind or personal actions. Focusing on these details can help law enforcement fill in the blanks to create a more accurate portrait of a person's location, contacts, and personal network. But the problem with this approach is that sometimes the circumstances and context for the content can be seen as damning, especially if the entities or organizations surveilling are already predisposed into believing you are up to no good.

More worrisome, the amount of metadata collected is staggering and borders on the incomprehensible. In 2006, according to one source, the NSA predicted that its metadata collection efforts would grow by six hundred billion records each year, with roughly one to two billion new telephone calls collected every day. Just a few years later, the Snowden documents released through WikiLeaks implied that the NSA in 2009 had the capacity to record *twenty* billion communications per day and almost 1.7 billion from American citizens. In 2012, twenty trillion transactions of U.S. citizens were successfully tracked overall, while nearly three-quarters of all Internet traffic was monitored and recorded in some fashion by the NSA, and one trillion pieces of metadata were processed. The Snowden papers have led Greenwald to conclude that our government has "built a system that has as its goal the complete elimination of electronic privacy worldwide" (Greenwald, 2014).

After WikiLeaks' release of the Snowden files in 2013, more revelations about the scope and scale of U.S. government surveillance occurred in quick succession, helping to shed more light on these very opaque machinations. On March 7, 2017, WikiLeaks released "Vault 7," a collection of documents that reveal some of the CIA's covert activities and some of the "hacking methods that many experts already assumed the agency had developed" (Miller and Nakashima, 2017). This "trove" of hacking tools allowed the CIA to compromise ordinary, commonly used consumer devices (ibid.). This includes most wired devices used for personal computing and mobile communications.

This is not to be taken lightly, or swept under the rug, as a necessary evil in an age of growing terrorist threats. When a society is unable to trust itself, it will destroy itself. Making things worse, the wounds of the Snowden leaks are still raw. Americans are torn, even now, between seeing him as a traitor or a true American patriot. One suspects the truth is somewhere in between, though with the release of his autobiography in September 2019, get ready for more of this heated and likely unresolvable debate. As Snowden asserts, "We've been forced to live naked before power for a generation" (Greenberg, 2019). Yet, as long as he lives in exile in Russia, one of the United States' main geopolitical adversaries, he will remain open to the charges that he is either working on their behalf or at least providing them valuable insight into American surveillance capabilities.

SURVEILLANCE AND THE PRIVATE SECTOR

Contrary to the general public view that corporations are the unwitting victims of the intelligence community's rapacious need to surveil, government surveillance cannot be carried out entirely through its own inventions. In fact, the U.S. federal government has worked directly with telecommunication companies to extend its reach (Greenwald, 2014). And, as Shoshana Zuboff notes, corporations are finding ways to incorporate the tools and methods of the spying and surveillance they helped to create in order to improve their bottom lines (Zuboff, 2015).

Quite a number of private, for-profit companies provide support for surveillance activities as subcontractors to the U.S. government and its intelligence organizations. Agencies have reportedly spend 70 percent of their budgets on these private-sector contractors (Greenwald, 2014). The data-collecting initiative PRISM gathers data from the servers of the *nine largest* Internet companies (Greenwald, 2014). One company in particular, Stratfor, calls itself a "geopolitical intelligence platform and publisher" (Stratfor, 2017). The partnership between them and the CIA shows just how closely the corporate world and government are entwined in their efforts to gather data on citizens and non-citizens alike.

The list of participating contractors goes on and on, even as public knowledge of their workings is limited. The relative silence about these private-sector collaborations in surveillance is intentional, both to protect the reputations of the companies and to provide openings for further surveillance. For example, Microsoft, which cooperates with the NSA, publicly asserts that its Outlook e-mail program is private. "Only the recipient who has the private key that matches the public key used to encrypt the message," the company explains, "can decipher the message for reading" (Microsoft, 2017). But the Snowden files reveal that Outlook is *not* secure. Access to its encryption technology exists through a backdoor that allows government agencies to bypass it (Greenwald, 2014). WikiLeaks' Vault 7 also shows that numerous companies that work as contractors for the government provide so-called zero day services, which are defined as security flaws found in devices *not yet disclosed to the public or the companies that own them*. These flaws or bugs are more easily exploited if no one is aware of them. David Ignatius of the *Washington Post* reports that "more than 200 zero-day exploits studied by Rand went undetected for an average of 6.9 years, with only 5.8 percent discovered by competitors within a year" (Ignatius, 2017). The length of time these remain undetected provides ample opportunities for spying. There is a clear motivation to keep these vulnerabilities secret despite the potentially negative effects on users.

INTERNATIONAL SPYING PROGRAMS

The United States is hardly the only player in this game. The United States works in collaboration with several allies to form the "Five Eyes" alliance as well as PRISM, ECHELON, and other surveillance and espionage projects. Other countries, of course, conduct their own spying programs in opposition to the United States, including China and Russia. Both countries have found ways, like the United States, to incorporate the whole of the Internet and its communications systems for an all-out total information war. According to James Hughes, in the *Journal of Social, Political and Economic Studies*, both China and Russia have attempted to map key infrastructure systems, including the electric grid, water, and sewage systems. "China," he writes, "has a sophisticated cyber warfare program, and numerous intrusions can be traced to Chinese sources . . . using an array of methods: spies, phone tapping, and the Internet to steal industrial secrets" (Hughes, 2010).

These countries have highly developed initiatives designed to spy on people within their countries as well as outside them. The well-publicized and documented interference into the 2016 U.S. presidential election is but one example of the results of this spying, as Russian hackers gained access to Democratic Party e-mails, releasing both Hillary Clinton's and John Podesta's private messages to WikiLeaks, and also installed malware on adversaries' computers. Additionally, in 2018 the Chinese telecommunications firm Huawei was singled out for its suspicious actions related to hacking and spying technologies. The company allegedly maintains ties with Chinese security services, and governments internationally—including the United States—are publicly worrying about adopting Huawei's fifth-generation (5G) mobile network (Taylor, 2019). As De La Bruyere and Picarsic (2019) report, "The goal is to build a 'ubiquitous and universally used information network system.'" They believe that "China wants to lace all these systems together . . . to make Chinese technology a foundation for the global flow of information and transactions—and thus to expand the Chinese Communist Party's leverage, influence and power worldwide." The point is for China to keep an eye on predicting and controlling world events in real time through a *Chinese-grown* operating system capable of dominating geopolitics.

These countries have similar goals in terms of spying on the United States and attempting to hack and interfere with private citizens. In his 2019 update to Congress, Daniel R. Coats (2019), director of national intelligence for the Trump administration at the time, testified that China, Russia, Iran, and North Korea "increasingly use cyber operations to threaten both minds and machines in an expanding number of ways—to steal information, to influence . . . citizens, or to disrupt critical infrastructure." It is clear from both the evidence compiled by journalists and the testimony of government leaders that international efforts to spy and impact our information infrastructure are reaching a fever pitch.

THE IMPACT OF SURVEILLANCE ON THE SURVEILLED

It is not clear how or when this ends. One can easily speculate that the result will be warring factions that wind up surveilling everyone who happens to be online in one form or another. That may be what we are experiencing now, but we just don't feel it yet. What is clear, however, is that this is unsustainable. People will eventually catch on. How, I have to ask, will people react to knowing that *everything* they do is monitored? My guess is not too well.

The scenario of complete surveillance and total information war leads me to ask: What happens when we *are* surveilled? What does it do to us? Perhaps we are already seeing the effects of this total information war in the hyperpartisan Twitterverse and blogospheres. While some are able to spout misinformation with impunity, others feel the weight of millions of eyes and coordinated attempts at public shaming. Indeed, the chilling effect of surveillance is that it directly affects whole populations and their ability to hold or investigate unpopular opinions and topics (Cushing, 2016). Jon Penney has shown in his own research that people are *less likely* to search for subjects that are seen as controversial if they are more aware of spying efforts. The chill on people's interest is clear. Searching for topics in Wikipedia not only declined immediately following the revelation of the NSA's spying programs, but the effects of this lingered for weeks and even months afterward (Penney, 2016).

Another danger of surveillance is that people will begin to mistrust *all* institutions, even those just tenuously aligned with or even completely independent of culprit organizations. This is not dissimilar to the effect that spreading fake news has had on legitimate news organizations. The scale of spying is vast, and if this mistrust continues, people will question the legitimacy of all institutions aligned with the dominant power structures, even if they exist to help those people. This applies to national as well as state and local organizations.

Another negative impact is the "boiling frog" principle, where people slowly get used to a gradual decline in quality of life and accept poor conditions if they come slowly rather than abruptly. In this case, the slow encroachment on our privacy and the quietly expanding areas of surveillance, where it once seemed inappropriate, serves to normalize its previously menacing presence. Eventually, surveillance starts to seem like the best and only solution to any number of societal ills. For example, several horrifying school shootings over the past decade have provoked strong responses for arming teachers with guns, keeping armed guards on school grounds, and implementing extremely tight security measures that include installing surveillance cameras, "deploying facial recognition, license plate readers, microphones for gunshot detection and even patrol robots" (Waddell, 2019). Decades ago, surveilling classrooms would have been seen as an Orwellian ploy straight out of *1984*. Now it unfortunately for many people seems like the only possible solution to the proliferation of guns and concerns about school safety.

Finally, as we discussed briefly in chapter 3, relying on surveillance to watch neighbors or to encourage certain behaviors can backfire. Observing people often results in faulty data and erroneous assumptions made about the observed, if the subjects are aware of it. The "Hawthorne Effect," as this phenomenon is known as, originates from a series of studies done at the Hawthorne Works, an electric plant in Illinois, whose managers wanted to find out whether workers could become more productive under higher or lower levels of light. During the observations, they noticed that workers' productivity improved when slight increases to light levels were made. Yet this improvement was short-lived. Once the study ended, productivity returned to previous levels. It is believed that the workers in the plants had changed their behavior because they *knew* they were being observed and wanted to make a good impression. But this change in behavior obviously skewed the results. The observers, unaware of their own impact upon the workers, erroneously attributed the changes in productivity to the changes in the light levels. Applying this principle to surveillance, there is a risk that those you are spying upon may actually be aware of it. What might result from this is a whole slew of problems, including erroneous data collection, false assumptions, and poor decision-making. Unfortunately, when those who make poor decisions also hold significant power and influence—like the CIA or NSA—it may be detrimental to the whole of the society.

SO WHO WATCHES THE WATCHMAN?

In a screen-mediated world, privacy will not exist so long as the opaque glass is pointing one way and we are unable to see what's on the other side. We will need to find ways to resist the total surveillance of all our activities, be it for the sake of keeping our daily routines private or for the sake of protecting national security. On both a small scale and a large scale, we will need to find ways to resist encroaching technologies until unequivocal transparency exists for how data is generated from and implemented on users. For the future we are facing is one of *total privacy loss*. As Whitaker (1999) writes, "The totalitarian vision is so compelling because it represents the architectural skeleton of modern power." The root of our problem, then, is that this power often remains hidden and therefore unchecked until it is too late. The Church Commission in the 1970s proved that without oversight, abuses *will* occur. We need that transparency returned to us.

REFERENCES

Coats, D. (2019). Statement for the record: 2019 worldwide threat assessment of the U.S. intelligence community. Office of the Director of National Intelligence. www.dni.gov/index.php/newsroom/congressional-testimonies/item/1845-statement-for-the-record-worldwide-threat-assessment-of-the-us-intelligence-community.

Cushing, T. (2016). The chilling effect of mass surveillance quantified. Techdirt. www.techdirt.com/articles/20160429/07512934314/chilling-effect-mass-surveillance-quantified.shtml.

De La Bruyere, E., and Picarsic, N. (2019). Why Beijing wants to dominate the Internet. *Japan Times.* www.japantimes.co.jp/opinion/2019/01/25/commentary/world-commentary/beijing-wants-dominate-Internet/#.XFD1ic2IZaR.

Dyson, G. (2019). Childhood's end. *Edge.* www.edge.org/conversation/george_dyson-childhoods-end.

Ferris, T. (1989). *Coming of age in the Milky Way.* New York: Anchor Books.

Greenberg, A. (2019). After six years in exile, Edward Snowden explains himself. *Wired.* www.wired.com/story/after-six-years-in-exile-edward-snowden-explains -himself/.

Greenwald, G. (2014). *No place to hide: Edward Snowden, the NSA, and the U.S. surveillance state.* New York: Henry Holt.

Griffiths, J. (2019). When Chinese hackers declared war on the rest of us. *MIT Technology Review.* www.technologyreview.com/s/612638/when-chinese-hackers -declared-war-on-the-rest-of-us/.

Hughes, J. H. (2010). China's place in today's world. *Journal of Social, Political and Economic Studies, 35*(2), 167+. Retrieved from link.galegroup.com/apps/doc/ A235406712/EAIM?u=csunorthridge&sid=EAIM&xid=e2297a04.

Ignatius, D. (2017). The real shocker in the WikiLeaks scoop. *Washington Post.* www.washingtonpost.com/opinions/the-real-shocker-in-the-wikileaks -scoop/2017/03/14/a464f9aa-08f2-11e7-a15f-a58d4a988474_story.html?utm _term=.65914704a1ba.

Koehler, J. (1999). Stasi: The untold story of the East German secret police. *New York Times.* www.nytimes.com/books/first/k/koehler-stasi.html.

Microsoft. (2017). Encrypt email messages—Outlook. Support Office. support .office.com/en-us/article/Encrypt-email-messages-373339cb-bf1a-4509-b296 -802a39d801dc.

Miller, G., and Nakashima, E. (2017). WikiLeaks says it has obtained trove of CIA hacking tools. *Washington Post.* www.washingtonpost.com/world/national -security/wikileaks-says-it-has-obtained-trove-of-cia-hacking-tools/2017/03/07/ c8c50c5c-0345-11e7-b1e9-a05d3c21f7cf_story.html?hpid=hp_hp-top-table-main _wikileaks-11a%3Ahomepage%2Fstory&utm_term=.a79de7d93488.

Miller, R. (2008). *US national security, intelligence and democracy: From the Church Committee to the War on Terror.* London: Routledge.

Penney, J. (2016). Chilling effects: Online surveillance and Wikipedia use. *Berkeley Technology Law Journal, 31*(1), 117. Available at SSRN: ssrn.com/ abstract=2769645.

Rosenberg, S. (2007). Computers to solve Stasi puzzle. BBC. news.bbc.co.uk/2/hi/ europe/6692895.stm.

Stratfor. (2017). About Stratfor. www.stratfor.com/about.

Taylor, A. (2019). The list of countries with espionage fears about China's Huawei is growing—fast. *Washington Post*. www.washingtonpost.com/world/2019/01/12/list-countries-with-espionage-fears-about-chinas-huawei-is-growing-fast/?utm _term=.035c2fc64536.

U.S. Congress. (1976). Select committee to study governmental operations with respect to intelligence activities. Library of Congress. Congressional Research Service. Final report of the Select Committee to Study Governmental Operations with Respect to Intelligence Activities, United States Senate : together with additional, supplemental, and separate views. Book 1. archive.org/stream/finalreportofsel01unit#page/524/mode/2up.

———. (2001). Uniting and Strengthening America by Providing Appropriate Tools to Restrict, Intercept and Obstruct Terrorism Act of 2001. www.congress.gov/bill/107th-congress/house-bill/3162.

Waddell, K. (2019). AI surveillance goes to school. *Axios*. www.axios.com/ai-video-surveillance-schools-a5845755-9c68-480a-a4d6-5e075a4d17b4.html.

Whitaker, R. (1999). *The end of privacy: How total surveillance is becoming a reality.* New York: New Press.

WikiLeaks. (2017). Vault 7. wikileaks.org/ciav7p1/.

Zuboff, S. (2015). Big Other: Surveillance capitalism and the prospects of an information civilization. *Journal of Information Technology, 30*(1), 75–89.

9

Disinformation, Misinformation, and "Reality"

Falsehood flies, and the Truth comes limping after it.

—*Jonathan Swift*

MIND OVER MATTER, OR MATTER OVER MIND?

Confusion is a part of life. We spend much of our lives trying to construct a clear vision of reality, testing daily whether something is true or untrue. Our senses, of course, help us to determine this. Look outside. Is it raining? Sunny? Cloudy? How does the rain feel? Some of this is important for survival. It's good to know that you shouldn't touch the hot stove. Fire *burns*. The cold can cause frostbite or hypothermia. *Watch out for that first step; it's a doozy!* And so on.

Yet our senses and our minds are notoriously fickle, too. Sometimes, depending on our mood, we feel things differently. People with depression sometimes feel aches and pains more acutely than those without it. Our internal feelings about something can directly impact how we perceive something, even if it is generally considered to be indisputably real. On any given day, at any certain hour, the glass "half-empty" can become the glass "half-full." Even more strangely, creating false memories is apparently a natural part of human life. Our memories of events are compromised by our feelings about and the lingering perceptions of something that occurred (Makin, 2016). It's not uncommon for witnesses to remember the same event differently. More than a hundred years ago, Ryūnosuke Akutagawa pointed that out in his short story "In a Grove" (*Yabu no Naka*), which most know from the film adaptation *Rashōmon*.

Many things in everyday life, similar to this tendency to over-rely on faulty memory, prevent us from seeing the truth. So far in this book we have examined a number of these factors in detail. We discussed, for example, how information can be used to nudge or alter desired behaviors. We examined how people can be overwhelmed by too much information, causing them to shut out new competing ideas for those already known, regardless of whether they are true or not. We examined how people can become skeptical of reality itself, like Descartes's "brain in a bottle" thought experiment, as if living in their own real-life Matrix. We've seen how people act differently when they know they are being watched.

Yet despite our constant vigilance and raising awareness, these pathologies of the mind and of information—both in terms of behavior and in skewed perceptions—persist. Some of the pathology is built in. We are imperfect, and our senses fail us. Our minds and emotions cloud what we see. Our nature pushes us into extreme positions or into adversarial relationships and the need to create a capital-O "Other," an enemy, a scapegoat. Conspiracies and political conspiracy theories also bleed into this sense of information as a pathology as well. People, perhaps out of deep-rooted fears of unequal power, believe the worst of the governments that they live under. But power is a concept that pervades all manner of human society. How it is distributed and shared can either alleviate the mistrust or exacerbate it.

This chapter will examine two concepts contributing to this sense of mistrust that are very similar—and often interchanged—though they are distinct themselves: *misinformation* and *disinformation*. Each of these phenomena works to prevent us from learning something true but has unique causes and specific impacts on people and societies.

HOW FALSE INFORMATION IS MANUFACTURED

Misinformation and Disinformation

Let's start with mistakes and how easily we can fall for them or create them on our own. We've all played "the telephone game" at one time or another. In primary school, I remember being surprised at how much the words changed from the beginning of the line to the end. How did a word or phrase so easily morph among twenty schoolkids into something totally different? All of us found it both hilarious and mystifying. We could never really pinpoint who was to blame for the mistakes, but sometimes we thought we knew who messed it up and let them have it.

Thinking back on it now, the fault was usually not on one person. And here's what our seven-year-old brains couldn't quite grasp: it's a *systemic* failure that speaks to the flaws of the whole group. Any number of factors can contribute to this system breakdown. It could be that the original concept from the child at the front of the line was unknown to some of the rest of the kids; it could be that someone mispronounced a word; perhaps some kids just guessed, unwilling to ask for the word again; other kids may have been overconfident and thought they knew the words but really didn't. Again, it takes a number of people to fail at a game like that, and sometimes many small failures add up to a major fail. *It's not all on one person!*

That is why the concept of misinformation, which is somewhat similar in *effect* and *results* to the telephone game, is also difficult to both define and stop as it represents as much a problem of the system as the individual. Much like a virus spreads among populations, sometimes changing from host to host, misinformation can spread among people genuinely invested in and credulous of it. Indeed, some characterize misinformation to be an *"honest* but *mistaken* belief that the relayed incorrect facts are true" (Kumar et al., 2016). Factual error does, of course, explain some of what makes up misinformation. We have all at some point unwittingly erred about one fact or another, since we're obviously not omniscient beings. Another factor is the belief put into how credulous something is or is not. This can often be both easy to pinpoint in others and impossible to correct in oneself. Research on overconfidence suggests that the people most likely to be incompetent are the ones with the *least* amount of awareness about themselves, making it harder to self-correct mistaken beliefs in the people most susceptible to them!

There is one quibble I have to make with this basic definition, however. Mistakes are not always as innocent as they appear on the surface. Sometimes mistaken ideas are caught up in specific worldviews that do not allow for dissenting ideas. When these so-called mistakes are caught up in a group's identity, it will be very difficult to counteract the spread of false information among them. For example, the people who genuinely believe the earth is flat and tell others about it (high-profile flat-earthers like NBA star Kyrie Irving come to mind) aren't necessarily gullible in that they haven't verified the facts in the normal sense. More often, they are instead pushing back against what they see as uneven, even abusive, power structures, while using erroneous ideas to point them out. In this case, skepticism about the shape of the globe is as much a critique of science and our ability to discern truth from our fallible observations—and the all-too-human scientists who make them—as it is about their erroneous understanding of geology. To them, their motives are pure. They want to show others "the truth" about science. Of course, the results are damaging not only to themselves in terms of their reputations but also to others who are genuinely confused by the error. Other motivations for misinformation, then, need to be considered in more complex ways than merely as "an honest mistake" passively accepted and retold to their unwitting counterparts.

At another extreme, however, we find *disinformation*, which "denotes false facts that are conceived in order to deliberately deceive or betray an audience" (Kumar et al., 2016). The important concept, of course, is that there is a deliberate attempt to deceive another person. The overlap with misinformation is telling, however. One person's disinformation campaign could become another person's unwitting relay of misinformation. It may be hard to tell the difference sometimes. But I would suggest that disinformation is probably easier to detect and police than misinformation, which has a lot more variables to consider. Bad actors generally intend to spread false information in order to damage the credibility of their enemies. That motive is often painfully clear to anyone taking the time to investigate the source of false information.

The FBI's indictment of the Russian-linked Internet Research Agency (IRA) in 2018 shows how the IRA's disinformation campaign was intended to impact the 2016 U.S. presidential election. As one report on the election suggests, Hillary Clinton was not merely running for president against Donald Trump, "she was involved in a global information war" (Korecki, 2019) and, as a result, was running against Putin-supported Russian disinformation campaigns as well. And, tellingly, that war was fought on one side only.

Despite the indictment of the IRA, evidence shows that attacks on Democratic Party candidates are actually starting up again ahead of the 2020 election. Like a game of whack-a-mole, if you shut down one malicious chatbot or troll farm, another one takes its place. When Elizabeth Warren announced her run for the Democratic nomination for president at the end of 2018, disinformation efforts also ramped up on cue. Significant increases were seen in the amount of insulting comments or posts calling Warren "Fauxcahontas," a riff on the well-known insult instigated by Donald Trump. Twitter in particular saw more than four thousand posts using that slur in the days immediately following her announcement to run for president. Aside from Twitter, fringe platforms such as 4Chan and Gab, where posters and their associations can remain anonymous, were some of the most prolific sharers and posters of anti-Warren commentary (Jones, 2019). But ultimately, these attacks originated from "a relatively small cluster of accounts—and a broader group of accounts that amplify them" (Korecki, 2019). Amplification of a minority viewpoint in order to reach mainstream numbers of viewers and readers seems to be the intent. If enough people at least *entertain* the idea of false or misleading information—though not necessarily accept it—then the mission to disrupt mainstream thinking or to manipulate attitudes about a targeted person has been accomplished.

The hardest part, though, is combating how misinformation, disinformation, and belief become inextricably tied in a person's mind. While it is certainly getting easier to combat disinformation through various vetting technologies that provide provenance or demonstrate clear evidence of tampering, the misinformation problem is more basic: how does one convince a *believer* of something that it is, in fact, *false*? These days it is becoming harder and harder for many people regardless of their education levels to distinguish between truth and lie. The Pew Institute calls this, with not a little bit of hyperbole, "the 21st century's threat of a 'nuclear winter'" (Anderson and Rainie, 2017) but without a non-proliferation agreement in place to contain it.

The corrosion of trust and the subversion of norms that people used to take for granted can be best seen in the problem of fake news. Fake news as a genre of disinformation attempts to mimic the conventions of traditional journalism by copying its communication style as well as its visual cues, in order to fool people into believing false ideas or to spread specific *slanted* perspectives about unclear or ambiguous past events. Fake news, of course, has dominated the public discourse the past few years due to frequent and irresponsible references to it by Donald J. Trump via Twitter, campaign rallies, interviews, and other wholly misleading public statements. Subjects that fall outside his own perceptions (e.g., decreasing immigration and effective border policing) or subjects that expose an inconvenient truth (such as global climate change or Russian interference in the 2016 election), the president has a well-documented tendency to declare a "hoax" or "fake news." (Keith, 2018). His persistent labeling of journalism as "fake news" demonizes the legitimate mainstream news sources, while promoting alternative news sources (e.g., InfoWars, Breitbart, RT, and the like) whose slanted, right-wing viewpoints maintain slim tethers to established fact or spread propaganda for Russian or other extremist group interests (Stone and Gordon, 2017). By calling into question the real media while propagating right-wing echo chambers, Trump does real damage to the concept of credibility. This makes it easier to fool people already susceptible to questionable ideas.

It also makes it easier for him to lie without consequence. The *Washington Post* has documented more than 13,435 false or misleading claims over the first one thousand days of his presidency, about *thirteen lies a day* (*Washington Post*, 2019). This is in stark comparison to President Barack Obama, who was called out by the *New York Times* for making "demonstrably and substantially false statements" eighteen times *in eight years* (Leonhardt et al., 2017). Yet the amount of lies seems to not affect Trump's standing among his staunchest supporters. This stumbles upon a truth about human psychology: people respond in exaggerated and heightened ways to news that is false, lurid, or just plain stimulating. As one recent study suggests, "A false story is much more likely to go viral than a real story. . . . A false story reaches 1,500 people six times quicker, on average, than a true story does" (Meyer, 2018). Perhaps we are hardwired to be attracted to the things that stimulate and confront rather than calm and soothe us. These things certainly hold our interest far more than the mundane, and we often revel in the sharing of that stimulation—whether it be excitement, happiness, anger, outrage, or surprise—with others in our social circles. Perhaps people are OK with lies so long as they are *entertaining*.

Coupled with social media's inherent ability to amplify and accelerate information sharing and the salacious or titillating natures of some content, the Internet has brewed a perfect storm of factors that allow for the rapid spread of misinformation and disinformation at a worldwide scale. Computer technologies and communications platforms have converged upon the highly malleable world of digital information, making regulation and standardization of information increasingly difficult, even as they transgress national borders. As one report suggests, the IRA "created a broad online ecosystem where divisive political messages were reinforced across multiple platforms"; they posed as members of Black Lives Matter and used the main social media platforms (e.g., Facebook, Twitter, YouTube, even Pokémon GO) "in an effort to exploit racial tensions and sow discord among Americans" (O'Sullivan and Byers, 2017). To combat such ploys, Facebook, Twitter, Google, and other social media platforms must play a direct part in preventing the spread of false information, especially as their technological advances continue to impact our society negatively while our ethical and legal practices lag behind them. International law is currently too weak to combat this, leaving corporate responsibility and national laws to fight an international problem.

Though the United States introduced a cyberwarfare division in 2018 to protect the mid-term elections from hacking and interference, dubbed "Cyber Command," it was obviously too late to counter the impact on the 2016 election (Nakashima, 2019). Calling out the bad actors like IRA is a good start, but the potential for the manipulation of the truth remains high. Indeed, the *next* development in weaponized information, the "deep fake" video, promises to be even more challenging to neutralize. Deep fakes are digitally altered videos placing other people's faces or bodies to create controversy and outrage in viewers. Ill-equipped as we are to deal with the current round of disinformation technologies, this new generation of info-weapon will require that we have ever more vigilance on what is true and what is fabricated.

In sum, the social media companies need to step up.

Strategies of Make-Believe: Kayfabe, Mockumentary, Infomercials, and Reality TV

Fake news incorporates more than just factually starved faux news stories. It also operates within the realms of parody, satire, and what some call "political kayfabe" (a term pulled from professional wrestling stagecraft) through the similar genres of mockumentary, infomercials, and so-called reality television.

Parody and Satire

Fake news occasionally falls under the wider phenomenon of parodic news stories, as it tends to imitate the form and look of legitimate news to fool readers and viewers. Parody performs a distinct function in literature as a way to ridicule not only genres and literary conventions but also wider societal values, while also giving distinct homage to the source material. Satire also imitates its source material's forms and conventions, but with the aim to shine a light specifically on people and to present their behaviors in a critical light. *Saturday Night Live*'s "Weekend Update" segment is perhaps the best example of this conflation of both parody and satire working in tandem, allowing its creators to entertain viewers with the familiar setting of a television news desk, while also conveying commentary and jokes that skewer public figures. Yet no one would reasonably assert that *SNL* is attempting to spread fake news through its show. Its over-the-top approach and clear comedic context provide viewers with the cues to understand the jokes.

Some have pointed out that the differences between satire and fake news are often difficult to discern (Golbeck et al., 2018). That line gets blurred easily, it is true. The key, really, is that the loss of context—especially on the Internet—accounts for this conflation of satire and false news stories. A few lawmakers, for example, have notably mistaken fake stories in the satirical online magazine the *Onion* as truthful. Once they realize what the *Onion* is, they surely realize the joke. Mockumentaries fulfill this role as well, sometimes parodying the source material, sometimes satirizing the milieu surrounding their topics. *This Is Spinal Tap*, with its look at rock stardom through the struggles of a fictional has-been rock group, is a prime example of using the documentary form to mimic real rock bands while providing clear satirical and parodic elements. Some might call it fake, but the intention is to get at deeper truths about the nature of stardom, the shallowness of some rock music or the music business in general, and so on. The ridiculous, in other words, can easily become the sublime. Ultimately, though, we might argue that distinguishing between satire and fake news is as much about discerning the intentions of the creators as it is the actual implementation of the news stories.

Infomercials and "Reality" Television

We also can't ignore another aspect of the culture of false information: the collision between information, fact-finding, and staged "reality" through the framing techniques of television production. We're all familiar with the ubiquitous infomercial, an extended riff on a product often taking the forms and conventions of a television talk show, with a "live studio audience" watching and participating in the spectacle. While most of us can pretty quickly tell the difference between the infomercial and a regular talk show, lately the lines between the two have been blurred quite masterfully. Pieces in journalism, produced ostensibly for the sake of sharing information in a dispassionate or objective manner, are actually turning out to be sponsored by businesses or organizations intent on selling a product or a service. These have morphed into a newer form, called "advertorials," which are "paid segments with legitimate features about community projects and personalities. Each segment, paid or otherwise, is moderated by one of the program's hosts, blurring the distinctions between straightforward editorial content and advertising" (Farhi, 2019). While there is nothing especially egregious or harmful on face value about this practice, as long as it is clearly stated as such, it does show the ongoing blurring between the practices of objective journalism and information sharing with the practices of business, selling, and advertising.

Unfortunately, this further serves to confuse people. If they were already skeptical of factual information, or if they were inclined to believe that the news is staged, this will only exacerbate the problem. Additionally, the debasement of the word "reality" as it is applied to staged fake documentary-type programs, such as *Keeping Up with the Kardashians*, *Bridezillas*, and the like, further erases the distinctions between what is real and what is fictional. While many of us might not be shocked to find that reality television shows contain staged confrontations, hyped-up and falsified interviews, or outlandish personalities chosen through central casting, some viewers still fall for the illusion. Ultimately, the forms are lifted straight out of documentary filmmaking, a well-respected genre that uses specific techniques, but staged—and therefore *subverted*—to boost ratings and improve advertising revenues. So much for a shared "reality."

Kayfabe

Yet there is more to it than mistaken contexts, misunderstood jokes, and mimicked or co-opted genre conventions used to signal a quasi-reality. In this regard, we must turn to a different way of looking at things: something out of pro-wrestling stagecraft, *kayfabe*. The term is defined as "the accepted substitution of reality and willing suspension of disbelief that allows fans to buy into often fictionalized storylines" (Stodden and Hansen, 2016). Make-believe is an accepted aspect of the ultimate goal of entertainment and theatrical catharsis; it is especially relevant to a sport like professional wrestling, which is seen by most as "more a form of entertainment than an actual sporting contest" (ibid.). Political discourse and political campaigns run on similar rituals and pretensions as wrestling stagecraft. In that regard, fake news might also sometimes fall under "political kayfabe," where the voters or consumers of a fake news story know it to be as far-fetched as a UFO story in the *National Enquirer* magazine. But the story provides the reader with an excuse for *catharsis*, a convenient chance to vent frustrations about political adversaries and exult in their enemies' defeats.

This may help to explain why the tall tales, outright lies, and willful misstatements that Donald J. Trump routinely spreads are acceptable to his hardcore following. It is not necessarily, then, about the absolute truthfulness of these statements and promises for his followers. It is, instead, more about the adversarial nature of the political show, and the catharsis that comes with it, as the rituals wrapped in staged spectacles are carried out until political rivals are vanquished. The disinformation and lies spread by the president are a central part of the ritualism that comes with the performance, allowing supporters to revel in the spectacle of their opponents (aka the "heels" in wrestling parlance) being taken literally and figuratively to the mat by any means necessary.

SOWING CONFUSION TO REAP PROFITS: IDEAS, KOMPROMAT, AND REALPOLITIK

"Info Wars," Spy Games, and the Marketplace of Ideas

Disinformation campaigns are also disrupting the democratic norms that have existed in the United States for the past two hundred years, turning our long-standing political beliefs and assumptions on their heads. By turning false speech into a weapon with information technology, Russia has found a way to destabilize a perceived rival and threat, especially as "false speech . . . can distort the democratic process" (Chemerinsky, 2018). Destabilizing your rival allows you to take over in terms of geopolitics and winning the hearts and minds of your rival's citizens. This attempt at turning ideas into a weapon is not entirely new. Propaganda has been used significantly during wartime efforts to manipulate public opinion both at home and abroad against enemies. Dropping pamphlets into East Berlin during the height of the Cold

War is one prime example of this. The use of Facebook ads exploiting racial fears is another.

We can see that part of Russia's intent for spreading disinformation and subverting shared assumptions about reality is to exploit the fault lines in American society for the sake of stoking disagreement and hostilities. Disinformation campaigns are turning specific American ideologies—namely free-market capitalism, neoliberalism, and Second Amendment rights—into weapons against themselves. The problem with all ideologies, regardless of where they fit on any political spectrum, is that they often rely on narrow interpretations of truth to perpetuate them. If one believes too blindly in something, one can very easily be exploited by that belief. This has been obvious from how the Russians have been manipulating one side of the political spectrum in the United States over the past decade—especially the National Rifle Association and the Russian spies that infiltrated it. How believable is it, we must ask ourselves, that an attractive young Russian woman would be allowed to start a gun-rights advocacy group in an authoritarian country that does *not* guarantee that private citizens can own guns?

Furthermore, American political discourse over the past thirty years has focused on the neoliberal idea of "the marketplace of ideas," where concepts supposedly vie with each other not only in terms of reality and truth, but also in terms of power, influence, and commerce. The best ideas, the reasoning goes, will win out and the worst will fail—just like an efficient business will succeed and an inefficient one will go bankrupt. There are some problems with this concept, however. Aside from the obvious fact that a market is not a consistently rational place of exchange (tulip mania, anyone?), this unique perspective is also easily subverted and twisted through disinformation campaigns, making it easier for bad actors to exploit its fundamental weaknesses as a political philosophy. If information is viewed primarily in terms of its commodification, then we are very much at the mercy of forces that have nothing to do with *facts* and everything to do with *influence*.

Deregulation is a central tenet to free-market ideology. But deregulating information results in severe problems. Spin, info wars, and spy games are the direct results of vying for the power and influence that comes with specific interests dominating the hypothetical marketplace of ideas. Cornering "information commodities" becomes much like cornering the market in wheat futures or 5G phone service, but with the added downside that truth and facts become subservient to *realpolitik*.

In this regard, we can see that transnational corporations, oligarchies, and organized crime are starting to dominate this very exploitable mode of thinking, using it to hide some very nefarious activities. Former FBI director Robert Mueller, who looked into interference in the 2016 presidential election as special counsel, gave a speech in 2011 that provides deep insight into what may be happening worldwide in terms of the spread of misinformation and disinformation and the motives behind it.

Mueller describes our world as feeling the "ripple effects" of globalization and technology, where the use of information technology has helped to spread the flow of negative and damaging practices worldwide. In his speech, which now seems incredibly prescient, he identifies "iron triangles" within the world of finance, government, and organized crime, whose sole purpose is greed and the consolidation of power. He describes them as follows:

> They are capitalists and entrepreneurs. But they are also master criminals who move easily between the licit and illicit worlds. And in some cases, these organizations are as forward-leaning as Fortune 500 companies.
>
> This is not "The Sopranos," with six guys sitting in a diner, shaking down a local business owner for 50 dollars a week. These criminal enterprises are making billions of dollars from human trafficking, health care fraud, *computer intrusions*, and copyright infringement. They are cornering the market on natural gas, oil, and precious metals, and selling to the highest bidder. (Mueller, 2011; italics mine)

What's important to note is that these "iron triangles" move unhindered in a coordinated fashion between legal and illegal business dealings, all in the name of free-market competition, while simultaneously breaking the law and sowing confusion in the process. They are developing multipronged strategies to steal and manipulate information, especially through "computer intrusions," that can result in holding personal or institutional data ransom or exploiting people through blackmail and *kompromat*. The role of misinformation and disinformation within these dealings cannot be understated. The confusion and spin they generate provides cover for further illicit activities, such as human trafficking, money laundering, and fraud. The role of Russian money, for example, in funding those YouTube and Facebook videos sup-

porting NRA causes or sowing dissention among African American voters
are prime examples. People are riled up and fighting against each other, while
the root causes of America's social problems, such as income inequality or
worse corruptions like money laundering and tax evasion, persist unnoticed.

Digital Noise and Monetized Confusion

When free markets are deregulated, there's supposed to be a boon in the
exchange of money: less regulation equals more competition, which equals
better products and services for the consumer. But the same does not occur
with the deregulation of information and ideas. Instead of freer and (somehow) truer information, the unfettered commodification of information
flow and idea evaluation results in a rise in noise and confusion, restriction,
and misdirection. For not only do the underbellies of organized crime and
Mueller's "iron triangles" benefit from the chaos, but smaller organizations
also gain financially in the everyday practice of disrupting and subverting
the Internet with misinformation and disinformation. Regulating the flow of
verifiable information becomes subservient to the manipulation of user time.

We can see these disruptions in the annoying increase of misdirection
ploys and clickbait articles now so common online. We're all familiar with the
set up: "Click here to learn one weird trick." Or, when scrolling down Yahoo!
or other search engine result lists, we find, as in figure 9.1, odd headlines
paired with strange-looking people and unexpected images. The success of
the "weird trick" or odd-headline stories stems from delaying the payoff, forcing users to wade through page after page until reaching the desired "information need" (Kaufman, 2013). Instead of an efficient marketplace of ideas,
we are subjected to the nickel-and-diming of an unequal power relationship,
where the holder of the content (or ideas) gets to dictate how and when we
finally reach satisfaction (if at all).

Lately, there's also been a rash of "nickname" stories about people who
may or may not exist doing controversial, taboo, or just plain offensive things:
BBQ Becky, Permit Patty, Cornerstore Caroline, Golfcart Gail, ID Adam, and
a whole motley crew of other similar foolish people (knowyourmeme.com).
Trading on the trend of shaming people online, many of these stories play
up the shocking and the lurid, or perversely flatter the reader's sense of su-
periority, just to gain views of the real content: *advertisements*. These memes
point people to websites that don't seem to go anywhere or fail to provide the

Sponsored UpBeatNews.com

These Movie Secrets Expose What Most People Missed

You'll be shocked to hear some of the wild secrets from some of your favorite movies!

Unusual Movie Secrets Even Fans Didn't Know About
UpBeatNews.com

Ever Wonder How This Was Filmed? Read More Here!
UpBeatNews.com

Sponsored Curious Historian

Strange Medical Techniques Now Banned By Hospitals

56 Strange Medical Practices In History

56 Bizarre Medical Practices Doctors Once Swore By
Curious Historian

Awful Medical Photos That Would Be A Lawsuit Today
Curious Historian

FIGURE 9.1
Screenshots from Yahoo! front page news story feed showing sponsored ads using misdirection, surprise, oddity, non sequiturs, and "doctored/photoshopped" images to attract attention and lure in viewers. *Yahoo!*

promised content. If they do provide it, it usually comes at the last possible moment after a flurry of other distractions meant to monetize your attention. The misdirection in the form of non sequiturs, clickbaiting, and distractions ensures that we remain online, trapped in repeating loops going back to the same sites, while constantly taking in more and more advertisements. The clickbait phenomenon of attempting to confuse and string out users is the result of the monetization that comes from deregulated confusion and misdirection. As with all false promises, the reality is a little more mundane than the hype.

This attempt at misdirection and distraction contributes further to the muddied Internet environment. Information is not there for the taking without giving up something in return. In this case, it's your time and attention. These are, of course, *deliberate* attempts at getting money from Internet users or Internet advertisers. In one telling article, Daniel Cristo, who claims to be "director of SEO Innovation at Group M's Catalyst, a thought leader in the organic, paid and social space," writes about using misdirection in Internet marketing campaigns. In his push to sell the obvious to his potential client base, he tells us that the "main goal of content for search marketers is to attract views, links and engagement, and that is sometimes better achieved by not creating content about what you're trying to sell directly, but instead, by creating something completely unexpected" (Cristo, 2015).

We see this attempt at grabbing attention through the surreal ad campaigns of insurance companies that feature cavemen, green lizards, or mayhem or in the images from the Yahoo! feed above. We see this in the Internet shaming stories about those obnoxious BBQ Beckys; the "one weird trick" that everyone needs to know; the doctored photos showing grotesque or embarrassing images; and the images that don't fit with the headline's text. All of this is designed, as Cristo asserts, by engaging people and vying for their attention with "a consistent diet of interesting and share-worthy material until you've trained them to open and read every piece of content you send their way" (ibid.). These attempts at misdirection, confusion, and shock have but one goal: to groom your attention for long enough that you'll buy something from them and keep coming back for more.

The irony of advice like Cristo's is that years before these proclamations about the advantages of misdirection, scholars and researchers were *already* pointing out the flaws in the attention economy's tactics. As figure 9.2 shows,

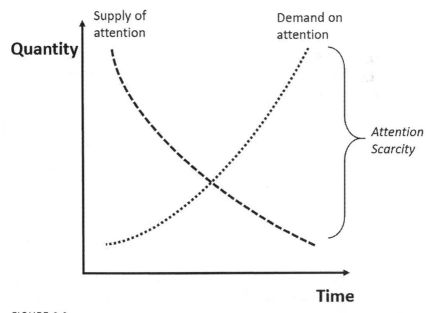

FIGURE 9.2
Graph showing the supply and demand for a person's individual attention and its diminishing returns. *MacMaster (2016); redrawn by author*

there's only so much attention out there. It's a finite resource. Over time, a person's ability to provide that coveted attention to advertising decreases as the demands to access it increase, resulting in a large-scale resource deficit. *This effectively kills the attention economy.* Eric Clemons (2009), a professor of operations and information management at the University of Pennsylvania Wharton School of Business, argues that this economic model is "doomed to fail" since "it is not scalable; [and] it is not possible for every website to earn its revenue from sponsored search. . . . Ultimately at least some of them will need to find an alternative revenue model."

Unfortunately, however, most of the marketing world seems to be ignoring Clemons and jumping on the SEO speedwagon. The problem with too much misdirection, confusion, or shock is that it kills trust in advertising, which is the golden goose of marketing. Without trust or loyalty, no one would consider purchasing from any specific brand more than once. Doubling down, instead, on suspect strategies, these marketers wind up destroying brand loyalties by their association with such tactics. These tactics might temporarily result in short-term gains due to distraction and mistakes, but people will catch on, if they haven't already, leading to long-term losses.

DIGITAL FUTURES: AI AND THE PROMISE AND THREAT OF MACHINE LEARNING

Finally, all of this is but a tip of the iceberg of what's to come in terms of automatically generated online content. In a screen-mediated, human-dominated world, there's only so much time and attention we can give to all the content out there, but at least autonomy is still with us. We can choose to turn things off, go somewhere else, and seek newer, greener pastures. We can still seek the unknown and the unknowable, without relying entirely on the unseen forces of our digital decision-making crutches. We also generally create and write content for each other, person to person. But factor in artificial intelligence, a computer-mediated world of bots, chatbots, and neural networks, and we start to enter the realm of cyberpunk, where the "ghost" in the machine calls the shots. We need to ask ourselves, then, what it means to be human in an increasingly computer-mediated world. What does it mean to be human in a world where decisions are increasingly made as a result of algorithms' choices? Are our choices—be they about music, books, art, learning, shopping—made of our own free will? Are we still human if we lack the power to make decisions or create things on our own *for* our own?

Putting these basic philosophical questions aside and getting back to the practical matter of how to sift through and decide what is fake or what is real, artificial intelligence also has the capability of creating confusion at a massive scale. Alan Turing's eponymous test of checking whether an artificial intelligence is real or not is slowly reaching the point where AI may be indistinguishable from real people. The only saving grace we have is that right now much of the artificially generated *creative* content from an AI still strikes us as strange. It's not quite realistic or idiomatic enough that we can forget its artificial origins. As an AI reaches a certain level of human-like qualities but fails, we become aware of its *innate* foreignness. It is stuck in an "uncanny valley," the point that all man-made objects or artificial intelligences reach as they become increasingly human-like and "actually become less trustworthy in the eyes of users, and remain that way until they are developed to full or near-full levels of realism" (Templeton, 2017).

As we can see in figure 9.3, if a healthy person is seen as 100 percent like a human and most familiar to us (at the top right of the graph), a fictional

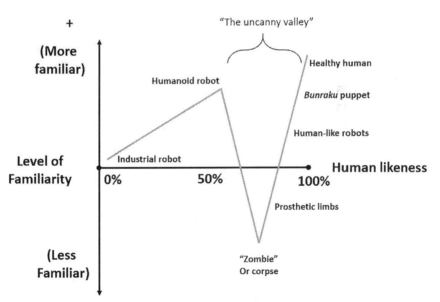

FIGURE 9.3

The "uncanny valley" diagram shows how people's perceptions about the realism an object change based on how familiar it is compared to how realistic it is; very close to human-like but not close enough results in the "uncanny valley" that distracts from an object's perceived realism. *Templeton (2017); redrawn by author*

monster like a zombie might be seen as the least familiar, at the bottom of the "uncanny valley," despite its closer *physical* resemblance to a person than, say, an industrial robot, which is on the far left of the human-likeness axis.

It is also notable that the humanoid robot (i.e., clear human-like elements but also stylized—like Honda's Asimo robot), even as it begins to rise in terms of both familiarity and human likeness, nevertheless rises along the same familiarity level as a typical Japanese *Bunraku* puppet, but on opposite sides of the uncanny valley. Bridging that gap between actual familiarity to and likeness of humans will be the main challenge for AI developers in the future. Right now, our humanoid robots look less human than zombies but seem more familiar to us. As they develop a greater likeness to us, however, the more human-like robots will fall into the uncanny valley until people can figure out ways to make them seem perfectly realistic.

Beyond just robotics, there are also some well-publicized advances of AI programs and neural networks attempting to mimic human creative endeavors. These include AI creating paintings or devising slogans for heart candy (Molina, 2019; Shane, 2018). Researchers are also developing AI capable of generating increasingly convincing "human-like" prose. AI is truly on the verge of major breakthroughs. As a 2019 Microsoft paid advertisement in the *New York Times* asserted, "Soon, interacting with A.I. will become much more natural and seamless: A.I. will eventually be layered into our work environments, so people won't have to be tethered to devices to access it" (Microsoft, 2019). What is interesting about the PR copy here is that the key concept seems to be "seamlessness": they want people to be unaware that they are engaged with programs and machines. Indeed, their whole philosophy could be summed up as an attempt to bridge that uncanny valley so that "you'll be engaged with people, not a machine" (Microsoft, 2019).

Yet, if AI finally moves beyond the uncanniness of near-realism, more issues will arise. Given how well chatbots disrupt online life now, such an AI could be employed to further increase the already-problematic fake news glut. Designed to create convincing articles, an AI could "fool people on a mass scale" (Knight, 2019). Here, again, we are confronted with the fact that not only is the technology reaching a point where it can mimic human behavior and fool even the best and brightest, it is also a problem of the size and scope of its implementation and reach. An AI—unlike the most prolific human-troll out there who still needs to eat and sleep—could conceivably crank out fake news stories and fabrications one after another, every minute of every day.

We are currently flooded with the degradation of open commentary sections in online venues such as newspapers, news aggregators, social media, and the like. The number of tweets and retweets, likes and shares of your online comment is probably not an accurate gauge of real people's interest. It is more likely a reflection of how many fake bots and artificial followers you have. The public discourse is irredeemably polluted and overrun by the methods employed by these non-human entities. We are at the mercy of the code as it raises us above the wave or drowns us out. As Lawrence Lessig (1999) so presciently predicted twenty years ago, "Left to itself, cyberspace will become a perfect tool of control."

REFERENCES

Anderson, J., and Rainie, L. (2017). The future of truth and misinformation online. Pew Research Center: Internet, Science & Tech. www.pewInternet .org/2017/10/19/the-future-of-truth-and-misinformation-online/.

Chemerinsky, E. (2018). Fake news and weaponized defamation and the First Amendment. Berkeley Law. scholarship.law.berkeley.edu/facpubs?utm _source=scholarship.law.berkeley.edu%2Ffacpubs%2F3002&utm _medium=PDF&utm_campaign=PDFCoverPages.

Clemons, E. (2009). Why advertising is failing on the Internet. TechCrunch. techcrunch.com/2009/03/22/why-advertising-is-failing-on-the-Internet/.

Cristo, D. (2015). Why content "misdirection" can be a viral homerun. Marketing Land. Blog post. marketingland.com/when-content-misdirection-can-be-a-viral -homerun-122871.

Farhi, P. (2019). Is it news you can use? An ad? Both? On some morning TV programs, it's hard to tell. *Washington Post.* www.washingtonpost.com/lifestyle/ style/is-it-news-you-can-use-an-ad-both-on-some-morning-tv-programs -its-hard-to-tell/2019/03/03/9c7541e4-3b79-11e9-a2cd-307b06d0257b_story .html?utm_term=.8a7b58820feb.

Golbeck J., Mauriello, M., Auxier, B., Bhanushali, K. H., Bonk, C., Bouzaghrane, M. A., Buntain, C., Chanduka, R., Cheakalos, P., Everett, J. B., Falak, W., Gieringer, C., Graney, J., Hoffman, K. M., Huth, L., Ma, Z., Jha, M., Khan, M., Kori, V., Lewis, E., Mirano, G., Mohn, W. T., Mussenden, S., Nelson, T. M., Mcwillie,

S., Pant, A., Shetye, P., Shrestha, R., Steinheimer, A., Subramanian, A., and Visnansky, G. (2018). Fake news vs satire: A dataset and analysis. In *Proceedings of the 10th ACM Conference on Web Science* (WebSci '18). ACM, New York, NY, USA, 17–21. doi.org/10.1145/3201064.3201100.

Jones, K. (2019). Fringe sites amplify conversation after Warren announces possible 2020 bid. Storyful. Blog post. storyful.com/blog/conservative-sites-junk-news -pages-amplify-conversation-after-elizabeth-warren-announces-possible-bid -for-2020/.

Kaufman, A. (2013). How "one weird trick" conquered the Internet: What happens when you click on those omnipresent ads. Slate. slate.com/business/2013/07/how -one-weird-trick-conquered-the-Internet-what-happens-when-you-click-on -those-omnipresent-ads.html.

Keith, T. (2018). President Trump's description of what's "fake" is expanding. NPR. www.npr.org/2018/09/02/643761979/president-trumps-description-of-whats -fake-is-expanding.

Knight, W. (2019). An AI that writes convincing prose risks mass-producing fake news. *MIT Technology Review.* www.technologyreview.com/s/612960/an-ai-tool -auto-generates-fake-news-bogus-tweets-and-plenty-of-gibberish/.

Korecki, N. (2019). "Sustained and ongoing" disinformation assault targets Dem presidential candidates. *Politico.* www.politico.com/story/2019/02/20/2020 -candidates-social-media-attack-1176018.

Kumar, S., West, R., and Leskovec, J. (2016). Disinformation on the Web: Impact, characteristics, and detection of Wikipedia hoaxes. In *Proceedings of the 25th International Conference on World Wide Web* (*WWW '16*). International World Wide Web Conferences Steering Committee, Republic and Canton of Geneva, Switzerland, 591–602. doi.org/10.1145/2872427.2883085.

Leonhardt, D., Philbrick, I. P., and Thompson, S. A. (2017). Trump's lies vs. Obama's. *New York Times.* www.nytimes.com/interactive/2017/12/14/opinion/ sunday/trump-lies-obama-who-is-worse.html?mtrref=undefined&assetType=opi nion&mtrref=t.co&assetType=REGIWALL.

Lessig, L. (1999). *Code and other laws of cyberspace.* New York: Basic Books.

MacMaster, K. (2016). The attention economy: Why marketers are killing, not capturing, attention. Vidyard. www.vidyard.com/blog/attention-economy -marketers-killing-not-capturing-attention/.

Makin, S. (2016). What happens in the brain when we misremember. *Scientific American*. www.scientificamerican.com/article/what-happens-in-the-brain-when-we-misremember/.

Meyer, R. (2018). The grim conclusions of the largest-ever study of fake news. *Atlantic*. www.theatlantic.com/technology/archive/2018/03/largest-study-ever-fake-news-mit-twitter/555104/.

Microsoft. (2019). Can A.I. make work seem less like work? (Paid Post by Microsoft from NYTimes.com). *New York Times*. www.nytimes.com/paidpost/microsoft/can-ai-make-work-seem-less-like-work.html?cpv_dsm_id=192198493&sr_source=lift_ed&tbs_nyt=2019-March-nytnative_ed.

Molina, B. (2019). Christie's sells painting created by artificial intelligence for $432,500. *USA Today*. www.usatoday.com/story/news/nation-now/2018/10/25/painting-created-ai-going-auction-block-christies/1759967002/.

Mueller, R. (2011). The evolving organized crime threat. FBI Speeches. Federal Bureau of Investigation. archives.fbi.gov/archives/news/speeches/the-evolving-organized-crime-threat.

Nakashima, E. (2019). U.S. Cyber Command operation disrupted Internet access of Russian troll factory on day of 2018 midterms. *Washington Post*. www.washingtonpost.com/world/national-security/us-cyber-command-operation-disrupted-Internet-access-of-russian-troll-factory-on-day-of-2018-midterms/2019/02/26/1827fc9e-36d6-11e9-af5b-b51b7ff322e9_story.html?utm_term=.8b9bf03a5059.

O'Sullivan, D., and Byers, D. (2017). Exclusive: Even Pokémon Go used by extensive Russian-linked meddling effort. CNNMoney. money.cnn.com/2017/10/12/media/dont-shoot-us-russia-pokemon-go/index.html.

Shane, J. (2018). Candy Heart messages written by a neural network. AI Weirdness. aiweirdness.com/post/170685749687/candy-heart-messages-written-by-a-neural-network.

Stodden, W., and Hansen, J. (2016). Politics by kayfabe: Professional wrestling and the creation of public opinion. docstodden.com/storage/files/wrestfin.pdf.

Stone, P., and Gordon, G. (2017). FBI's Russian-influence probe includes a look at Breitbart, InfoWars news sites. McClatchyDC. www.mcclatchydc.com/news/politics-government/white-house/article139695453.html.

Templeton, G. (2017). Researchers have discovered a second uncanny valley. Inverse. www.inverse.com/article/28995-ai-uncanny-valley-robots-artificial -intelligence-mind-creepy.

Washington Post. (2019). Tracking all of President Trump's false or misleading claims. www.washingtonpost.com/graphics/politics/trump -claims-database/.

10

The Antisocial Network

Dealing with Online Social Media Misbehaviors and Pathologies

WHEN LIFE IS STRANGER THAN FICTION

As I began to write this chapter in March 2019, I was shocked and saddened by news feeds across the country recounting the terrorist attack that occurred at a mosque in Christchurch, New Zealand. The fallout from this event as the weeks unfolded afterward occurred in two areas: one was in the area of gun control and the actions that the New Zealand government unilaterally took to ban assault rifles and other heavy weapons from their society. *Some glimmer of hope out of unspeakable evil, at least*, I thought. The other thing that came out of this event was the blame—or at least the partial blame—that social media companies absorbed for failing to regulate their online domains and for perpetuating the hate-mongering that contributed to this attack. YouTube and Facebook in particular were seen as negligent in their failures to respond quickly or reasonably enough as the streaming video of the violence spread through their services in real time. A month later, as I was still writing this chapter (thanks in part to my tendency to procrastinate), I was surprised again as the British government arrested Julian Assange at the Ecuadoran embassy in London, pledging to extradite him to the United States for his role in hacking and posting CIA-related materials in coordination with Chelsea Manning in 2010. Of course, the specter of Russian meddling in the 2016 election and the subsequent Mueller investigation likely had an effect on this as WikiLeaks has had an outsized impact on both the Trump and Clinton campaigns. Julian Assange, founder of WikiLeaks, has been directly linked to the Russian-hacked e-mails from the Democratic National Committee as well as Hillary Clinton's campaign chairman, John Podesta. The release of the redacted Mueller report on April 18, 2019, provided clear evidence of the impact of these information warfare tactics.

It's hard, then, not to see that virtual behaviors can be truly intertwined with consequences in the real world. People tend to focus on the non-threatening, self-interested uses of social media (e.g., the vanity and preening aspects, the shopping, and the messaging), but the much darker sides—the personal problems, the anxieties, the arguments, the invasiveness—also become magnified by social media. As one writer laments, "A platform that claims to bring people closer together is helping derail and destroy some of the few remaining places that actually do" (Pelly, 2019). In this case, Facebook exacerbated one group's real-life problems, magnifying the divisions among a group of people living together, while failing to find ways to reconcile the social contract through their platform. It may very well be that division keeps people hooked online more so than unity. Passion pays, it seems, and anger lasts longer than joy. The pathologies we witness every day include not only the typical trolling and "flame war" arguments that occur so often in online comment forums, but also the more serious cyberbullying, doxing, swatting, astroturfing, sock puppeteering, and so on.

This chapter will focus on the way in which the online world's misbehaviors and transgressions can spill over into the real world. For it all boils down to this: the honeymoon period of the dot-coms, Silicon Valley, and even the Internet itself is over. We are seeing the clear toll that these online information pathologies exact upon *everyone* that comes in contact with them, like real viruses or diseases. Even Congressional Rep. Alexandria Ocasio-Cortez (D-NY), herself a heavy user of Twitter and Facebook, has called social media "a public health risk" (Shaban, 2019). This impact involves neither a subset of obsessed Internet users nor an esoteric group of technologically advanced countries and people. This involves everyone online, *billions* of people, whose tolerance for new technology ranges from minimal to full-on saturation. The scale is daunting. It even starts to impact those charged with *protecting* Internet users from these pathologies. Moderators, investigators, law enforcement, politicians, and everyday public-minded citizens, are starting to see their quality of life declining in the face of online abuse. It is, therefore, worthwhile examining these transgressions in detail and finding ways to prevent them.

ANTISOCIAL NETWORKS: USING INFORMATION TO BREAK LAWS, FIND LOOPHOLES, AND GAME SYSTEMS

Beyond Hacking: Manipulation, Phishing, Cat-Phishing

Hacking, which was first coined during the 1960s, is central to the development of computer systems and, ironically, essential to their future growth. At first, hacking merely referred to someone who was skilled at programming and phone-line or mainframe manipulation, a kind of self-deprecating nickname for those who could work magic on these massive, complex electronic systems. But along the way, the concept began to morph. By the mid-1970s, the personal computer arrived, but just barely. It was the domain of a few obsessive tech-advanced hobbyists and home enthusiasts. These were "hackers" in a more literal sense: hobbyists or engineers tooling around in the garage or basement, making and breaking, fixing and modifying mail-order home computer systems. Later on, as the home computer became mass-produced and the dial-up modem became standard, the image started shifting to the isolated prodigy—usually male, usually a teenager—working in secret, attempting to break into a large computer network, say the CIA's or the FBI's, or the local high school (like Ferris Bueller changing his grades).

Of course, hacker culture and the so-called hacker ethic are in reality more complicated than this. Hacking now incorporates a significant number of subcultures and unique practitioners, who have evolved from these humbler, narrower, and more juvenile concerns into more serious issues, involving security, integrity, and freedom. Contrary to the stereotype of the self-interested or malicious actor, hacker culture and ethics involve sharing, openness, decentralization, the free access to computers, and a desire to improve the world. Even the proposed emblem of hackers, a spaceship called the "glider" taken from the early programming game Conway's Game of Life, hints at the deeply philosophical and ethical concerns central to these subcultures: cooperation, complexity, and the emergent properties of decentralized systems. Conceiving of computers as a force for goodness and equality, rather than for cybernetic control, absolutely stems from their original anti-authoritarian roots.

So hacking and hacker culture in general should not be seen as a primary vehicle for many of the online misbehaviors we are witnessing. Indeed, these groups, especially white hat and grey hat hackers, may be the only ones capable of saving us from malicious intent. The flood of ill-operators has only grown over the years as access to computers has increased. We are watching in real time as Internet use devolves into more antisocial and disruptive patterns associated not only with general mayhem but also with organized crime. Online manipulation now includes any number of techniques designed to break into systems, steal passwords, or generally create havoc among normal people in order for specific teams or organizations—usually illicit—to profit materially.

Phishing

Phishing has become so widespread that probably all of us have been contacted at some point in our online lives by a Nigerian prince, an assistant to a wealthy dowager, the personal accountant for a now-deceased rich banker, or an alleged "official" representing a foreign government or agency, promising to send you millions of dollars that you absolutely (somehow!) deserve. That these e-mails, known as "419 scams" after the section of the Nigerian penal code that addresses fraud, still find their way to our mailboxes is a testament to that one in a thousand or one in a million person who falls for them (419 Eater, 2019). Most of us just ignore them, seeing the ruse for what it is. Some have gone to the extent of fooling and leading on phishers, to comic effect, but also to intentionally waste the scammer's time so that others are not bothered (Crampton, 2007)—a kind of trolling-in-reverse public service.

Unfortunately, even with awareness and counter-strategies in place, online fraud continues to persist. It's not isolated to just Nigerian phishing groups, either. It is a worldwide scourge, comparable to the long-running phone scams that attempt to part money from their marks. It's not just the gullible or easily fooled. Most of these scams can only work by exploiting the mark's inherent greed or other vices. If a person were able to see beyond their greed, the scam would probably be more easily noticed. For some, however, the lure of or desire for easy money is just too strong.

Spear-Phishing

Phishing, however, is a broader term for attempting to get sensitive information from victims, including passwords, usernames, and credit card numbers. A variation on this, *spear-phishing*, however, is even more perverse.

It attempts to target a specific person by pretending to be a close friend or trusted person within their sphere of influence. The spear-phishers then try to get into their marks' e-mail or social media accounts or get access to bank and financial information. As a member of a large state-supported public university, I can attest to being targeted—along with hundreds of my faculty and staff colleagues—by spear-phishing e-mails at least a few hundred times over the past eight years. The e-mails are often suspiciously similar to our institution's e-mail addresses, using CSUN or familiar on-campus names but with strange variants. The names are familiar, but the contents of the e-mails are often a little off, full of grammar mistakes, wrong titles, malapropisms, or misused academic terms. There have been many types of these scams over the years, but the most common one is the "password is expiring" e-mail, coming from "Campus IT," that requests recipients to click on a link and then enter their username and passwords. Other variants also include warning me that my computer is vulnerable and that I need to immediately send my computer information and my institution password to the sender.

Regardless of the method, the true aim of these attempts is to get into my online accounts and allow malicious users to access my correspondences or to secure my financial information. It has never been very successful and has generally tapered off with greater safeguards enacted at my university, but it still contributes to an occasional compromised user account. The reason it persists, despite the low percentages of fooled people, is that it is ultimately "the most successful form of acquiring confidential information on the Internet, accounting for 91% of attacks" (Giandomenico, 2019).

More Types of Phishing

Taking this a few steps further, *angler-phishing* and *cat-phishing* have become more widespread, bringing more sophisticated attempts at manipulating people through online fraud. With angler-phishing, the perpetrator uses social media to create a fake online brand and support pages to redirect people to websites that function as phishing sites. Essentially this is a form of impersonation, imitating the look and feel of a legitimate web page, like a bank, for example, in order to feign trust to steal the sensitive data that is divulged to them (Bloomberg, 2017). Similarly, cat-phishing aims to present false information about an online persona but with a specific manipulation in mind: the human need for companionship. Cat-phishing attempts to defraud

people based on the romantic or familial feelings they might develop for another. It essentially finds ways to exploit certain human weaknesses, especially
"emotional cons that target older women, and sexual cons targeting men of
all ages" (ibid.). The endgame is usually the same: the manipulator gains a
victim's trust through deception and then builds up to the big ask, which may
be a request for money on the pretense of travel or a family emergency.

The manipulations described above are sometimes used to gain access to
private institutions or organizations, especially those that handle sensitive information. Typically, someone in a position of power privy to business secrets
or other privileged information is targeted by cat-phishers in order to gain
access to those secrets. Industrial espionage is not just the subject of movies
or pulp novels. The boundaries that once existed between business and government are increasingly blurred, especially with regard to China's businesses
or in the case of subcontractors in areas of the U.S. government. According
to the U.S. Senate Intelligence Committee's 2018 report, 90 percent of the
corporate espionage cases handled by the Department of Justice from 2011
to 2018 were China-related (Maza, 2018). The techniques used to steal this
information from both businesses and government agencies involved these
more sophisticated phishing techniques.

Manufacturing Dissent: Sock Puppets, Astroturfing, and Memes

Fraud and deception are used not only to steal money or sensitive information from people. They are also used to manipulate how people react to or
perceive events. Obviously, surveillance, espionage, propaganda, and other
widespread misinformation/disinformation campaigns have been in play for
some time now, as we covered in chapters 8 and 9. However, the online world
has developed even more methods of "manufacturing dissent" that overlap
with political and social positions.

We hear about the methods taken to persuade public opinion through
public relations campaigns and mass media blitzes, as Edward Herman and
Noam Chomsky (1988) point out in *Manufacturing Consent*, where the
media function as "effective and powerful ideological institutions that carry
out a system-supportive propaganda function . . . *without overt coercion.*"
The worst of these were the cigarette companies who blatantly covered up
damaging research that showed the link between cancer and smoking, while
widely broadcasting the benefits of smoking in commercial media. Of course,

they lost out in the end, but not without untold damage done to millions of people's health—and not before the actual "smoking gun" was found.

But the online world is vastly more complex in terms of how information is disseminated and consumed. Traditional mass media have been subverted by online media, as their print and broadcast means are no longer the only ways in which information can be shared. But they have adapted to this and enhanced their power by adopting online message and comment boards. Here, the online boards function as arms of various agendas and organizations, and instead of attempting to create consensus, they instead invite *dissension*.

Perhaps some of this is a result of the fragmented media structure and the realization that the days of suppressing information are long gone. But this manufactured dissent is also an obvious attempt to merely sow disagreement for the sake of disagreement, to sow contention regardless of whether one side is right or wrong on an issue. Sometimes the motivation is political, to confuse voters into supporting or at least doubting certain ideas. Sometimes the motivation is merely "kicks and giggles" from the troll set in an attempt to goad or instigate online users. Many of these new wedge issues have evolved into deep chasms within American life, including abortion rights, gun control and permissiveness, blue vs. red states, liberal vs. conservative viewpoints, and so on. As a result, whole organized campaigns that attempt to manipulate levels of obstruction and dissent come to dominate vast areas of the web, including web pages, web forums and discussion sites, and the ubiquitous comment sections in newspapers, online magazines, journals, blogs, and social media platforms. The result has been a steep decline in people communicating with each other in rational and empathetic ways (Rosin, 2019) and an increase in the deliberate muddying of the waters.

Another negative tendency in online "rabble-rousing" and antagonizing is the practice of *astroturfing*, which is "the attempt to create an *impression* of widespread grassroots support for a policy, individual, or product, where little such support exists" (Bienkov, 2012). We see the negative impacts of this from any array of organizations pretending to espouse specific viewpoints, or attempting to discredit them, while really existing to provide support for something else. One notorious example of this stems from the Russian government's attempt to swing the 2016 election in Candidate Trump's direction.

Page 31 of the redacted Mueller report (see figure 10.1) shows how the Krem-lin-backed Internet Research Agency (IRA) promoted the Trump campaign by advertising rallies in the name of "miners" or other blue-collar workers, while hiding the fact that they were actually Russian operatives (Mueller, 2019). The deception is telling, for it pretends that real-live people, purported free-thinking Americans, independently supported a cause or a person, while in reality it merely promoted the interests of a *hostile and adversarial government*. In the end, there is no evidence that these rallies ever occurred, further hammering home the point that these messages were created for the sole purpose of deception. This type of deception is also accomplished through "sock puppets," which are online identities used to fool other users. It references the simple hand puppet made from a sock but is a pejorative term for anyone assuming a false identity and pretending to be another person.

Obviously, without clear mandates requiring people disclose all their personal information for an online identity, the problem will persist. Yet part of the appeal of online life for many people is the very ability to mask one's

U.S. Department of Justice

~~Attorney-Work-Product // May-Contain-Material-Protected-Under-Fed. R. Crim. P. 6(e)~~

From June 2016 until the end of the presidential campaign, almost all of the U.S. rallies organized by the IRA focused on the U.S. election, often promoting the Trump Campaign and opposing the Clinton Campaign. Pro-Trump rallies included three in New York; a series of pro-Trump rallies in Florida in August 2016; and a series of pro-Trump rallies in October 2016 in Pennsylvania. The Florida rallies drew the attention of the Trump Campaign, which posted about the Miami rally on candidate Trump's Facebook account (as discussed below).[86]

Many of the same IRA employees who oversaw the IRA's social media accounts also conducted the day-to-day recruiting for political rallies inside the United States. Harm to Ongoing Matter

[87]

IRA Poster for Pennsylvania Rallies organized by the IRA

FIGURE 10.1

Screenshot excerpt of Robert Mueller's redacted report, page 31, as released to the public on April 18, 2019. *Mueller (2019)*

identity, to assume another identity at times even, and move freely without negative social consequences or the shame that accompanies much of real-world living. All of us perhaps engage in at least withholding of information, even our real names. Some, however, take it much further, developing alter egos or elaborate avatars for their online lives. There is nothing harmful in this, to a certain degree. It is harmful, however, when the deception is used to breed mistrust or to manipulate. This was another one of the tactics used by the IRA, which in 2017 "used 133 fake Instagram accounts to spread disinformation, gaining more than 183 million likes and 4 million comments" (Martineau, 2019). This egregious breach of trust erodes online communities and forces people to question whether their online counterparts are actually who they say they are. This ultimately eliminates the possibility of rational and truthful communication.

On the Memefication of Our Discourse

The word *meme* has been around since Richard Dawkins's 1976 book *The Selfish Gene*. In it, he defines a meme as a piece of information copied and then transmitted to another recipient. He conceives the idea in terms similar to how genes transmit their information from cell to cell to create complex organisms. He envisions them as "the cultural equivalent to genes" (Rogers, 2019). The meme's basic concepts—its ideas, information, wisdom, etc.—are shared among various people, then transmitted generation by generation to future descendants via verbal or visual means, especially electronic communications, books, television, e-mail, or the Internet.

Nowadays, however, the meme has morphed from the rather broad theoretical concept of cultural information passed down from generation to generation into a specific formalized *genre* of Internet communication, unique in both its format and layout and quite clearly bound to its time. Often using an image and a brief all-caps headline, like figure 10.2, the Internet meme conveys attitudes, emotions, and viewpoints in a compact manner. In the first one, a full understanding of the cultural references is expected, including part of a famous quote from the *Lord of the Rings* films (not the books), the advertising slogans of candy bars, and the parodic intent of mixing the two together. Though referred to as a meme, one could argue that this is not at all a stripped-down version of a transmittable idea. It is instead an elaborately constructed socially specific form, incapable of being stripped out of

FIGURE 10.2
An example of a typical Internet meme, showing the image with headline fonts, non sequiturs, and a clear punchline. *Google Image Search*

its cultural context and not easily transmittable beyond this current generation. It's hard to imagine future readers (in ten years, let alone one hundred)
fully grasping all that is implied by the meme or why it's even supposed to
be funny.

These memes convey, in essence, a strong point of view, a specific perspective on an issue, and quasi-political intent. A well-known meme shared on
Facebook by Iowa's fourth congressional district representative Steve King
(see figure 10.3), implies his support for a hypothetical civil war in the United
States and the impact that support of gun rights will have on one side of the
issue. Ironically, as many pointed out on various social media platforms, Iowa
sided with the Union during the Civil War and is shown below as being on
the same side as California. The fact that Iowa fought for the North during the
American Civil War seems to be lost on the various people who "liked" the
meme, not least of which the representative of Iowa himself. *Oops!* But details
like that are really *beside* the point. The meme was nonetheless effective at
antagonizing Mr. King's opponents while satisfying and flattering his supporters, especially as it conflated two contentious political issues: gun control
and LGBTQ gender equality rights (gender-blind bathrooms).

FIGURE 10.3
A well-known meme shared on Facebook by Iowa representative Steve King. *Washington Post*

What impact, though, does this "memefication" of the Internet have on our society? While the meme is an effective communication form to be sure, it also simplifies facts, perpetuates falsehoods, exacerbates polarized opinions, and elicits bullying and antagonistic behaviors, all for the sake of short-term emotional impacts dependent upon high levels of cultural fluency and large cultural blind spots. The meme, as it is currently constructed and deployed online, is used to shut down dissenting opinions, suppress rebuttals, and distort facts.

Cyberbullying

This leads us directly to bullying and shaming, which have become epidemic online over the past ten years. While these types of negative behaviors predate the online world and are an inherent part of human society in all forms, they seem to be exacerbated online. The act of bullying itself includes name-calling, spreading rumors, receiving explicit images, stalking behaviors, physical threats, and sharing images or information online without consent. Many of these behaviors exist in the real world, too, but the reach of the bullying has expanded beyond the proverbial mobs with pitchforks to online mobs with Facebook pages and Twitter feeds.

In 2007, the Pew Research Center studied the impact of online bullying and found some interesting results. At that time bullying seemed to happen a lot less online than in real life, according to the teenagers they surveyed. Girls surveyed then were more likely to report being bullied online than boys. Second, and importantly, Pew found that social media *significantly facilitated* bullying, with nearly 40 percent of respondents who used social media experiencing bullying of some form versus 20 percent for those who did not use social media. As Pew wrote at the time:

> The impulses behind [bullying] are the same, but the effect is magnified. In the past, the materials of bullying would have been whispered, shouted or passed around. Now, with a few clicks, a photo, video or a conversation can be shared with hundreds via email or millions through a website, online profile or blog posting. (Lenhart, 2007)

Following up in 2018, Pew found cyberbullying was even *more* pervasive. Fifty-nine percent of the respondents at this time reported they had been subjected to some form of cyberbullying online. But the difference now is that the likelihood of being bullied for boys or for girls was essentially the same. There is now no longer a gender gap in bullying, and there has also been an overall increase in the amount of bullying (Anderson, 2018). One obvious reason for this increase is that significantly more people are now on social media than there were in 2007. Facebook, for example, had from twenty to fifty million users worldwide at the time. Now it has approximately 2.3 billion. Twitter rose even more precipitously in that same time period, growing from a few thousand in 2007 to 321 million by 2019. The share of teens on social media has grown with this rise—and for a time, teenagers *drove* this rise. As a result, it is not surprising that incidents of bullying would increase as well.

Online Shaming

The other side of bullying is shaming. One of the more interesting looks at how shame has come to dominate social media is Jon Ronson's 2016 book *So*

You've Been Publicly Shamed. In the book, Ronson recounts numerous people who have been called out for transgressions, dishonesty, or poor choices of words on social media and describes the impact it has on their careers, personal lives, and reputations (online and offline). In one telling example, Ronson details how one woman tweeted something marginally offensive, boarded a plane for an eleven-hour flight, and arrived at her destination to a full-blown online assault and roast on Twitter. In the end, she was fired from her job and left with a sense of injustice that lingered on for months and years afterward (Ronson, 2016). Her reputation was essentially destroyed by the public shaming. Ronson suggests that "with social media, we've created a stage for constant high drama. Every day a new person emerges as a magnificent hero or a sickening villain" (Ronson, 2016, p. 79). And this occurs at alarming frequency. A recent story in the *Washington Post* discussed how a woman, Yovana Mendoza Ayres, posed as a vegan for years online, traveling and espousing the "glamorous" lifestyle of veganism, while secretly eating a regular diet (including fish protein) because veganism had caused health problems. The online shame machine was swift and brutal. Like many preachers caught in sin against their congregations, Ayres attempted to rectify by coming clean, while at the same time rationalizing it to hold onto the golden goose: her followers.

We can derive some lessons, at least, from these public shamings. Some people certainly deserve their fates for deceiving others and taking money or property based on that deception. Yet some might suggest that the *users* of these systems are also victims. These "algorithm-driven systems . . . [are] forcing them into a never-ending quest for viewers, ad money, sponsorships and engagement against dwindling attention spans" (Rosenberg, E., 2019). The technology exerts its own pressure on people to act in ways that we might otherwise see as shameful and would typically avoid. In the case of Ms. Ayres, we can see that the drive to uphold her image online as the fit and beautiful paragon of the so-very-rich-and-vegan lifestyle clearly clouded her judgment. While a regular person might actually abandon their stance of strict veganism in the face of legitimate health problems, the benefits of that social media mirage were too great to abandon. Despite the threat of public shaming, people still risk it all to acquire online notoriety. They are willing to deal with the slings and arrows of an online mob for the sake of real-world financial and social capital. But isn't that similar for many of us? We might sometimes take up positions online that may, in fact, be adopted for a like or a retweet, just to increase what we see as our online social standing.

Cultural appropriation has become another trend in public shaming, with many people growing upset over perceived thefts of ideas or art from other cultures. A few years back Katy Perry, the pop singer, was abused online and shamed for wearing a kimono in a music video. Accusations of yellow-face were leveled at her as she appeared to not have the consent of the owning culture (Feeney, 2013). Of course, it is not my intent to judge whether these grievances are legitimate or not or to criticize postcolonialism and other useful theories for analyzing culture and power. The centuries- and decades-long aftermath of the era of colonialism absolutely still has scars that will persist until effort is made to heal them. But we should also keep in mind that the sharing and stealing of ideas from others is something that *all* humans do, regardless of the dominant power structures, which, as we see with Japan's postwar reintegration into the world economy, can change over time.

But I digress. What is more relevant to this discussion is the technological mechanism fueling the growth of online antagonism and shaming. The increase in accusations of cultural appropriation may be linked to the ability for a message to be spread more quickly through social media, allowing outrage and the anger to flare up more intensely than ever before. While cultural exchange, and yes, even appropriation in the form of "unauthorized" copying, has happened before in the past—for millennia, even—it has never occurred in such a widespread manner so quickly. Exchange has usually happened much more slowly. The current pushback against appropriation may be driven partly by technological advances resulting in a kind of techno-fundamentalism. We should be reminded that fundamentalism—like railing against cultural appropriation—is a form of pushback against societal change, both technological *and* behavioral. It is no wonder that fundamentalism often leads to positions of extremism and violence. Our attitudes exist along a continuum from complete tolerance of behavior to complete intolerance, regardless of one's personal politics or one's pet ideas. It is entirely possible—and incredibly ironic as well—that one can be intolerant of intolerance, exhibiting the same extreme behavior of disliking or hating (or shaming) someone who is themselves intolerant. Publicly shaming someone in the name of cultural appropriation exhibits this same unfortunate irony.

Another irony that stems from this is that extremists—especially white supremacists and Islamic terrorists—in the modern world have adopted the very tools created by the society they want to eradicate. Perhaps nothing would give such people greater satisfaction than to use the tools of the society they hate to literally bring it down. However, extremism not only polarizes and exacerbates the problem of online communication, it also forces people to take adversarial positions where none used to exist, or where only fringe elements cared to take up the fight. We are shoehorned into believing the world is at its roots adversarial or that the world is full of unresolved conflicts waiting to flare up. As the *Washington Post* has reported, in the wake of the New Zealand terrorist attacks (and prior to the retaliatory Easter attacks in Sri Lanka), the opposing viewpoints of white supremacy and Islamist terrorism have fueled each other. They are strengthening their ranks by fixating on the conflicts, both virtual and real, between them. De-escalating this conflict requires that *both* sides be diminished, not just one (Anderson, 2019).

Ultimately, though, there is more to the world than a faux-Manichaean struggle between the forces of good and evil. Not everything is a zero-sum game. The battle lines are sometimes clearly drawn online, as some issues appear to be "either-or," but the technology itself may actually exaggerate, facilitate, and encourage these differences. Researcher danah boyd introduces the term *agnotology* to describe the forces that artificially construct these adversarial sides to an issue, which ultimately turns it into a political act (boyd, 2019). We should, therefore, be well-reminded of this context before we engage in online arguments and be more cognizant of how the technology may be encouraging us to adopt adversarial roles.

On Internet Trolls

In addition to ongoing technological manipulations and bad-faith actions, as well as the manufactured polarization of opinion and communication itself, online conflicts are further exacerbated when adding another factor, the Internet troll. Like adding gasoline to a fire, the troll exacerbates the heated argument, thickens the fog of war, and spews out the confusion of irrational and irrelevant debate. The point is the disruption of legitimate rhetoric and the sidelining of reason, all to stoke anger. Now the etymology of the troll is interesting. It draws its name from the Scandinavian mythological creature

that lives under the bridge blocking passage and generally annoying wayfar-
ers. Of course, that tells part of the story. The first real documented use of
the term appeared in 1992, in an online newsgroup, where one poster com-
mented, "If I didn't know better I would *swear* that this post bears the mark
of the inevitable Peter van der Linden in *troll* mode" (OED, 2019). The intent
seems to be clear: someone deliberately causing trouble, blocking safe passage
to reason, forcing people into argument and disagreement online.

American politicians have absorbed the general adversarial nature of online life, too, as we saw in figure 10.3. The intent was to antagonize a specific
group of people. In this case it was "liberals" and "gun control nuts." But there
are millions of other examples where the antagonizing parties are reversed,
and liberals poke fun at the ignorance of rubes or the religious. Regardless of
party affiliation, however, the dynamic remains the same: the person deliberately posts something provocative in order to antagonize. It's unclear if the
troll really believes the message, or if it's just for show. Indeed, researchers
have pointed out that online behaviors on new social media platforms "cloud
judgments of intent and intentionality" (DeAndrea, 2012). It's easy to mis-
interpret what people are trying to say online, and trolls find ways to exploit
this weakness by making it seem like they're fully vested in the outrageous
ideas they espouse.

Usually, though, the troll doesn't have a dog in the fight. Instead, the troll
prefers to take a contrary stance just for the sake of it, a form of intellectual
hipsterism with malevolent intent. The ultimate goal of the troll is to dumb
down or to destabilize a conversation and disrupt attempts at communication. Success is then measured by how much the troll can goad others into
irrational and angered responses, to force them into "self-destructive" acts
that undercut their own best interests or reputations. The way these ends are
met are through employing basic rhetorical tricks to anger people. This might
include things such as ad hominem attacks, which are personal insults about
someone's personality to discredit them, or anecdotal fallacies in which a
personal story—likely fabricated—is used to prove the opposition wrong. The
point is to discredit opponents by any means necessary and to disrupt normal
social interactions.

It's entirely possible, too, that trolls are acting out with classic psychopathic behavior or antisocial disorders, disrupting normal communication

and collaboration in order to feel more in control of their own lives. One researcher identifies the source of this problem as a reaction to the alienating and distancing effects of online technology itself. Being online, according to the theory, causes a physical and psychic distance from others, known as "de-individuation," where no one exists to take blame or get hurt (McDermott, 2012). Indeed, the people perpetuating online trolling *never* risk their own necks. Their livelihoods, reputations, or even friendships are never threatened by societal retributions that might otherwise happen in real life. The troll hides behind a wall (or under that bridge). However, when real stakes are added to online identities, perhaps trolling will fade out, and personal responsibilities will rise.

WHEN THE ONLINE WORLD OF THE UPSIDE-DOWN SPILLS INTO THE REAL WORLD

The relatively good news in all this is that online misbehaviors can be ignored just as easily as they can be carried out. All we need to do is turn off the computer or the phone and move on with our lives. And generally, we do. Even among politics, where the rhetoric is heated and logical fallacies routinely fly in the face of reality, social media still must contend with reality. Many make the mistake of assuming that political views shared on Twitter represent the views of a general population, or "a clear window into pure public opinion" (Mounk, 2019). In truth, they do not. Real voters aren't always the members of the Twitterverse. And often real-world events turn out to contradict or refute what was happening online.

But here's the rub: as we have increasingly seen, the boundaries between the real world and the digital world are becoming more blurred. Technology in the form of Google Glass, cell phones, the Internet of Things, and wearables assures that we have increasingly less time offline. Much of what we do now remains online whether we want it to or not. The clear demarcation between our digital life and our real-world, analog, flesh-and-blood life *is no longer there.* Just as there is no distinction between some people's Facebook accounts and their social lives—meaning their online friends *are* their real-life friends—there also is no distinction between the love and hate online and in real life. It is when online worlds collide with reality that the greatest damage and danger, both physical and psychological, takes hold.

Real-World Impacts: A Timeline in Real Time

Back to March 2019. It started when a terrorist killed fifty-one people and injured forty-nine in separate attacks on two mosques in New Zealand. The terrorist was inspired by online hate speech but took things a step further by broadcasting the attack in real time on Facebook Live, while people (in horror or morbid curiosity) watched online. *Axios* reported later that same day that "the New Zealand mosque shooter leveraged social media channels to spread both a race-hatred manifesto and a horrifying live video of his killings, throwing a harsh light on online platforms' continuing role in propagating extremist violence" (Rosenberg, S., 2019). The live video feed makes the incident even more visceral, more shocking. It is possible that such events may occur more frequently as the large impact felt from this one will spur others on.

One month later, in retaliation from Islamic terrorist groups on Easter Sunday, 2019, Christians were killed as they worshipped in Sri Lanka. The organization aligned with the suicide bombers took credit for the attack and claimed they were revenge for the New Zealand attacks one month earlier. As we saw in the previous section, the adversarial nature of online life seems to be feeding the hatred of both these groups. Their actions have spilled over into real-world events, making the tolerance of their views less and less sustainable. And the views become more extreme until it devolves into open conflict. As P. W. Singer and Emerson Brooking (2018) in their excellent book *LikeWar* describe it, "Conflicts of popularity and perception began to merge with conflicts of flesh and blood. As the stakes of these online struggles increased, they began to look and feel like war. Soon enough, they would *become* war" (p. 4). Spurred on by the desire to bring fame and notoriety for their group and their twisted principles, they hatch more shocking and diabolical plans for violence, resulting in a strange online viral arms race of who can out-shock their rivals. It doesn't end until most everyone in the groups is dead or someone backs down.

This is not only the case with white supremacist and Islamist jihadist groups, but also with gangs and gang violence. Their violent behaviors have been further exacerbated by online social media, so much so that new slang has grown around it to better describe them. "Wall banging," "Facebook drilling," "cybertagging," and "cyberbanging" each describe real-world attacks and killings of rival gang members—or other bystanders—instigated by online feuds and arguments. For those neither up on their social media or gang terminology, "wall" refers to someone's Facebook profile page, and "banging" is a slang term for overall gang violence or murder. Instead of leaving the trolling and taunting online, some gang members become bent on real-world retaliation.

But what causes a virtual insult to spill over into physical violence? Without any regulations to crack down on insult and baiting language, social media effectively allows any person to start up a feud, almost without warning (Singer and Brooking, 2018). The result of poorly regulating the hate and instigation of rival gangs or criminals "is a cycle of confrontation in which the distinction between online and offline criminal worlds has essentially become blurred" (ibid., p. 14). A person, insulted online, decides to exact revenge on a rival in the real world. It escalates from a war of words and reputations to gunfights and murders. Chicago's stubborn persistence in gang violence, even as crime in American cities has mostly declined, may be a result of these cyber-exacerbated behaviors, where reputation and standing depend on shows of strength, to "goad foes and brag about their crimes" (AP News, 2018). Simply speaking, a person's virtual reputation is intertwined with their physical one. Any failure to address challenges to it shows weakness. The result is the zero-sum game of gang warfare, openly broadcast for all to see and judge and leave a Facebook "Like." And so, the cycle of violence continues. Retaliations for virtual slights spill over into the physical world in an ongoing pattern that mimics the sharing patterns and memes of social media itself, only delivered with violence. Imagined slights can turn into volatile anger and grievance at any time.

Whose Life Is It Anyway? (or, the Need for More Oversight)

We must ask ourselves whether the online world is as transparent and benevolent as it once seemed twenty-five years ago. Its original promise has morphed into something totally different than the free exchange of information between scholars and researchers. While the freedom of expression of ideas is paramount in American life, there are unresolved questions with this freedom. Where, for example, are the lines drawn between censorship and responsibility? Where does responsibility begin for the *platforms* providing and facilitating online content creation and content sharing?

Margaret Sullivan, a media columnist, writes, "As violence goes more and more viral, tech companies need to deal with the crisis that they have helped create" (Sullivan, 2019). But what is the responsibility of a platform like You-Tube or Facebook Live, which did indeed help to perpetuate the New Zealand terror attack video in real time? Why isn't Facebook held more responsible or partially liable for some of this? Isn't it time that they are held responsible for the negative content that they profit from? The Digital Copyright Millennium Act provides platforms and online content providers with a "Safe Harbor" in the case of copyrighted materials, meaning that they are not held liable for copyright infringement if a user posts a Disney video without its permission. But they are still required to comply with copyright law by taking down violating material. The same, however, cannot be said for the liability of Google or YouTube in light of terrorist videos that are broadcast on their platform. Despite the magnitude of the need for a solution, there seems to be no mechanism in place for holding Google or Facebook accountable for enabling the spread of information that leads to hate crimes or terrorist activity.

Related to this, people can be directly affected or manipulated by online content that implicates them or uses their images and identities without their permission. In some cases, this is criminal, as in the case of "revenge porn," when a jilted lover posts illicit home videos of themselves and their partners or releases illicit images intended for the recipient only. This is a more widespread problem, though, than it seems at first glance and can be used to blackmail or threaten people, either for purely monetary gains or for political gains.

Earlier in this chapter we saw the example of the rally event created by the Russian government cyberwarfare/troll farm Internet Research Agency to benefit the Trump campaign in the summer of 2016. The miner, whose real name is Lee Hipshire, was used in the IRA advertisement (shown in figure 10.1). The ad was posted on Facebook and other social media sites using his image without his permission. In fact, Mr. Hipshire's son claims that his father, who died in 1987, would not have approved of the use of his image, as he was a lifelong Democrat. Putting rights for personal privacy aside, as well as the legality of using someone's image without the publication rights, the fact remains that the image was used to manipulate the outcome of an important real-world event, the 2016 U.S. presidential election. More specifically, it was used to promote "dissension in the ranks of coal miners and working people in particular with misinformation" (Madej, 2019). But what happened to Mr. Hipshire's image, and even his reputation, is not an isolated incident.

Vietnam Veterans of America, a congressionally chartered organization, examines similar abuses of images and online accounts of U.S. military servicemen and women in their report, "An Investigation into Foreign Entities Who are Targeting Servicemembers and Veterans Online" (Wentling, 2019). They warn about the widespread co-opting of military veterans' online images or the use of their social media identities to defraud others.

Data breaches and the misuse of people's online identities also have a disproportionate effect on the lower class and the poor. For not only are the poor more likely to be targeted for criminal profiling and background checks, they are also more likely to encounter predatory lending and other borderline legal and exploitative practices while online. Data brokers assemble digital dossiers of people and break them into narrow categories, including such labels as "rural and barely making it" or "credit crunched: city families." The poor are then targeted with online advertisements for "predatory products such as payday loans, high-interest mortgages and for-profit educational scams" (Gilman, 2019). The ads contribute directly, and negatively, to the quality of a person's life. The result, much like the cycle of violence with gangs online, is generations of people caught in endemic poverty exacerbated by excessive loan terms, unreasonable penalties, and hidden fees designed to exploit those most in need of quick cash or desperate for a change in careers.

FIXING CRACKED MIRRORS AND DISTORTED GLASSES: VISUALIZING A MORE SOCIALLY CONSCIOUS MEDIA

I suspect that we all take the Internet's transparency for granted. We use it every day, and bad things generally don't happen to us. Or if they do, we just find ways to shut it off or shut it down. The Internet is a constant part of our life, part of the background hum informing our daily habits, waiting patiently for us to log on, post, or reply to someone in good faith and friendship. Social media has had a huge impact by bringing people together. But what if the screen is not really as transparent as it seems? What if, instead, we're entering an alternative to physical reality itself *pretending* to be real?

The Internet, I believe, has become a veritable digital looking glass that not only distorts what's within it but also manipulates our thoughts and perceptions about ourselves and the world. Perhaps this confusion accounts for some of the skewed and warped behaviors we see magnified online. By confusing this alternate reality within the looking glass for the real thing, some people are acting out in pathological ways. Instead of operating *within* reality, they are operating in an alternate version with its own rules of engagement. When the usual rules of engagement we're accustomed to suddenly do not apply, we are goaded into angered responses as a result. If we can take a step backward and realize that the rules of the game have changed, that others are in fact manipulating our behaviors for their own ends, then perhaps we can begin to push back and solve some of the pathological and antisocial problems that routinely occur online.

This may be more easily said than done, it is true. However, all hope is not lost. In fact, there are clear ways to combat these problems, if taken one step at a time and approached with multiple strategies. The next section of this book will look at how these ongoing and exacerbated information pathologies can be counteracted, starting with engaging and neutralizing the trolls and bots.

REFERENCES

419 Eater. (2019). Home page. www.419eater.com/.

Anderson, M. (2018). A majority of teens have experienced some form of cyberbullying. Pew Research Center. www.pewInternet.org/2018/09/27/a-majority-of-teens-have-experienced-some-form-of-cyberbullying/.

Anderson, S. (2019). The twin hatreds: How white supremacy and Islamist terrorism strengthen each other online—and in a deadly cycle of attacks. *Washington Post*. www.washingtonpost.com/news/posteverything/wp/2019/03/22/feature/how-white-supremacy-and-islamist-terrorism-strengthen-each-other-online/?utm_term=.b3fd778bd582.

AP News. 2018. The latest: New Chicago gangs case highlight social media. www.apnews.com/a99dd02184f64f92b6c31b59078d057b.

Bienkov, A. (2012). Astroturfing: What is it and why does it matter? *Guardian*. www.theguardian.com/commentisfree/2012/feb/08/what-is-astroturfing.

Bloomberg, J. (2017). Fear these three types of phish: "Catphishing" enterprise targets. *Forbes*. www.forbes.com/sites/jasonbloomberg/2017/10/14/fear-these-three-types-of-phish-catphishing-enterprise-targets/#38776a4379f1.

boyd, d. 2019. Agnotology and epistemological fragmentation. Points: Data & Society Research Institute. points.datasociety.net/agnotology-and-epistemological-fragmentation-56aa3c509c6b.

Crampton, T. (2007). Scamming the e-mail scammers. *New York Times*. www
.nytimes.com/2007/07/01/technology/01iht-scam.1.6428742.html.

DeAndrea, D. (2012). Participatory social media and the evaluation of online
behavior. *Human Communication Research, 38*(4), 510–28. doi.org/10.1111/
j.1468-2958.2012.01435.x.

Feeney, N. (2013). Katy Perry's "geisha-style" performance needs to be called out.
Atlantic. www.theatlantic.com/entertainment/archive/2013/11/katy-perrys
-geisha-style-performance-needs-to-be-called-out/281805/.

Giandomenico, N. (2019). What is spear-phishing? Defining and differentiating
spear-phishing from phishing. Digital Guardian. digitalguardian.com/blog/what
-is-spear-phishing-defining-and-differentiating-spear-phishing-and-phishing.

Gilman, M. (2019). Data insecurity leads to economic injustice—and hits the
pocketbooks of the poor most. The Conversation. theconversation.com/data
-insecurity-leads-to-economic-injustice-and-hits-the-pocketbooks-of-the-poor
-most-116231.

Herman, E., and Chomsky, N. (1988). *Manufacturing consent*. New York: Pantheon
Books.

Lenhart, A. (2007). Cyberbullying. Pew Research Center. www.pewInternet
.org/2007/06/27/cyberbullying/.

Madej, P. (2019). Son of man who was face of "Miners for Trump" flyers targeting
Pa. says dad would have been angry. Philly dot com. www.philly.com/politics/
mueller-report-miners-for-trump-philadelphia-russia-photo-20190423.html.

Martineau, P. (2019). The existential crisis plaguing online extremism researchers.
Wired. www.wired.com/story/existential-crisis-plaguing-online-extremism
-researchers/?utm_source=pocket-newtab.

Maza, C. (2018). China involved in 90 percent of espionage and industrial secrets
theft, Department of Justice reveals. *Newsweek*. www.newsweek.com/china
-involved-90-percent-economic-espionage-and-industrial-secrets-theft-1255908.

McDermott, I. (2012). Trolls, cyberbullies, and other offenders. *Searcher, 20*(10),
7–11.

Mounk, Y. (2019). The problem isn't Twitter. It's that you care about Twitter.
Atlantic. www.theatlantic.com/ideas/archive/2019/04/political-leaders-should
-stop-caring-about-twitter/588004/.

Mueller, R. (2019). Report on the investigation into Russian interference in the 2016 presidential election. United States Department of Justice. www.justice.gov/storage/report.pdf.

Oxford English Dictionary. (2019). www.oed.com/.

Pelly, L. (2019). The antisocial network. *Logic Magazine.* logicmag.io/06-the-antisocial-network/.

Rogers, K. (2019). Meme: cultural concept. *Encyclopedia Britannica.* www.britannica.com/topic/meme.

Ronson, J. (2016). *So you've been publicly shamed.* New York: Riverhead Books.

Rosenberg, E. (2019). Vegan YouTube star Rawvana went to Bali. A video by Pauvlogs helped bring her platform crashing down. *Washington Post.* www.washingtonpost.com/technology/2019/03/22/vegan-youtube-star-rawvana-gets-caught-eating-meat-camera/?utm_term=.abf7e98df796.

Rosenberg, S. (2019). New Zealand killings hatched and exploded online. *Axios.* www.axios.com/new-zealand-mosque-killings-social-media-56020d80-de41-4819-be2d-a202b6b1bc48.html.

Rosin, H. (2019). The end of empathy. NPR. www.npr.org/2019/04/15/712249664/the-end-of-empathy?utm_source=pocket-newtab.

Shaban, H. (2019). Alexandria Ocasio-Cortez quits Facebook, calls social media a "public health risk." *Washington Post.* www.washingtonpost.com/technology/2019/04/15/alexandria-ocasio-cortez-quits-facebook-calls-social-media-public-health-risk/?utm_term=.5cd360d59e56.

Singer, P., and Brooking, E. (2018). *LikeWar: The weaponization of social media.* New York: Houghton Mifflin Harcourt.

Sullivan, M. (2019). Social media platforms were used like lethal weapons in New Zealand. That must change now. *Washington Post.* www.washingtonpost.com/lifestyle/style/social-media-platforms-were-used-like-lethal-weapons-in-new-zealand-that-must-change-now/2019/03/15/aaeafbc8-471e-11e9-90f0-0ccfeec87a61_story.html?utm_term=.2bafd1591d17.

Wentling, N. (2019). Cybercriminals target military online to set up imposter "romance scams." *Stars and Stripes.* www.stripes.com/cybercriminals-target-military-online-to-set-up-imposter-romance-scams-1.599355.

IV

DRAINING THE FEVER SWAMP

11

Combating the Trolls and Bots

Today we think that what is false and artificial in the world around us is substantive and meaningful. It's not that loved ones and friends are mistaken for simulations, but that simulations are mistaken for them.

—*Robert Sapolsky*

There is no end of history; each generation must assert its will and imagination as new threats require us to retry the case in every age.

—*Shoshana Zuboff*

PATHOLOGIES AND THE PROBLEMS OF AN INFORMATION-WISDOM HIERARCHY

The term "pathologies" has been used a lot in this book. The word infers a kind of sickness, or at least a negative set of symptoms that are the result of external and internal obstructions. These are the negative *conditions* preventing the free exchange of ideas and the creation of shared and mutual trust. I am not suggesting that there is an "ideal" set of conditions that will create a perfect understanding of all the information that exists. "What is *truth*?" is a timeless question that resists an easy answer—and beware anyone who tells you otherwise. Testing and living within reality is a part of being human, even as we imagine something new or different, even as we struggle with first causes, the limits of our perceptions, and our own faulty senses. Some of this speculation is merely about pointing out where flaws may exist in the current theories about information (and how information functions/works) as well as in the technology transferring it from user to user. Even researchers who explore information and information technology have reached crisis points when it comes to the Internet, often seeing it as "an unreliable narrator," in which "any attempt to interpret online actions with the same sincerity afforded to those in the real world is fraught" (Martineau, 2019). Yet the breakdowns and failures to reach perfection may not even be the technologies' fault, but instead those flaws may stem from ourselves.

Although technology may exacerbate and worsen underlying problems, bringing them out more prominently into the forefront, the root cause is not *necessarily* technology itself. As one researcher suggests, "Without a sense of communal impact or personal responsibility, it's increasingly difficult to expect a shift towards less toxic behavior and amplification" (Martineau, 2019). Better online behavior starts with clearer social expectations, rewarding good behavior and penalizing the bad. It is not entirely social media's fault, for example, that people use those technologies to bully others. The tendency to bully stems from people themselves. By the same token, it is also not necessarily library search technology's fault that people prefer to take the easiest pathway to finding things. I sometimes hear academic librarians complain that students stop searching after the first few hits on a list, assuming that they are lazy or have procrastinated so much that they have too little time to thoroughly search through a library's deep resources. But the cause is not always laziness or putting things off. More often, it's pragmatism. The old joke is quite revealing: librarians love to search, but users prefer to *find*. "Why waste our time," the students are really saying to us, "when good enough only takes a few seconds?"

Of course, some of the problems we have always faced are made *much* worse than before. Information overload, a phenomenon noted over the millennia, is more potent than it has ever been. Spying and surveillance has reached undreamt-of heights of invasiveness—threatening to eliminate privacy for anyone, except for the very rich and very powerful. And that gets to the height of these issues. Everything we consider to be part of a good life, as Aristotle might have put it, including our access to information and the development of our own personal sense of agency, is subject to the misapplication of technology and the abuses of power that come with it.

As a result, by conceiving these imperfect information conditions as a se-ries of pathologies—like conceiving of diseases in terms of pathogen vectors rather than "ill humors"—we can perhaps better see where our assumptions about information may be erroneous. We do not need to approach these problems as dirges for the paradises of information lost or as laments for the limitations (or the laziness) of the human mind, but instead as a series of *conditions* that might be improved upon with the right approaches.

The remaining chapters in this book's final section, "Draining the Fever Swamp," will examine the practical and enforceable strategies that can be created to improve the information landscape. This chapter, specifically, will focus on how to neutralize some of the more irritating, obnoxious, and bad-faith online actors: the trolls, bots, and disruptors. The stakes are high, getting at the basic question of who gets to control our online world and why. To do so, we will examine ways in which we can make bad behavior online a little more accountable and online life a little more bearable.

DESIGNING AN ERA OF ACCOUNTABILITY

Mark Zuckerberg surprised people with an opinion piece in the *Washington Post* in 2019 outlining his proposal for four new Internet rules. He acknowl-edged up-front that mistakes were made by Facebook and other IT giants in the past. To rectify these mistakes, he proposed focusing on the following areas: (1) harmful content, (2) election integrity, (3) privacy, and (4) data portability. For harmful content, Zuckerberg recommended regulation from third-party, independent watchdog groups, suggesting self-published "trans-parency reports" from all IT companies outlining their efforts to remove and combat negative content. An independent group, he argued, would allow people to appeal decisions to remove content, thus better balancing consid-erations of personal harm versus the freedom of speech. Zuckerberg's second suggestion of protecting elections is well-taken in this political environment. He suggests new legislation to ensure that elections are free of outside inter-ference. This is certainly the most salient improvement for the near future, especially as important elections are looming. It is striking, however, that this idea is also the *least* fleshed out in terms of actionable items. In other words, the question still remains for us, not Facebook, to figure out: *what are we go-ing to do about it?*

In terms of privacy, Zuckerberg also suggested further regulation and legislation along the lines of the European Union's General Data Protection Regulation (GDPR), the well-publicized legislative attempt to rein in surveillance-capitalist practices, which collect and resell our data for the purposes of making money. If we have more control over our data, we can create a better online experience for ourselves. Directly related to protecting our privacy is data portability, Zuckerberg's fourth suggestion. It allows people to obtain and reuse their personal data for their own purposes. We are all familiar with how difficult it is to get the "full dossier" of our digital footprint across all the hundreds of Internet services and platforms we encounter daily on the Internet. Data portability, however, is meant to address this constant road-blocking of our information and is meant to facilitate and force data releases (Zuckerberg, 2019). Combining privacy regulations, which allow us to restrict who sees our information, with robust data portability regulations, which would allow us to dispose of our information as we see fit, might *together* provide people with more autonomy than they currently have. But it is not a foregone conclusion that either will even work on their own, let alone function coherently together as a protective body of legislation.

The open call for new regulations from Mark Zuckerberg ironically highlights the problems of dealing with big-data-driven social media platforms. The major social media companies, including Google and Zuckerberg's Facebook, have had a tendency to be disingenuous at worst and naïve at best about what they are doing. For example, despite Zuckerberg's insistence upon "election integrity," two months after his op-ed, Facebook *refused* to take down a doctored video (aka a "deep fake") of a Nancy Pelosi speech. The doctored video of Pelosi was slowed down to imitate slurred speech in order to make it look like she was drunk. Copies of this video were shared across all social media platforms, especially Facebook, Twitter, YouTube, and the usual suspects. More than two million hits occurred in the first few days (Harwell, 2019). The refusal to take it down directly contradicts their founder's earlier public stance about dealing with "harmful content." It's hard to say if the call for new Internet rules was just naïveté on the part of Zuckerberg or a calculated ploy to appease vocal critics without having to actually change.

Realistically, despite their idealistic rhetoric, these companies still have a long way to go to make good on their public promises, especially when they continue to obsess over the bottom line while reaping the benefits of minimal legal oversight. This is a case where we need to watch not what they say, but what they *do*. Pelosi, to her credit, did not mince words about Facebook: "They were willing enablers of the Russian interference in our election," she declared. Unfortunately, Facebook's defense of this incident was not exactly principled, as they merely reiterated their long-standing hands-off policy that they were in the "social media business," not the news business.

Fortunately, we don't have to take Mark Zuckerberg's unclear motives as the final word on how to remake the Internet to fit a better image of humanity. There are, again, always more solutions than the limited ones offered to us, especially the ones presented to us as false dilemmas. It's not *either* you have privacy *or* you have security, with one destined to elbow out the other. There is a need for both, and a nuanced balance in the form of regulation or legislation will help bring this about. We need not be bound by the compromise between two incomplete solutions when there may be a thousand other ways to solve these issues. Furthermore, there are other things to consider beyond the four areas that Zuckerberg suggested and subsequently ignored. The unspoken assumption by Zuckerberg (and all the other social media leaders for that matter) is that people will continue to be as openly trusting and extend the same amount of goodwill toward Silicon Valley as in the past. But what they fail to realize is that openness and trust will decline if the dominant online platforms don't get their acts together.

CREATING NEW DIGITAL PROVENANCES AND EFFECTIVE "RULES OF ONLINE ENGAGEMENT"

It has been noted that the Internet erased cultural and social boundaries and mores. These boundaries were usually established over time within the context of a social contract, but that sense of history and "provenance" for online life and behavior is now diminished. It has been reported that 89 percent of cell phone owners used their phones during their most recent social gathering (Rainie and Zickuhr, 2015). The implications for this are not immediately noticeable but are ultimately far-reaching. We wind up diminishing our "social connections to mere threads so that we can maintain as many of them as possible. This leaves us with signposts of familiarity that are frail remnants of the real thing" (Sapolsky, 2019). The focus of the quantity over the quality of relationships is damaging to our social fabric. Thinning and dwindling relationships with real people lead directly to an increased vulnerability to imposters and con artists. Without the bonds we make through constant interactions with real people, not their avatars, we lose practice in being able to verify whether or not someone is being truthful. Right now, it is especially important to create that much-needed provenance, much like it was important in the past to represent authority and trust through the development of the "seal of approval," the stamp, and other markers and monikers of trust. But how can trust be developed in an illusory online world that is constantly changing and can be mimicked and altered to look like the real world?

Social Credit Systems: So, Do You Want the Carrot or the Stick?

Obviously, one important way that trust can be built up on social media is by prioritizing and focusing on our *real* ties, the people we actually know and interact with in real life. The other way that has been developed over time, in the absence of a first degree of separation, is the creation of verification and certification systems. Brands and seals originate from our desire for consistency in the things that we buy. Our attachment to labels and brands very much originates out of this need for verification that we're not wasting our hard-earned money. Trust and reputation are still important. It cuts both ways, too. When banks require that we have good reputations garnered from credit scores, we are essentially telling them that we're going to be trustworthy enough to pay back the money we borrowed. We'll deliver on our promises, just like the Gucci label delivers. Current digital technologies have allowed this concept of reputational branding to expand further into more powerful digital systems that reward desired traits and marginalize those considered less desirable. But as we have seen, the devil is in the details. How this system is implemented would make a big difference in all our lives.

The social credit systems being developed in China, such as the National Social Credit System and Alibaba's Zhima Credit, show us one way of approaching crowd control: mass surveillance and control of behavior through incentives and punishments. If you behave desirably within this social credit system, you receive desirable perks. Trustworthy behaviors lead to benefits such as fast-tracked government visas, lower taxes, free health checkups, travel vouchers, even access to desirable dating web sites (Kostka, 2019)! One significant benefit lets people move to the top of medical care waiting lists. Another allows people to rent a car without a security deposit. If you are for all intents and purposes a non-threatening presence, you will likely thrive.

However, if your presence is or becomes threatening, whether because of personal beliefs, your racial profile, your looks, your job, your political affiliation, or the shifting whims of power, then you will have a much harder time succeeding. You might lose access to those desired perks. You might have to pay higher fees for some services, or you find you are now blocked from certain online dating sites.

Unlike Facebook, however, you can't really quit this type of system without negative consequences. It's too big to ignore, and it's getting bigger. As Paul Mozur reports in the *New York Times*, "With millions of cameras and billions of lines of code, China is building a high-tech authoritarian future. Beijing is embracing technologies like facial recognition and artificial intelligence to identify and track 1.4 billion people" (Mozur, 2018). For China, the ultimate goal appears to be "algorithmic governance," which they believe will solve the problems of controlling human behavior through tracking, assessment, and prediction. But this avenue, tempting as it is to any dime-a-dozen Silicon Valley techno-utopian or power-hungry politician, is fraught with peril.

China has expressed interest in adding blockchain technology to their banking system, allowing the government to track its citizens' financial transactions. As reported by Bernard Zand (2018) for *Der Spiegel* in 2018, China has already created a prototype for their nationwide surveillance system in their Xinjiang region, which is home to an Islamic majority:

> The surveillance infrastructure in Kashgar is state of the art, but the Chinese government is already working on the next level of control. It wants to introduce a "social credit system" that rates the "trustworthiness" of each citizen, to reward loyalty and punish bad behavior. While the rollout of this system in the densely populated east has been sluggish and spotty, the Uighurs are evidently already subjected to a similar point-based system. This system primarily involves details that could be interesting to the police. . . . Every family begins with 100 points, one person affected by the system tells us. But anyone with contacts or relatives abroad, especially in Islamic countries like Turkey, Egypt or Malaysia, is punished by losing points. A person with fewer than 60 points is in danger. One wrong word, a prayer or one telephone call too many and they could be sent to "school" in no time.

Beyond the privacy aspects of this undertaking, the racism and abuses of power against minority cultures, in this case Uighurs, Kazakhs, Mongolians, and Chinese-speaking Muslim Hui, appear to be one of the main catalysts for the projects. Appallingly, if one wanted to stamp out or control a problematic subgroup within one's country, this would be an effective way to reach that end.

The cure, then, may indeed be worse than the disease, when the price to be paid for a world without trolls or disrupters is the complete lack of privacy both online and in the real world. Even if a system is run fairly and justly, these systems will still run into national and cultural barriers. It's nearly impossible to fully standardize human behavior so that multiple viewpoints and customs remain valued while none are subjugated or devalued.

Social media is at a unique place in this regard. It is now neither fully American nor fully international, but in the attempt to police content for the sake of the bottom line and shareholder confidence, social media has created "a mix of remarkably permissive (regarding threats and images of graphic violence) and remarkably conservative (regarding nudity)" values (Singer and Brooking, 2018, p. 232). The problem is that these are values acceptable to people in the United States and may not be considered acceptable in other countries. Generally, Americans are far more tolerant of excessive violence but far less so of nudity and sexuality. Americans are far more permissive of gun ownership than most other countries, while Japan, in steep contrast, is about as restrictive as a country can get. Building trust and establishing social credit systems not only nationally but internationally will be difficult in the face of these wildly divergent customs and worldviews.

To combat trolls, we can take a less *invasive* approach while still maintaining a kind of "social credit" or social responsibility system. People can still remain anonymous while their online reputations are awarded or punished by their online behaviors. This is in play already at some websites. Scribophile, which is a writer critique site, relies on a small-scale approach to content moderation, with internal enforcement of locally decided policy in a relatively small community of similarly motivated individuals. While the main purpose of the site is the sharing and critiquing of creative writing (novels, short stories, poems) in a members-only space, the site has an active writer's forum section, where users discuss writing in general (e.g., grammar), the state of publishing, or even current issues. In these forums, however, they require that users refrain from discussing politics, religion, and other hot-button issues, upon penalty of removal from the site if users persist in generally abusing other users or ignoring the rules. People there are generally anonymous, with a few choosing to provide real-world details. However, what sets this site above others is the use of a "karma" system that awards people for good behavior (in this case good behavior means writing and critiquing another writer's works). Once enough karma is gathered, it can be spent for the privilege of your getting own work critiqued. This is a promising approach as it provides people with their right to withhold information about themselves from others, while at the same time they can receive and give benefit to others within the community. Rather than merely receiving "likes," which often don't translate into anything more than an ephemeral mood boost, the more karma I receive based on my own labor as a reviewer of others' pieces, the more I can post my own work for review. It's a good example of how a subculture can thrive on a mutually beneficial quasi-social contract. It's win-win and reciprocal, not lose-lose and asymmetrical.

Online Harmony through Mindfulness?

People's actions and interactions with each other are essential for improving and combating online misbehaviors. Researchers looking into some of the extreme elements and bad actors online—for example, extremists espousing violence and hate—could provide us with some insight. But this insight comes not from success but from their own sense of failure. Researchers have butted up against the limits of regulating people online. Whitney Phillips, researcher at Syracuse University, suggests that to surpass these limits, "we need to think more holistically and more humanely about how we get folks to think about how they fit amongst other people" (Martineau, 2019).

Phillips envisions an online "Copernican revolution," which could reframe the discussion of how the Internet is conceived. She argues that we should be moving away from the idea that we are the center of the online universe and our own sense of "liking" and reputational "scoring," and toward a more holistic realization that "there are other people . . . and that could change how you interact with the people around you in your world more broadly" (Martineau, 2019). Other researchers suggest similarly that we need to meet the challenge of online problems "with our best thinking, not our quickest" (Fraser, 2019). Rather than rely on social-media-generated online reputations, that would surely become misunderstood across different cultures, we should focus, instead, upon a kind of self-developed internal mindfulness to "counteract the rush to judgement, the bullying, and the trolling . . . [and to] learn methods of distinguishing between the serious and the unserious, between the learned and the ignorant" (ibid.). Much of this sounds quite close to information literacy, which provides people with a clear protocol of steps and skills to responsibly use (and share) information. These skills are important for not only verifying the information we consume, but also for helping to establish trust among all users.

Our Better Angels: The Moderator Confronts the Worst of Humanity

In the absence of self-regulation and holistic or mindful approaches, independent parties remain essential components for improving online social conditions. One of the earliest methods of improving online life has been the most effective: the use of moderators to police, curb, or shape online behavior. They represent some of the more selfless actors online, often hidden behind the scenes and usually, like all referees, abused for doing their jobs correctly.

The positive impact of moderators online cannot be overstated. We have probably all dealt with abusive and trolling behaviors online, with people challenging what we have written or insulting us for no good reason. Sometimes our tempers flare and we "flame" up and attack other users online in a sort of cyber road rage. One way to conceive of cyberspace, chatrooms, message boards, and social media itself is as a kind of "contact zone," which is defined by its creator Mary Louise Pratt (1991) as "social spaces where cultures meet, clash and grapple with each other, often in contexts of highly asymmetrical relations of power, such as colonialism, slavery, or their aftermaths as they are lived out in many parts of the world today." No one is more attuned to the contact zone playing out in terms of conflict than the online website moderator. What these people provide is an essential service, much like educators and teachers, in moderating the contact and channeling it into something non-destructive.

Interestingly, the methods by which moderators best function revert to older, *traditional* practices of establishing and maintaining social order. As information science researchers David Wall and Matthew Williams (2007) describe it, "[Online] community members prefer the use of vigilante justice, peer pressure and ostracism to maintain order." Methods for one online community were found to hearken back to "the medieval practice of 'charivari' in 13th and 14th-century France," which involved groups of people parading about town to shame or make an example of someone. This perhaps gives new meaning to the term "going medieval" on someone. Putting it another way, people are organizing their online lives in ways that are surprisingly old, stemming from long-standing tried-and-true traditions that were effective, if harsh and pre-modern, in the real world.

The worst punishment seems to be old-fashioned banishment. Alex Jones and many other conspiracy theorists or extremists have been removed from Facebook and other social media platforms, rendering them less harmful (Schwartz, 2019). To be sure, banishment sometimes turns into a game of whack-a-mole, with new accounts taking the place of the old ones. But, overall, moderation tactics end up being very successful when the moderators are able to enforce rules within clear sets of user guidelines with no exceptions (Broderick, 2019).

One major problem, however, remains unsolved: scale. The growing numbers of user accounts have literally outstripped social media platforms' ability to supply sufficient labor to effectively moderate user behavior. By the end of 2018, Facebook had roughly 2.13 billion monthly active users and approximately 20,000 "safety and security specialists," some with the fancy name "News Feed integrity data specialist" (Lev-Ram, 2018). This is a ratio of about 106,500 accounts per Facebook moderator, who has to keep tabs on all of the videos, images, messages, and general interactions with countless others. YouTube in 2018 had about 10,000 moderators, while Twitter planned to add moderators for the first time (ibid.). The moderators perform functions in a variety of ways, but generally check that people work within the safe-use guidelines set up by their websites.

The 1:106,500 moderator-to-user-account ratio for Facebook looks incredibly large to me, and I would guess it is likely very ineffective. Scaling up is probably one of the biggest underreported dilemmas of the Internet. It is a problem not only in terms of the type of content added or the outrageous choices people broadcast to others, but it is also problematic in terms of developing reasonable regulation and providing general moderation. No one wants to admit they are victims of their own success, so it remains a mostly silent issue for IT companies to regulate as long as it doesn't impact the bottom line. But there are unfortunately just not enough eyes on what is being put up on the web (Broderick, 2019).

Not only is the scale of content moderation outrageously large, so is the scope and speed with which content is shared and re-shared. Moderators are now required to view an increasing amount of content every day, with the subject matter expanding as well. Additionally, moderators are having trouble with the online cat-and-mouse game, where moderators attempt to limit problem behavior with "more refined comments filters, but toxic users are constantly finding new ways to circumvent them" (Brassard-Gourdeau and Khoury, 2018). The result is an artificial intelligence and technological arms race, with more technology created or obscure slang invented to counteract AI-enhanced moderators.

Moderators are also just as vulnerable to toxic and extreme content as regular users. The result of the constant exposure to online strife, disturbing rhetoric, and violent or abusive images includes such problems as PTSD, depression, and anxiety (Singer and Brooking, 2018, p. 247). Given the low status of this work, moderators also tend to be paid less and hired as part of outsourcing efforts, much like Google paid low-wage workers to mass-digitize tens of millions of books in its Google Books project. The working conditions are bad, but the toll on mental health is worse. Sometimes moderators might see something relatively harmless, but the next thing could be shocking. They are asked to make decisions on emotionally charged and emotionally taxing content thousands of times per shift (Chotiner, 2019). These are essentially "digital serfs" (Singer and Brooking, 2018, p. 244), who, due to the rigors of the job and the constant exposure to negative content, become especially vulnerable to burnout and apathy. As Brian Burlage (2019) writes about his experience as an online moderator on Reddit, working under the characteristically provocative <dickfromaccounting> username handle,

> Emptying the site of all hatred and apathy is impossible. Every time I open the moderation tab, no matter how many times a day, new posts and comments have been reported for one reason or another. The cycle never stops, and how could it? Users wield their anonymity like a regenerative get-out-of-jail-free card, continually renewing the choice to be selfish and inconsiderate without facing any immediate consequences.

The problems he describes are daunting. The toll of this toxic content lies heavy on moderators, who themselves are simultaneously users, facilitators, and gatekeepers of the information and communication occurring in their online communities. The scale of these problems and the relative weakness of their corresponding punishments add to this feeling of futility. Better conditions and a greater effort at hiring more people to better moderate the massive scale of content would be a good start, but they can't do it without improvements in user accountability, content verifiability, and technology.

VERIFICATION STRATEGIES AND REQUIREMENTS

Some of the problems facing moderators as outlined above have stemmed in part from the immense scales and scopes of the problems. The labor of Internet moderation needs to be augmented, then, with better strategies to enforce these rules as well as improved technological advances to detect and curtail harmful content and bad-faith behavior. But online moderation also suffers from companies trying to fit strategies that work for one company but not for another. Such strategies will be better implemented if the problems are anticipated in terms of the localized needs of users in specific platforms.

In her report *Content or Context Moderation?* Data & Society affiliate Robyn Caplan (2018) outlines three types of content-moderation strategies that might more effectively improve our online experience. The strategies include three broad areas: "artisanal" content moderation, "community-reliant" content moderation, and "industrial" content moderation. These strategies would then be implemented by Internet organizations after determining what approach would work best for them. So-called artisanal strategies would involve teams that operate on a smaller scale in terms of company and user-base size. Moderation is generally, then, an in-house affair, relying far more on manual labor than algorithms or automation. The development of moderation policies and their enforcement would happen simultaneously in the same locale. Some examples of companies implementing artisanal moderation would include Vimeo (a video-sharing site), Medium (a writing/publishing site), and Scribophile (the author critique site mentioned above).

Community-reliant moderation strategies, on the other hand, would utilize a much greater number of moderators, but the distinction is that these are volunteers from a community of practice, drawing especially from heavy site users and those with good reputations. The policies are often set up by a smaller policy-implementation team employed within a larger organization, and the volunteers set the normative values for their sub-communities.

Wikimedia Commons (an online content/knowledge site) and Reddit (an online messaging/discussion board) are examples of this type of strategy. The research cited above from Wall and Williams likely looked at this type of strategy, which employed very medieval-like shaming and banishment approaches to moderating content. These community-based approaches are also seen as a "kind of federal model" (Council on Foreign Relations, 2018), relying on an overarching structure to unify the platform or site, while employing those within a localized area to enforce the policy.

Finally, industrial strategies for content management are the ones that are the most publicized in the media. These are the largest platforms, the ones sharing content on a global scale and tasked with moderating vast amounts of big data. For these platforms, they are generally forced to develop automated technologies to stem the tide of negative and undesirable content. There appears to be clear separation between the policy developers, who likely exist within the confines of the company itself, and the enforcers, who are usually outsourced to third-party contractors. Facebook and Google represent two primary examples of "industrial strength" content managers (Caplan, 2018). As mentioned earlier in this chapter, the flaws in this approach are evident in the toll taken on the moderators and the poor ratio of moderators to users.

Overall, the smaller-scaled platforms and sites are generally more manageable. Look at how different the tone and content of message boards are for an online newspaper like the *Washington Post* compared to Yahoo! News. Artisanal and community-based strategies do have their hands full at times, it is true, but are overall able to manage and police the amount of negative content. The problem is much more troublesome on the industrial scale, and that is what we will focus on next.

Algorithms for Content Flagging in an "Industrial" Setting: Benefits and Pitfalls

One of the ways in which online content is flagged and then referred to moderators is through the deployment of mathematical algorithms. These algorithm-based AI have been used for some time now on YouTube as a way of finding content among millions of postings that violates the copyright of creative works, especially music, films, and images. But there is more to it than just flagging content. Google's Content ID system, which is a series of algorithms designed to find and notify the company about potential copyrighted material violations, seeks to solve some of the issues of merely "taking down" content, by also identifying areas of user interest and *mediating* them by applying fees and payment for content use. In fact, nearly 98 percent of "copyright management," as Google describes it, occurs through their Content ID system. Tellingly, only 2 percent of the flagged content originates from real people filing removal notices.

The result has been a not-insignificant amount of money (nearly $5 billion!) generated for traditional record labels through this notification system (Alexander, 2019). Google also reports that "the music industry opts to monetize more than 95 percent of its copyright claims" (Popper, 2016). In other words, the labels choose to leave nearly all the videos up on YouTube—despite not posting the works themselves more than half the time—in order to make money from them. Looking at the statistics Google cites, it is obvious that recouping such a large amount of money would not be possible without the use of the algorithm. Yet, despite this windfall, the music labels nevertheless accuse Google of underreporting copyright violations! However, they haven't resorted to litigation in the way that the Authors Guild did with the Google Books project, which says as much about the record labels' ultimate motivations (hint: $$) as it does about the overall power of Google.

However, some interesting high-profile mistakes in copyright violation flagging have come to light that cast some doubt on an AI's ability to accurately analyze the often ambiguous and loosely defined tenets of copyright law. One especially vexing case occurred when a gamer made a home video tutorial of the old Nintendo NES system basketball game Double Dribble, demonstrating an exploitable flaw in the game's play. Later, the *Family Guy* cartoon used the home video clip as part of a gag in one of their episodes. The original homemade video was then flagged on YouTube for copyright infringement (Shephard, 2016)! Obviously this is all backward. As we see in figure 11.1, the algorithm assumed that Fox, or its affiliates, owned the home video clip since it appeared in the show, despite the fact that the company has no claim on an original home video made by another person featuring a game developed by yet *another* company (Konami). YouTube, once it recognized the mistake, restored the video, and blame was assigned to a faulty algorithm.

Unfortunately, aside from a viral online outcry (and yes, sometimes they are beneficial), there is little recourse for those in similar situations who have been erroneously flagged for copyright violations. YouTube tends to strictly follow Digital Millennium Copyright Act takedown and safe-harbor proce-

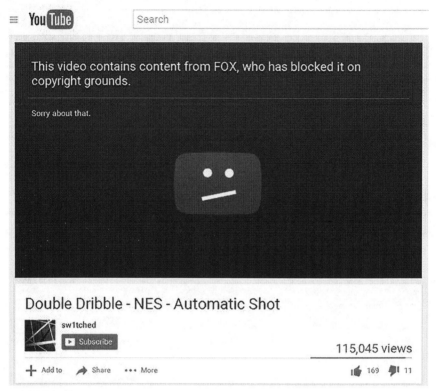

FIGURE 11.1
Double Dribble video game from NES, blocked by FOX on erroneous copyright grounds. *YouTube*

dures by complying with notices first and asking questions later. Content posters have to either stick to their guns and try to appeal the takedown decision or relent in the face of the algorithm's final result.

Despite their obvious flaws, algorithms are nevertheless being used for identifying hateful and damaging content. Rather than identifying potential infringements of intellectual property, the algorithms instead are employed to identify infringements on the rules of online behavior. Content moderation is somewhat easier for platforms and content hosts with such assistance. They do not have to rely as much on human moderators and could, perhaps, affordably regulate the content that appears in their forums and comment sections. Yet the reliance on algorithms leads to problems.

Much like the Double Dribble situation, algorithms can be fooled when the situations are overly complex or ambiguous. Facebook reports that only 38 percent of the posts they have taken down were identified by an AI-driven algorithm, suggesting that a lot of content slips through the cracks. People, as they do, have found clever ways to confuse algorithms to avoid flagging, exploiting the gaps they find in the programming. Some, for example, have started adding numbers and symbols to potentially loaded words in order to mask them. Known as "leetspeak," this involves changing a word like "newbie" (or "noob," which rhymes with "rube")—slang for newcomer (and by implication, idiot)—into something like <n00b> or changing the eminently flaggable word "porn" into <Pr0n>, and so on. Humans whose native language is English could probably figure out these inversions and substitutions almost instantly, but algorithms much less so. Another trick people have adopted to fool algorithms is jamming words all together like so: <MartiansAreDisgustingAndShouldBeKilled>; or sometimes for good measure they'll add the word <love> right next to that offensive string, as in: <MartiansAreDisgustingAndShouldBeKilled *love*.> It may be enough to fool an algorithm as the word <love> probably appears on its list of acceptable terms. As these examples show, the concept of hate speech is a very slippery idea, capable of being seen as simultaneously non-threatening by one group or threatening to another, depending upon the context in which it appears. This shifting context and evolving code-speak makes policing hate speech even more difficult (Matsakis, 2018).

Regulating Speech, but Institutionalizing Bias

Generally speaking, finding ways to regulate speech online is moving forward along well-established constitutional and mercantile ways. There are two well-defined types of speech regulations in the United States. The first is the government-sanctioned, constitutional guarantee of free speech, which is bound by its long history of established precedent. The second is corporate regulation, which is usually proscribed and bound by the terms of a service or licensing agreement. This can be quite restrictive in comparison to free speech but bound by signed agreement. If I violate YouTube's policies, for example, I would have to accept their decision to remove anything that breaks their rules, as I had initially agreed to their terms of service upon uploading content. These limitations on our rights are standard practice in many areas, including copyright license agreements, other boilerplate online licensing agreements, and contracts in general.

Interestingly, a third area of speech regulation is beginning to form online as well, as outlined by Tiffany Li, resident fellow, Information Society Project, Yale Law Schools. This new form of regulation appears to be a mixture of the first two types and part of a developing "triangle model of speech regulation," as she describes it in a panel discussion held by the Council on Foreign Relations (2018). Governments increasingly appear willing to dictate to social media companies the violations of their own terms-of-service agreements. This is leading to some interesting enforcement of online speech, suggesting that there may be a need for clearer regulation and law in the area of online communications, especially if social media is unable or *unwilling* to enforce its own standards.

Related to this, it appears to be quite easy for people to have their content misinterpreted and erroneously removed, either as a violation of the terms of service or as a transgression of free speech (e.g., libel or slander). The unwitting mistakes made by poorly functioning or badly designed algorithms compound these issues. Algorithms reflect their creators' worldviews, as they are the ones instructing what the algorithm should count or discount. The creators are the ones making the decision-rules for the formulas. As legal scholars Margot Kaminski and Andrew Selbst (2019) report, "When creating a machine-learning algorithm, designers have to make many choices: what data to train it on, what specific questions to ask, how to use predictions that the algorithm produces. These choices leave room for discrimination, particularly against people who have been discriminated against in the past." In the case of the Double Dribble home video, no one was harmed. Little financial loss would have occurred to anyone. The outcry against the video's removal was far more about the *principle* of the thing than any one person's loss or injustice.

People are harmed far more by the mistakes made by algorithms designed to distinguish certain types of people from other ones. As Safiya Umoja Noble has shown in her book *Algorithms of Oppression*, which shows numerous examples of how minorities are misrepresented and discriminated against online, "racism and sexism are part of the architecture and language of technology" (Noble, 2018, p. 9). This is easily demonstrated. If you type in the word <professor> into a Google Image search, you will largely get back images of older white men. Conversely, if you type in the word <poverty>, you will mostly get images of African children in slums. But don't take my word for it. (Try it!)

A picture tells a thousand words. Look at figures 11.2 and 11.3. You'll be struck by the stark differences between the results of these two searches.

In the aggregate, this institutionalized bias may impart significant harm on how people communicate and interact online, driving some people further underground, alienating others, while allowing hate, dissension, or apathy to fester. We would much rather not have our words flagged and curtailed for saying things in the heat of an argument, yet sometimes people cross the line from normal discourse into threats. But this line is so fine sometimes that even humans have trouble with drawing a distinction between the two. AI definitely isn't ready to moderate that fine line either.

Along the same lines as stifling the fair use of copyrighted materials, moderating user-generated content for rules-of-use compliance in a similar large-scale automated way may come to stifle people's ability to express themselves, especially if the algorithms are built in ways that favor certain groups

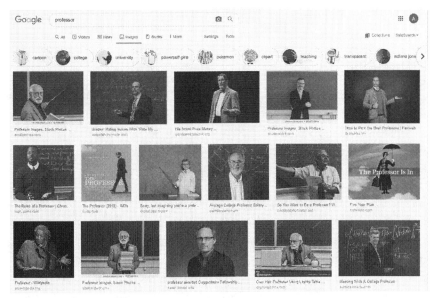

FIGURE 11.2
Results of Google Image search for pictures associated with the word "professor."
Google Image Search

FIGURE 11.3
Results of Google Image search for pictures associated with the word "poverty."
Google Image Search

over others. When these larger companies turn to automated takedown systems, user speech is curtailed more easily. Though, as we saw above with "leetspeak," any flaws in a system can be ultimately exposed and then worked around—they are human-made, after all.

One effective way to avoid systemic bias, unintentional or not, is to provide clear public policy on how algorithms are created and deployed. Establishing significant and effective avenues to recourse for those wronged by erroneous decisions or results will go a long way to alleviate the problem. Better public policy such as the Algorithm Accountability Act might provide some balance to the situation. This act aims to require companies that use algorithms to make decisions, to preempt negative behaviors in online forums, or to make predictions about a person's work, finances, or health, to provide clear assessments of their algorithms' outcomes (Kaminski and Selbst, 2019). This will hopefully encourage companies to track and document their methods of algorithm design. By taking a proactive approach to designing the better algorithm, especially by focusing on soliciting and utilizing feedback from the public, this focus on assessment can help to avoid some of the pitfalls we have seen.

To improve algorithms, transparency also needs to be central to the accountability process. Data about an algorithm's effectiveness and functioning within legal guidelines must be made public, so that a true accounting of an algorithm's societal impact can occur. Without this openness, we may fall prey to poorly or maliciously designed programs and might never be the wiser. Indeed, looking at the two Google Image searches above was eye-opening for me. I have come to seriously doubt the objectivity or the overall usefulness of the Google Image search algorithm. The excessive scale and scope of these companies has forced them to rely on somewhat faulty algorithmic technologies at the expense of a healthier social contract (in Rousseau's sense) as we see in the contrasting successes of the smaller and mid-sized content moderation approaches.

It is, furthermore, unsustainable for a pluralistic society to stand aside and do nothing about the implicit bias built into these highly influential, widespread technologies. To allow free rein for bullying and pathological behaviors without regulation will consume the Internet in hatred, causing it to eventually implode. Worse, if left unchecked, the Internet will be abandoned in disgust by those who can afford to use a more selective system, leaving a combination of the worst abusers and the most apathetic, a twenty-first-century "tragedy of the commons."

Like many of the issues outlined in this book, there are numerous solutions. The problems we are facing are unfortunately too often envisioned solely within the false dichotomies of polarized political discourse that allow for only two approaches, usually taken up cynically just to oppose the other party. Fortunately for us, it is almost never the case that there are only two ways to look at something. There are always multiple solutions to our problems, as long as we have the imagination to visualize them and the will to carry them out. As we have seen in previous chapters, extremist thinking from *any* end of the political spectrum—right or left, authoritarianism or anarchy—is a failure of cognition, a failure to vigilantly test and retest one's assumptions. We *can* find multiple solutions to all our problems as long as we keep our minds open and prize reason.

REFERENCES

Alexander, J. (2019). YouTubers and record labels are fighting, and record labels keep winning. *Verge.* www.theverge.com/2019/5/24/18635904/copyright -youtube-creators-dmca-takedown-fair-use-music-cover.

Brassard-Gourdeau, E., and Khoury, R. (2018). Impact of sentiment detection to recognize toxic and subversive online comments. Arxiv. arxiv.org/abs/1812.01704.

Broderick, R. (2019). The comment moderator is the most important job in the world right now. BuzzFeed. www.buzzfeednews.com/article/ryanhatesthis/the -comment-moderator-is-the-most-important-job-in-the.

Burlage, B. (2019). Confessions of a Reddit "karma whore." Vice. www.vice.com/ en_us/article/3k359n/confessions-of-a-reddit-karma-whore.

Caplan, R. (2018). Content or context moderation? Artisanal, community-reliant, and industrial approaches. Data & Society. datasociety.net/output/content-or -context-moderation/.

Chotiner, I. (2019). The underworld of online content moderation. *New Yorker.* www.newyorker.com/news/q-and-a/the-underworld-of-online-content -moderation?utm_source=pocket-newtab.

Council on Foreign Relations. (2018). Moderating online content with the help of artificial intelligence. www.cfr.org/event/moderating-online-content-help -artificial-intelligence.

Fraser, G. (2019). The Twitterization of the academic mind. *Chronicle of Higher Education.* www.chronicle.com/article/The-Twitterization-of -the/245965?cid=cr&utm_source=cr&utm_medium=en&cid=cr.

Harwell, D. (2019). Pelosi says altered videos show Facebook leaders were "willing enablers" of Russian election interference. *Washington Post.* https://www .washingtonpost.com/technology/2019/05/29/pelosi-says-altered-videos-show -facebook-leaders-were-willing-enablers-russian-election-interference/?utm _term=.347316031c6e.

Kaminski, M., and Selbst, A. (2019). The legislation that targets the racist impacts of tech. *New York Times.* www.nytimes.com/2019/05/07/opinion/tech-racism -algorithms.html.

Kostka, G. (2019). What do people in China think about "social credit" monitoring? *Washington Post.* www.washingtonpost.com/politics/2019/03/21/what-do -people-china-think-about-social-credit-monitoring/?utm_term=.86341d8b109a.

Lev-Ram, M. (2018). Why thousands of human moderators won't fix toxic content on social media. *Fortune.* fortune.com/2018/03/22/human-moderators-facebook -youtube-twitter/.

Martineau, P. (2019). The existential crisis plaguing online extremism researchers. *Wired.* www.wired.com/story/existential-crisis-plaguing-online-extremism -researchers/?utm_source=pocket-newtab.

Matsakis, L. (2018). To break a hate-speech detection algorithm, try "love." *Wired.* www.wired.com/story/break-hate-speech-algorithm-try-love/.

Mozur, P. (2018). Inside China's dystopian dreams: A.I., shame and lots of cameras. *New York Times.* www.nytimes.com/2018/07/08/business/china-surveillance -technology.html.

Noble, S. U. (2018). *Algorithms of oppression: How search engines reinforce racism.* ebookcentral.proquest.com.

Popper, B. (2016). YouTube to the music industry: Here's the money. Verge. www .theverge.com/2016/7/13/12165194/youtube-content-id-2-billion-paid.

Pratt, M. (1991). Arts of the contact zone. *Profession, 33–40.*

Rainie, L., and Zickuhr, K. (2015). Americans' views on mobile etiquette. Pew Research Center. www.pewInternet.org/2015/08/26/americans-views-on-mobile -etiquette/.

Sapolsky, R. (2019). To understand Facebook, study Capgras syndrome. Nautilus. getpocket.com/explore/item/to-understand-facebook-study-capgras -syndrome?utm_source=pocket-newtab.

Schwartz, M. (2019). Facebook bans Alex Jones, Louis Farrakhan and other "dangerous" individuals. NPR. www.npr.org/2019/05/03/719897599/facebook -bans-alex-jones-louis-farrakhan-and-other-dangerous-individuals.

Shephard, J. (2016). Family Guy "stole" a video of Double Dribble from YouTube then claimed the original video breached copyright. *The Independent.* www.independent.co.uk/arts-entertainment/tv/news/family-guy-stole-a -video-of-double-dribble-from-youtube-then-claimed-the-original-video -breached-a7042026.html.

Singer, P., and Brooking, E. (2018). *LikeWar: The weaponization of social media.* Boston: Houghton Mifflin Harcourt.

Wall, D. S., and Williams, M. (2007). Policing diversity in the digital age:
Maintaining order in virtual communities. *Criminology & Criminal Justice*, 7(4),
391–415. doi.org/10.1177/1748895807082064.

Zand, B. (2018). A surveillance state unlike any the world has ever seen.
Der Spiegel International. https://www.spiegel.de/international/world/chinas
-xinjiang-province-a-surveillance-state-unlike-any-the-world-has-ever
-seen-a-1220174.html.

Zuboff, S. (2019). *The age of surveillance capitalism.* New York: Public Affairs.

Zuckerberg, M. (2019). The Internet needs new rules. Let's start in these four areas.
Washington Post. www.washingtonpost.com/opinions/mark-zuckerberg-the
-Internet-needs-new-rules-lets-start-in-these-four-areas/2019/03/29/9e6f0504
-521a-11e9-a3f7-78b7525a8d5f_story.html?utm_term=.f97ca95be419.

12

How to Keep Your Privacy—and Still Live in the *Real* World

They're doing it as we sit here. And they expect to do it during the next campaign.

—Robert Mueller, on election interference by the Russian government, July 24, 2019

INSISTING ON PRIVACY DOESN'T MAKE YOU A LUDDITE

As we've examined the impact of information technologies throughout this book, the shift from living an "analog" life to a digital one significantly alters how we can look at privacy. As it stands, privacy in the digital age is now at a critical juncture, so compromised by the Internet and "smart" devices that it is now possible to envision a world that is erased of the concept. Lost in the chaos of sudden change, though, is the realization that the world doesn't need to adopt every new technology without a fight. Neither should people have to feel like they are fossils, veritable Luddites, if they don't immediately adopt every new change wholesale.

New technologies that wind up being rapidly adopted often do one or another main thing better than their predecessors. When digital cameras took over the industry in the early 2000s, photography became easier in nearly all aspects. Printing was easier. Photo editing was easier. Erasing mistakes was easier. Deleting was easier. The convenience was great. There's no denying just how useful and pervasive digital photography has become—even to the point that most mobile devices now have a photo lens installed. In business, you have to adapt or die, so it became an obvious advantage to get images out within minutes or hours instead of days or weeks.

But not everything is better. From another perspective, there is still no better alternative—in my eyes at least—to a film negative printed on silver-gelatin paper. The print lasts longer than inkjet prints. Film itself is more stable than a hard drive, which has yet to be proven as a viable long-term preservation technology. The range of tones elicited from a film negative and transferred onto a print can be breathtaking in its subtleties. It takes longer to make an image this way, but it is infused in *teinei*, a Japanese term meaning the dedicated and careful attention given to something. Photographers have largely given up some of these slower but deeper aspects and, in some ways, superior results for the speed and convenience of digital photography.

New technologies can also lead to unforeseen consequences down the line, as with the music business in the early 2000s. Compact discs became the new music standard almost overnight in the mid-1980s. The industry shifted partly for the sake of cost-cutting. CDs were cheaper, and since they were new, they could also charge more for them. A win-win. They were also supposedly better in terms of sound and flawless playback and were marketed to audiophiles until they became the most popular format. But for all their convenience, portability, and clear sound quality in comparison to vinyl records, they nevertheless opened a Pandora's Box of digital music. For they were also far easier to copy in mass quantities than vinyl records ever were. Once the Internet took off, people could easily engage in file-sharing from music ripped from CDs onto their PCs—leading first to mass file-sharing with Napster and then eventually to iTunes, YouTube, Spotify, Pandora, and other music streaming services.

Yet even with these less-than-ideal consequences frequently occurring with new technologies, we are made to feel like Luddites if we don't adopt these new things quickly enough. For a modern person to be called a Luddite is to endure the ultimate insult. It is to be lumped in with the stereotypical, head-in-the-sand laggard or off-the-grid lunatic. But why? Luddites as a group certainly get a bad rap. Their historical stereotype is one of dour anti-technologists, resisting change with reactionary violence; brutes who failed to understand that they were on "the wrong side of history." If only they had been just a little more prescient in their thinking, the modern take on them goes, and used "foresight" or acknowledged the "bleeding edge" of scientific progress—or any other term that exists today to paint them negatively in as broad a stroke as possible.

But that's a fantasy.

Luddites are more than just a historical punchline, more than just poster children for the hopelessly left behind and the technologically "challenged" among us. They are, at root, a humanistic movement, concerned with how technology directly affects our quality of life. What the Luddites really fought against wasn't technology itself, but our ability to control *how* we use it and incorporate it into our lives. What also lurks beneath the stereotype are our own false assumptions of what it means to be *modern*—itself a term that is in constant need of evaluation and redefinition. To be modern in the Enlightenment sense of the word is to throw off past un-reflected traditions and to use reason and evidence to strike up new ideas. In that regard, we are, as long as we adhere to Enlightenment ideals, perpetually evolving, culturally speaking, *as* the modern, not *into* it. What the Luddites wanted, in the end, *we* want too. What the Luddites were, *we* are too:

> The original Luddites would answer that we are human. Getting past the myth and seeing their protest more clearly is a reminder that it's possible to live well with technology—but only if we continually question the ways it shapes our lives. It's about small things, like now and then cutting the cord, shutting down the smartphone and going out for a walk. But it needs to be about big things, too, like standing up against technologies that put money or convenience above other human values. (Conniff, 2011)

The point, of course, is that just because we don't immediately and blindly accept adopting all the flash and tech that the online IT companies provide, it does *not* automatically make us Luddites in the sense of being laggards. It's about us deciding what "to live well with technology" actually means.

Indeed, given the fact that the online browsers, platforms, and apps that allow us to communicate online can *actually track our every move*, we would be prudent to show a little restraint. We have been conditioned, as we have seen earlier in this book, into accepting more concessions to our privacy in exchange for rather meager returns. One researcher did a basic test of the Google Chrome browser and found that the software program allowed more than eleven thousand "tracker" cookies into his browser "in a single week"

(Fowler, 2019). This is astounding! In the context of regular life, and the general assumption of Google as a benign "older brother" role in our lives, it seems relatively normal. As we have become quite used to it, the concept of being tracked barely registers with us anymore. Yet, if we hadn't gone so gradually into this surveillance-state twilight, then we might instead all be protesting in the streets about the excessive tracking Google routinely subjects us to. Historians will look back at us one day, and perhaps the best they might say about us will be "At least it was a *gradual* fall."

Establishing Privacy for the Digital Age

It may already be a contradiction in terms to call for such a thing as "digital privacy." It may be that the computer technologies and telecommunication systems we've created are so hopelessly compromised that no ideas or concepts with the words "e-" or "digital" appended to them can ever be trusted to be entirely private. I hope this is not the case; we have to at least try. To that end, there needs to be an interlocking set of policies, actions, and advocacy guaranteeing privacy within three areas: information technology itself; our current, and future, legal frameworks; and special protections for democratic systems based on universal human rights.

In examining future political systems, we can see that privacy will have to be central to the development and maintenance of a democratic society, regardless of what shape or character it assumes in various countries. Researcher Martin Hilbert has outlined some important ways in which we might better conceive of future democratic governance in a digital era. In figure 12.1, we see eight different "flavors" of a democracy, ranging from the traditional Polis democracy (Athenian) (1) and the republic model of Rome (7), to some newer models including what he calls "Deliberationware" democracy (8), "pushbutton" democracy (6), and "cyber" democracy (2). Add to that concepts of "big brother" democracy (4) and "economic" democracy (5), and we have a full range of potential models to choose from. In the next chapter, we will examine these e-democracy models in more detail in order to reach a clearer idea of how we might devise a sustainable future system.

Though it is not clear where America stands at this point within such a diagram, one can reasonably argue that the current state of American democracy lies somewhere in between the laissez-faire policies of an economic democracy and the republicanism of Roman-republic-era democracy. But

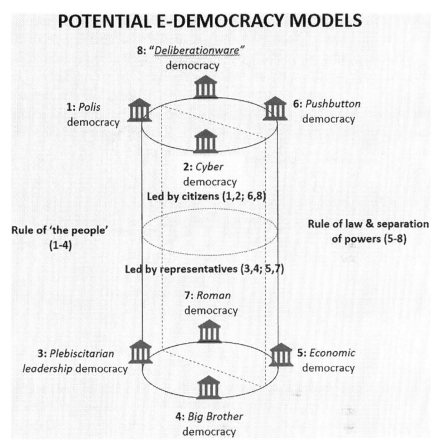

POTENTIAL E-DEMOCRACY MODELS

8: *"Deliberationware"* democracy

1: *Polis* democracy

6: *Pushbutton* democracy

2: *Cyber* democracy

Led by citizens (1,2; 6,8)

Rule of 'the people' (1-4)

Rule of law & separation of powers (5-8)

Led by representatives (3,4; 5,7)

7: *Roman* democracy

3: *Plebiscitarian leadership* democracy

5: *Economic* democracy

4: *Big Brother* democracy

FIGURE 12.1
Various models for democracy in the past and present, including newer models based on computer and information technology. *Hilbert (2007); redrawn by author*

regardless of the specifics of any of these models, the main issue is that "separation of powers and a tight law structure must protect people's privacy lest the available information be used to manipulate democratic processes and centrally steer the shaping of public opinion" (Hilbert, 2007, p. 10). Without strong guarantees of privacy, any democratic model is doomed to fail. And this is partly what we are seeing today with the shaping of public opinion through online social media as well as through the surveillance and tracking of people—both as willing and unwilling participants in their own observation. As Hilbert argues, "The rule of law in the information society faces two major challenges: safeguarding the principle of equality among all interest groups and *protecting the privacy of the individual*" (p. 120).

In other words, it all hinges upon safeguarding equality and privacy. How we do this in the real world will be the main question. It certainly starts with ensuring that our technology allows for privacy to exist; that our policies for privacy remain flexible and adaptable to the changing technology; and, finally, that social advocacy remain strongly clear on its support for the institutions that allow for democracy in an electronic age.

Differing and Evolving Ideas of Privacy: Creating a Unified Theory and Practice of Privacy

Some of the problems we are facing stem from the mutable but fragmented ways of viewing the concept of privacy itself. Ask Google what it means by privacy and, once we delve into its actual practice (not its surface policies), it likely will differ from our own conceptions or assumptions. Ask what Google values in comparison to what we value, and we are likely to find very widely differing perspectives. We will find the same thing with other IT companies, such as Facebook and Apple. Journalist Scott Rosenberg (2019) argues that these companies generally do "agree that privacy is a good thing, that [the] government should protect it, and that you can trust them to respect it," but the catch is that "each [IT] company defines privacy differently and emphasizes different trade-offs in delivering it." Unfortunately, as we saw with the disconnect between Mark Zuckerberg and Facebook in the previous chapter, the public face of their rather conservative privacy policies belies their actual beliefs in gathering as much information about us as possible.

Rosenberg suggests that for Apple, privacy means "keeping your personal data between you and your device" (ibid.). This means that keeping your device encrypted and inaccessible to others without your consent is priority one. This is not without some controversy. In the December 2015 San Bernardino shooting that killed fourteen and injured twenty-two, the FBI famously attempted to hack into the perpetrators' phones without Apple's help. In cases like this, Apple seems to have taken a public hit in order to preserve this feature of their phones, in order to tout them as unhackable devices. Yet other IT companies may approach this differently. Facebook, in contrast, is mainly concerned with "limiting who can see what you post or send" (ibid.). They are less interested in personal privacy and security than they are in the public- or private-facing interactions people have with others, as that is their ultimate bread and butter. Finally, in Google's case, privacy seems strangely limited and vague, something they likely do not want to define too clearly beyond "an option that you can invoke" (ibid.). Of course, it's most likely that the companies have come to define and then handle privacy in the terms that are most beneficial to their businesses. It makes sense that Apple would focus on creating unhackable devices; that Facebook would want to quell your fears of being harassed or bothered online; that Google would downplay what it does to continue tracking you.

As we saw in chapters 4 and 8, however, there is a real need for a clear definition of what privacy means in all situations, especially in relation to tracking and surveillance. But beyond that too, there needs to be a clear set of policies that regulate all the IT companies nationwide. Currently, privacy is being considered on a state-by-state and case-by-case basis. California has some of the strictest privacy regulations in the United States, but most other states lag behind, essentially ignoring the needs of their users and consumers. The use of medical, financial, and student record information is rightly regulated, but other sensitive data about us needs the same protection at the federal, national, and even international level.

CREATING STRONGER PRIVACY POLICIES AND BEST PRACTICES: A ROADMAP FOR CHANGE

So, what can we do? What is being done to improve the state of privacy for people? Obviously, the Internet has changed significantly over the past twenty-five years since its debut. In simpler times, say 1999, Google just mentioned a few of the things it did with your online information, if you even bothered to think about it: for example, "aggregated search activity"; "personal information you provide"; "clickthrough information"; and "cookies" (Warzel and Ngu, 2019). Now, twenty years later, Google advises people in their privacy policy that they essentially track and collect information from eight main areas, and more than forty much more granular ones, including the following:

- **"Things you create or provide to Google"** (i.e., your name; password; phone number; payment information; content you create, upload, or receive from others)

- **"If you use Google services for calls or messages"** (i.e., telephone information; phone number; time and date of calls and messages, duration of calls, routing information, types of calls)
- **"Your activity"** (i.e., terms you search for, videos you watch, views and interactions with content and ads; people with whom you communicate or share content; Chrome browsing history)
- **"Apps, browsers, and device data"** (i.e., browser type and settings; device type and settings; operating system; mobile network information; IP address; system activity; date, time, referrer URL of your request);
- **"Data from publicly accessible sources"** (i.e., trusted partners; marketing partners; security partners; advertisers)
- **"Location data from GPS"** (i.e., IP address, device sensor data, wifi access points, cell towers, Bluetooth-enabled devices)
- **"Data from Android devices with Google apps"** (i.e., device type; carrier name; crash reports; which apps are installed) (Warzel and Ngu, 2019)

The changing nature and increased number of data types that Google collects shows just how sophisticated the Internet (and Google) has become, entangled with not only online search information but also our mobile devices, our content creation (text, image, video, etc.), the methods of payment we choose, and our online browsing and web-usage behaviors. Google also collects data about our locations, reports about devices crashing, and how long we spoke to someone via their Google call and message services. It is mind-numbing to see all the situations and scenarios in which Google can gather my information—including with what Google calls its "security partners." This last bit is slipped in, almost innocuously, between mention of Google's marketing partners and its advertisers, but it is chilling to this writer nonetheless. Who *are* these "security partners" exactly? Are they law enforcement? Government agencies? Other surveillance entities? All of the above?

It is clear from this list that the need for stronger privacy policies is paramount. The European Union famously enacted the General Data Protection Regulation (GDPR) to improve the rights to privacy for many users in the EU. As they describe it, the GDPR is "data protection by design and default" (GDPR, 2019), meaning that the protection of user data needs to be developed at the outset whenever a technology that processes personal data is designed, implemented, or operated. The GDPR mandates that "privacy standards [be] built into the technology and offered to the user by default" (ibid.). Essentially, this shifts the burden of protecting privacy away from the users, where it has been firmly entrenched in most other countries for decades now, and back to the IT companies where it should have been all this time.

However, despite its well-publicized fanfare as a new and powerful way for nations and governments to push back against and curtail the abuses of the largest IT companies, there have been mixed results so far. In the year since the GDPR was passed, 100,000 privacy complaints were filed against various online companies. Nearly 56 million euros in fines were levied against these companies. Seems like a lot. Unfortunately, 50 million of that was levied against Google in a one-time fine that has yet to be paid while the case is appealed. So, in essence, 100,000 privacy complaints, minus one big one, resulted in about 6 million euros in fines (or about 60 euros per complaint) (Scott et al., 2019). Without getting into the legitimacy or the merits of each case, it nonetheless seems puny for the amount of alleged and actual breaches in user privacy. Some of this ineffectiveness stems from a lack of understanding about what the GDPR will accomplish and what its aims are.

Many countries—especially the United States—don't require companies to provide blanket default privacy options. Generally, if you want to bolster your online privacy within a website or vendor, you have to be proactive about it. As we saw in chapter 4, companies routinely deemphasize such options or make them incredibly difficult to find. While California may soon have some of the strongest laws for online privacy in the form of the California Consumer Privacy Act, they are still allowing companies to lobby for exceptions to the types of data they can collect *without your permission or knowledge.* Of great concern is the following: "Lobbyists have until 2020 to soften the proposals' impact on the likes of Google and Facebook by adding industry-friendly provisions to exempt certain kinds of data collection. Companies also successfully petitioned local lawmakers to kill a bill that would have given citizens greater ability to sue firms for illegally collecting their digital information" (Scott et al., 2019). So while it may seem on the surface that we have stronger policies in the works for the United States, it is quite possible that the policies in reality are far more permissive than we think. Indeed, the laws proposed in the United States seem to be watering down the GDPR's main data protection "by design and default" principle and are essentially allowing

U.S.-based corporations to co-opt "Europe's privacy reboot [but] without offering the same fundamental rights to U.S. citizens" (ibid.).

It is clear from this that we need to be better advocates for our own privacy. It is likely that the laws cannot be trusted by the very nature of how these laws are created and settled. U.S. laws seem to be favoring businesses at the expense of regular people's rights to privacy. Our rights to privacy are partly an issue of consumer protection and partly an issue of constitutional and legal protections. When the laws favor businesses and allow them to manipulate our basic lives without us having true knowledge of it, we *all* lose.

It also becomes clear that there need to be new startups and new competitors to the established monopolies of Google and Facebook. Perhaps, and this may be far-fetched, a new Internet needs to rise up that prizes privacy at the expense of profiteering and incentivized snooping. Yet to do this, it is obvious that the asymmetries that have developed over the decades as tech companies have consolidated their power need to be broken up. Some, as we will see in chapter 13, have called for breaking up the tech giants. It is unclear to me whether such a drastic measure would be successful or if it would make things worse. At any rate, the rebalancing of power will be essential to ensure that privacy policies are actually enforceable and don't wind up being merely slaps on the wrist.

CYBER SECURITY AND THE FUTURE OF A FREE INTERNET AND A FREE SOCIETY

While ensuring that our privacy policies remain uncompromised by private interests, we will also need to implement technologies and countermeasures that improve our online election security. For not only does the well-documented Russian interference in the 2016 presidential election loom over us, it looms over the next election cycle as well. It will continue to do so until clear measures are taken to counteract it. Election security also gives way to general Internet privacy, too, and the growing need for an independent and balanced encryption technology and set of public policies that can handle it in a safe yet nuanced way. It may not all be high-tech, either. There are ways to resist the onslaught of surveillance through anti-technology countermeasures that on the surface may seem desperate, but they may ultimately preserve our freedom. However, the time to do this is *now*. Events have occurred over the past several years that show we are reaching a breaking point. We are at a crossroads that will determine the direction of the next ten to twenty years, not only in terms of political stability, but also societal well-being and personal psychological needs.

Election Security Measures

The first order of business is election security. Robert Mueller's congressional testimony on July 24, 2019, had some memorable moments, not least was the advice he gave, after much prompting from one member of Congress, about what has been happening *since* the 2016 election. He reiterated in person, from the evidence gathered in his written report, that he believed the Russian government interfered with the U.S. election and was going to do it again. "They're doing it as we sit here," he said, in his characteristically understated and muted style, "and they expect to do it during the next campaign" (Mueller, 2019). All but begging Congress to act, he asserted that the U.S. government and its agencies needed to start working together to cobble together a plan to counteract the meddling of the Kremlin and its army of hackers. Later on, he also asserted that it was *not just Russia* that was planning to meddle in the upcoming 2020 U.S. election. "Many more countries," he added, "are developing the capability to replicate what the Russians had done" (ibid.). Though he did not go into detail explaining which countries were developing these capabilities, it is assumed that they include North Korea, Iran, Saudi Arabia, Israel, China, the United Arab Emirates, and Venezuela (Timberg and Romm, 2019).

Unfortunately, members of Congress so far seem to be less concerned with the substance of Mueller's testimonies, and the alarming implications they bring forth, than with the delivery of his words. Case in point, even with a redacted Mueller report, it is clear to anyone who has bothered to read it (including me) that election security is a national security issue. Yet the Senate twice failed to advance bills "aimed at strengthening election security just hours after former special counsel Robert Mueller warned of the continued threat that foreign powers interfering in US elections" (Barrett and Collier, 2019). This failure occurred even as the Senate Intelligence Committee released its own report *in the same week* about how Russian hacking targeted election systems *in all fifty states* (Gazis, 2019). A bipartisan approach to shore up our elections would be the wisest thing to do, especially given the evidence gathered and the indictments handed down.

The Senate Intelligence Committee report outlines some important strategies that might be taken to counteract the cyberattacks on elections. Notably, they suggest developing an "overarching Cyber Doctrine" (p. 54) that would create clear definitions of what constitutes a cyberattack, cybercrime, and cyberespionage. In collaboration with allies, the United States could better counteract the threats coming from Russia, China, Iran, North Korea, and "other emerging hostile actors" in cyberwarfare (U.S. Senate, 2019). This should provide a basis for determining what hostile acts are being directed at the United States and the establishment of clear protocols for responding to such acts.

In addition to this conceptual framework or doctrine, the committee also provides clear actions, including methods to improve information gathering and sharing among agencies and states, secure election systems, and "secure the vote itself," which ironically and somewhat paradoxically asks states to resist pushes for online voting! Finally, they suggest providing even more funding to states as they need it, especially in regard to smaller and local governments. The report also describes the vastness of the Russian machine and the weakness of the response in the United States, pointing out that "we shouldn't ask a county election IT employee to fight a war against the full capabilities and vast resources of Russia's cyber army" (Demirjian and Itkowitz, 2019).

Unfortunately, like much surrounding the investigation into Russian interference in the 2016 election, a lot remains undisclosed, hidden behind a wall of classified information. The committee's heavily redacted seventh suggestion, as you can see in figure 12.2, cryptically suggests to "____ build a credible ____," further muddying what should be transparent communication to those most likely to be impacted: the American voter. The lack of action as well as transparency should be a concern for all citizens.

Another suggestion to protect elections is to combat cyberaggression by essentially "fighting fire with fire." According to the *Washington Post*, "a right-of-center Washington think tank has a novel recommendation for how the Trump administration can push back on Russian and Chinese hacking and disinformation campaigns: Strike back with its own information warfare operations" (Marks, 2019b). The think tank, the Foundation for Defense of Democracies, advocates a strong response in the form of creating "cyber task forces to synchronize defenses and options for offensive operations" (FDD,

7. ▓▓▓▓ **Build a Credible** ▓▓▓▓▓▓▓▓▓▓▓▓

[382] (U) SSCI Transcript of the Open Hearing on Russian Interference in the 2016 U.S. Elections, held on Wednesday, June 21, 2017, p. 114.
[383] (U) *Ibid.*, p. 119.

61
COMMITTEE SENSITIVE - RUSSIA INVESTIGATION ONLY
▓▓▓▓▓▓▓▓▓▓ ▓▓▓▓▓▓▓▓▓▓▓▓▓▓

FIGURE 12.2
Screenshot of Report of the Select Committee on Intelligence, U.S. Senate, on Russian active measures campaigns and interference in the 2016 U.S. election, volume 1, page 61. *Report of the Select Committee on Intelligence, U.S. Senate*

2019, p. 85). They even suggest holding "cyber war games" as a way to demonstrate America's might (ibid.). One understands that if this *were* real warfare, then the need to defend freedom at all costs should be obvious. But short of an all-out declaration of war, it seems that the more we fight back online with equally invasive and destabilizing attacks on adversaries who share the same cyberspace with us, the worse the situation will get. It might solve some problems in the short-term, but in the long run we will undoubtedly be subjected to more frequent and increasingly damaging attacks.

It would be better, instead, to focus on making our election systems and cycles resistant to attacks rather than striking back and destabilizing things further for everyone online. Approaches include creating an impervious cyber wall, as one of the minor presidential candidates for the Democratic Party floated (Moulton, 2019); helping to develop skills through education to counter these cyberattacks; and partnering with so-called ethical hackers, who can find leaks or weak spots in online systems.

The National Guard, for example, has created a cyber escape room as a training tool for students, in order to help the Guard better protect us from cyberattacks. The cyber room sets up real-life scenarios, forcing people to work as teams to solve some variation of cyberattack. Participants not only learn how successful cyber-protection teams should function; they are also tested individually on a range of challenges that include, for example, "writing a binary code that reveals a hacker's IP address" or "reviewing system logs to find suspicious activity and building a secure infrastructure that protects data as it moves from storage to a database" (Miller, 2019). The key is that people are learning practical and effective strategies to cope with behind-the-scenes aggressions. Because they don't seem as obvious as physical attacks, it is easy for people to discount or underestimate them. Such educational programs would help everyone to learn how to proactively protect themselves and others.

Developing an Election "Cyber Doctrine"

These approaches are very useful. However, an overarching cyber-protection policy is a key missing element. So, in absence of a real policy, let's speculate on what good security "cyber doctrine" for protecting democratic elections *should* look like.

First and foremost, an essential condition for voting is privacy. We need to be able to prevent others who are unauthorized from knowing how we voted. Without this, elections would be forever compromised. If that means keeping voting offline until electronic ballot machines can be proven secure and hack-free, then so be it. The best practice for election security must start and end with privacy. Second, some action must be taken by the federal government to ensure that elections remain fair for all people, regardless of party affiliation, race, and religion. Some progress had been made in 2018, when Congress earmarked approximately $380 million "for states to bolster election cybersecurity and replace vulnerable voting machines" (Basu and Uchill, 2019). The Federal Elections Commission also took a small step in bolstering election security in June 2019 by allowing campaigns access to free cybersecurity services from the non-profit organization Defending Digital Democracy Project (D3P). As the FEC says on its website, "Microsoft may offer the AccountGuard program at no additional charge on a non-partisan basis to election-sensitive customers, including federal candidates and national party committees, without incurring an in-kind contribution" (USFEC, 2019). Generally free services to campaigns are considered a violation of campaign finance law, as one might conceivably ask for a political favor in return. However, the FEC considers the potential damage from Russian and Chinese hacking to be far more destructive to free elections than the offer of a service, especially one meant to safeguard those elections (Marks, 2019a)! Third, independent non-profit "watchdog" groups are a good step to ensuring election freedoms. Bringing in the United Nations, or international non-governmental organizations (NGOs), to officially observe elections would help ensure that at least face-to-face, physical norms for elections are upheld. This may not help directly with cyber warfare. As a result, it may be necessary to create online independent (non-partisan or NGO) cyber-watchdogs that could help create neutral, hack-free "election zones" to ensure elections remain fair.

Encryption

One of the last remaining ways we have been able to preserve what privacy we still have has been through the use of encryption technologies. Modern encryption has been employed by digital computer algorithms to help with the transfer of private information across the Internet. But simple methods of encryption have existed for millennia, since at least the fifth century BCE, in the form of clay tablets requiring a basic "key" to unlock the message; ciphers, which are basic rules for obscuring information (essentially an algorithm); or the mysterious "scytale," which is a cylinder with a strip of parchment wound around it, which is believed to be an encryption device meant to hide information (Fundukian, 2012, p. 256). The point was, and is, to hide communications or sensitive information from prying eyes.

The process of modern digital encryption "prevents data from being exposed to unauthorized access and makes it unusable" for those without the key to decipher it (Kapoor and Pandya, 2014, p. 29). It works as follows: Starting with plain text, an encryption algorithm alters the text following specific rules, resulting in a seemingly garbled message. The algorithm then generates a key, which is really just a string of numbers that allows the holder of the key to decrypt the message (Fundukian, 2012). It's a simple concept made more complex and powerful by the development of computer science. It works to keep online commerce humming along. Without it, we wouldn't dare share information—especially credit card or other personal info—across the web for fear of it being stolen. Of course, that's still a risk, but minimized somewhat with the use of encryption technology.

But, like everything else, there's a double-edged sword to encryption. On one hand, we want to preserve our privacy, but it may come sometimes at the expense of security. If we're going to "fight fire with fire," as the FDD report suggests we do, by creating our own cyber aggressions, then encryption technology absolutely becomes an enemy not a friend in the fight for national security. The Department of Justice's push to weaken the regulations surrounding encryption in the United States is one recent example of this. In his examples, Attorney General William Barr (2019) suggests that through "the deployment of warrant-proof encryption" technologies, drug cartels have been able to avoid detection, plan assassinations, and transport opiates into the United States. Barr argues that this diminishes U.S. law enforcement's ability to prosecute cartels and other organized crime ventures when they break the law. He concludes by suggesting, "The Department would like to engage with the private sector in exploring solutions that will provide lawful access" (ibid.). What's missing from that statement about "engaging with the private sector," of course, is any reference to "the public" or to regular "people." We are effectively shut out of our own privacy concerns by political considerations and private corporate interests. In that regard, when certain people in the government recommend "fighting fire with fire" or advise us that security is more important than privacy, they are essentially advocating for the reduction of privacy technologies and diminishing their importance for private citizens. Unfortunately, this approach will likely not help us.

What we really need, instead, is strong advocacy for our right to encryption coupled with clear guidelines for what law enforcement can and cannot do when it comes to cracking encrypted messages or devices. I for one would prefer that this tool for privacy remain intact and uncompromised; the web should allow us to create a private space for ourselves, away from the prying eyes of others. To throw out encryption then in the name of cybersecurity at the expense of other strategies, or with agreements between government agencies and privacy companies, is to essentially throw in the towel for the fight for personal privacy.

Desperate Measures: Rejecting the Surveillance State

Not everyone is meekly accepting the loss of privacy, subtle and slow as the erosion has been. The 2019 anti-government riots in Hong Kong give us a good look at the contemporary strategies and precautions protesters must take to exercise their rights to protest within China's growing high-tech surveillance state. As some journalists reported at the time, protesters took extreme caution to avoid detection. They restricted their communications to secure digital messaging apps; they adopted non-digital ways to move around the city, including purchasing "single-ride subway tickets instead of prepaid stored-value cards, forgoing credit cards and mobile payments in favor of cash and taking no selfies or photos of the chaos." They hid their faces in order to prevent their identities from being determined through facial recognition software. To avoid detection through GPS satellites on their cell phones, they purchased "pay-as-you-go" SIM cards and threw them out when finished (Mahtani, 2019).

While these methods seem extreme to us right now in our everyday boring lives, it may be a portent of things to come. In light of these events, we may want to consider just how widespread our identities may actually be, and whether it will compromise us in the future. In a world where surveillance cameras are everywhere, where neighbors even have installed door cameras (e.g., Amazon's Ring), and where AI facial recognition is beginning to be implemented on the back-end far and wide, will we be able control how (and when) our identities are shared with others? When we are photographed at an intersection while the light is turning from yellow to red, are we having our privacy violated? Is it possible for us to reach a compromise with the implementers of the surveillance apparatus to carve out a private space for ourselves? It is unclear how extreme we will need to be to protect our privacy. Without a clear policy, however, we don't stand much of a chance.

A Final Word

Some of the lessons above suggest that we need to buttress existing privacy policies by erecting stronger barriers and developing clearer strategies advocating for them. We certainly need to go beyond just taking the large IT companies' word at face value and start developing our own requirements for privacy dictating what *we* will allow the IT companies to do with our information. Regarding cybersecurity, while the rhetoric has been getting heated lately, it is important to see the forest for the trees, even if they are burning. We need to cooperate in apolitical—or at least bipartisan—ways to solve the problems of election security. Encryption remains a hot-button issue, too, but in the case of security versus freedom, we need to again assert our desires for the freedom to choose whether or not someone can look at what we are doing. Taking away the right to encrypt or the use of fully encrypted information will make things worse for us, even if it alleviates short-term fears of the Other. Finally, the desperate measures people take to ensure their privacy in places like Hong Kong, as a full-fledged surveillance state is watching, should be considered a cautionary tale. While it is true that we are nowhere near the same level of surveillance state implementation, it is not that far-fetched to see the same things occurring here in the United States if we are not vigilant. In other words, live in the real world but, like true Luddites, fight to protect your well-being in the face of disruptive and invasive technological changes.

REFERENCES

Barr, W. (2019). Attorney General William P. Barr delivers keynote address at the International Conference on Cyber Security. Department of Justice. www.justice.gov/opa/speech/attorney-general-william-p-barr-delivers-keynote-address-international-conference-cyber.

Barrett, T., and Collier, K. (2019). GOP senators block election security legislation hours after Mueller warns of Russian interference. CNN. www.cnn.com/2019/07/25/politics/republican-senators-block-election-security-legislation/index.html.

Basu, Z., and Uchill, J. (2019). Senate Intel releases 1st volume of report on 2016 Russian interference. *Axios*. www.axios.com/senate-intelligence-russian-interference-report-d5077b7b-5b7b-48fc-8b14-ecceb8e4ed22.html.

Conniff, R. (2011). What the Luddites really fought against. *Smithsonian Magazine.* www.smithsonianmag.com/history/what-the-luddites-really-fought -against-264412/.

Defending Digital Democracy Project. (2019). About page. www.belfercenter.org/ project/defending-digital-democracy.

Demirjian, K., and Itkowitz, C. (2019). Russians likely targeted election systems in all 50 states, Senate intelligence report says. *Washington Post.* www .washingtonpost.com/national-security/senate-intelligence-panel-releases-first -chapter-of-bipartisan-report-into-russian-meddling/2019/07/25/63bce4f4-af0c -11e9-bc5c-e73b603e7f38_story.html?utm_term=.13cd00484af3.

Foundation for the Defense of Democracies. (2019). *Midterm Assessment: The Trump Administration's Foreign and National Security Policies.* Foreword by Lt. Gen. (Ret.) H. R. McMaster. Edited by John Hannah & David Adesnik. Washington, DC: FDD.

Fowler, G. (2019). Goodbye, Chrome: Google's web browser has become spy software. *Washington Post.* www.washingtonpost.com/technology/2019/06/21/ google-chrome-has-become-surveillance-software-its-time-switch/?utm _term=.67b00b58b7d3.

Fundukian, L. J., ed. (2012). Encryption. *Gale Encyclopedia of E-Commerce*, vol. 1 (2nd ed.). Detroit, MI: Gale, 256–257.

Gazis, O. (2019). Russian cyber actors targeted 2016 state elections with "unprecedented level of activity," says Senate Intel report. *CBS News.* www .cbsnews.com/news/election-security-report-on-russian-meddling-released-by -senate-intelligence-committee/.

General Data Protection Regulation. 2019. GDPR explained. gdprexplained.eu/.

Hilbert, M. 2007. *Digital processes and democratic theory: Dynamics, risks and opportunities that arise when democratic institutions meet digital information and communication technologies.* www.martinhilbert.net/democracy-html/.

Kapoor, B., and Pandya, P. (2014). Data encryption. Chapter 2 in *Cyber security and IT infrastructure protection*, 29–73. Waltham, MA: Syngress.

Mahtani, S. (2019). Masks, cash and apps: How Hong Kong's protesters find ways to outwit the surveillance state. *Washington Post.* www.washingtonpost.com/ world/asia_pacific/masks-cash-and-apps-how-hong-kongs-protesters-find

-ways-to-outwit-the-surveillance-state/2019/06/15/8229169c-8ea0-11e9-b6f4
-033356502dce_story.html?utm_term=.a6069c9aa165.

Marks, J. 2019a. The Cybersecurity 202: FEC approves free cybersecurity for
campaigns despite influence concerns. *Washington Post.* www.washingtonpost
.com/news/powerpost/paloma/the-cybersecurity-202/2019/05/24/the
-cybersecurity-202-fec-approves-free-cybersecurity-for-campaigns
-despite-influence-concerns/5ce73f5c1ad2e52231e8e7ae/?utm_term=.4a40c
368046c&wpisrc=nl_cybersecurity202&wpmm=1.

———. 2019b. The Cybersecurity 202: U.S. should counter Russia and China hacking
with its own influence operations, think tank says. *Washington Post.* www
.washingtonpost.com/news/powerpost/paloma/the-cybersecurity-202/2019/02/01/
the-cybersecurity-202-u-s-should-counter-russia-and-china-hacking-with-its
-own-influence-operations-think-tank-says/5c5341331b326b29c3778d3d/?utm
_term=.aa1ff5c2dcb5

Miller, S. (2019). The National Guard's cyber escape room. Defense Systems.
defensesystems.com/articles/2019/05/29/cyber-escape-room.aspx?utm
_source=IGI+Global+Products+and+Publishing+Opportunities&utm
_campaign=77e1379d0a-EMAIL_CAMPAIGN_Research_Trends_1_19
_wk1_COPY_01&utm_medium=email&utm_term=0_bcbd627034
-77e1379d0a-48965269.

Moulton, S. (2019). "We need a cyber wall, not a border wall." Twitter. twitter
.com/sethmoulton/status/914589490194386946?ref_src=twsrc%5Etfw%7Ctwcamp
%5Etweetembed%7Ctwterm%5E914589490194386946&ref
_url=https%3A%2F%2Fwww.washingtonpost.com%2Fnews%2Fpowerpost%2Fpa
loma%2Fthe-cybersecurity-202%2F2019%2F06%2F20%2Fthe-cybersecurity-202
-2020-hopeful-seth-moulton-is-calling-for-a-cyber-wall-here-are-the-details%2F5
d0acc51a7a0a47d87c56d9c%2F.

Mueller, R. (2019). Transcript of Robert S. Mueller III's testimony before the House
Intelligence Committee. *Washington Post.* www.washingtonpost.com/politics/
transcript-of-robert-s-mueller-iiis-testimony-before-the-house-intelligence
-committee/2019/07/24/f424acf0-ad97-11e9-a0c9-6d2d7818f3da_story.html?utm
_term=.2331d8f30db6.

Rosenberg, S. (2019). What Apple, Facebook and Google each mean by "privacy."
Axios. www.axios.com/what-apple-facebook-and-google-each-mean-by-privacy
-e2d82692-49bf-4a73-971c-b0bf62d3b2b9.html.

Scott, M., Cerulus, L., and Overly, S. (2019). How Silicon Valley gamed Europe's privacy rules. *Politico*. www.politico.eu/article/europe-data-protection-gdpr -general-data-protection-regulation-facebook-google/?utm_source=pocket -newtab.

Timberg, C., and Romm, T. (2019). It's not just the Russians anymore as Iranians and others turn up disinformation efforts ahead of 2020 vote. *Washington Post*. www.washingtonpost.com/technology/2019/07/25/its-not-just-russians -anymore-iranians-others-turn-up-disinformation-efforts-ahead-vote/?utm _term=.542ac34bc94a.

United States Federal Election Commission (USFEC). (2019). AO 2018-11: Microsoft may provide enhanced security to political committees at no cost. www.fec.gov/updates/ao-2018-11/?wpisrc=nl_cybersecurity202&wpmm=1.

United States Senate Select Committee on Intelligence. (2019). Report of the Select Committee on Intelligence United States Senate on Russian Active Measures campaigns and interference in the 2016 U.S. election, Volume 1. www .documentcloud.org/documents/6214167-Report-Volume1.html#document/p55.

Warzel, C., and Ngu, A. (2019). Google's 4,000-word privacy policy is a secret history of the Internet/How a nascent search engine became a tech behemoth, one edit at a time. *New York Times*. www.nytimes.com/interactive/2019/07/10/ opinion/google-privacy-policy.html?action=click&module=Opinion&pgtype=Ho mepage&mtrref=www.nytimes.com&gwh=46223AE5E3A7120362D1F372EECC6 90E&gwt=pay.

Wide Awake

The Future of Democracy, Digital Commons, and Digital Rights Advocacy

We inherited freedom. We seem unaware that freedom has to be remade and re-earned in each generation.

—*Adlai E. Stevenson*

PROGNOSIS UNCLEAR: TWO VISIONS OF DYSTOPIA

We are living in interesting times, as the old Chinese curse goes. From misinformation campaigns to the general debasement of the scientific process through the distorting influence of conspiracies and junk science, it is easy to feel besieged as well as confined and helpless all at the same time. Journalists, when discussing the impact of new technologies, bring up two specific models to explain our predicament: either George Orwell's *1984* or Aldous Huxley's *Brave New World*. A lot of times, it seems that these two writers have most accurately, and eerily, predicted our current lives. Extrapolating the then-current scientific progress and political and social models, both authors present us with rather bleak views of the world and our societies and the impact of technology upon them. But the value of speculative fiction such as this is not merely in the prognostic accuracy of these authors—as if these were Nostradamus's prophesies—but in the ability to truthfully show how *human beings* would behave in such conditions. For Orwell, it was about the ability of technology, information, and political power to control the lives of the weak and lower classes with brute force. For Huxley, it was about the ability

of technology to modify human biology and thus alter human societal structures and attitudes toward them. Often posed as "either/or" outcomes for our
societies, both writers together show our current world in equally powerful
and convincing fashion. Whether it is political *or* sociological, technologies
change us in shocking and brutal ways.

But what many may not realize about *1984* is that Orwell gave us some
light at the end of his dark tunnel. The narrative ends with Winston Smith
fully brainwashed, happy in his acceptance of Big Brother, no longer concerned with resistance or even truth. If the story ended there, it would be
a thoroughly depressing end. But the appendix at the end of *1984* takes a
sudden long view, as it discusses the minutiae of Newspeak, that implies
Big Brother's efforts to control thought and language failed and that he was
eventually defeated. This breather that Orwell gives us lets us feel that hope,
ultimately, does exist. Truth, once released from the repression of the powers
that control it, will come out. That the appendix is so dry and factual actually
comes as a breath of fresh air compared to the claustrophobic final scenes
where Winston Smith accepts the lie that two plus two really *is* five.

And that is what this final chapter is meant to convey: hope for the future
and our future abilities to push back against repression, invasive technologies,
and the narrow technocratic abuses of power. Instead, we can focus on how
Enlightenment values might be better promoted within our societies, focusing not on the information pathologies that have recently defined our online
lives but on the methods to combat these. We should focus on cures and the
alleviation of these pathologies, to encourage people to use the Internet and
information toward the development of peace and prosperity. In other words,
if we can identify the pathologies that ail us—if we can clearly identify and
delineate these potential information "disease vectors"—we might more easily find cures for them. But this requires a clear-eyed, non-partisan, systemic
analysis of the problems.

STRATEGIES TO "CURE WHAT AILS US"

Developing and Protecting a Viable Digital Democracy or e-Democracy

As we have seen throughout this book, information technology has trans-
formed our lives in distinct yet unanticipated and disruptive ways, especially
in the area of politics and the public sphere. In fact, we might even argue
that digital technology has severely curtailed or greatly damaged our current

democratic governance. With fascist, racist, and hate movements on the rise, Enlightenment ideals are coming under direct threat from not only external adversaries but also from within. Concepts that have been taken for granted among liberal first-world societies, such as freedom, equality, privacy, and personal autonomy, may be endangered.

Shoshana Zuboff, as mentioned in previous chapters, has been arguing that our lives are undergoing significant negative changes due to the impact of surveillance capitalism. "What is at stake," she writes, "is the human expectation of sovereignty over one's own life and authorship of one's own experience. What is at stake is the inward experience from which we form the will to will and the public spaces to act on that will. What is at stake is the dominant principle of social ordering in an information civilization and our rights as individuals and societies" (Zuboff, 2019, p. 521).

While I do not think we are yet definitively situated within this "Big Other" system, as Zuboff dubs it, we would be well-advised to consider how technology is impacting our government systems. We need not accept the "draconian" quid-pro-quo terms given to us by IT companies or the governments that prop them up. Instead, we must answer these important questions for ourselves: *"Who knows? Who decides? And who decides who decides?"* (Zuboff, 2019, p. 521). In other words, who gets to know about our lives? Who controls who knows about our lives? And who controls the narrative—including both personal goals and personal reputations—about themselves? It is high time to establish what we want and need through developing appropriate and fair systems of self-government to meet these ends.

In the previous chapter, we briefly looked at researcher Martin Hilbert's e-democracy project, with its various established and hypothetical democratic models (see figure 12.1). At bottom, for all of the models discussed, privacy was the single most important element for the success of each. As seen in table 13.1, the basic definitions as well as strengths and weaknesses of these models can be easily seen. The risk of a Big Brother system in Hilbert's list is the "manipulation of individual and public will" leading to a kind of "informational dictatorship" (Hilbert, 2007). This is something that Zuboff also warns us against quite vehemently, especially in light of the unbalanced and asymmetrical power structures that exist between people online and corporations that control the online environment.

Hilbert describes seven more models of democratic government, both historical and theoretical ("digital"), starting with the Polis, or city-state democracy of Athens, and the republic model of Rome. The Framers' favored Roman republican model was built into the checks-and-balances system of the U.S. model, with an emphasis on the "rule of law" and "separation of powers." But over the years, we could argue that the U.S. system has drifted away from this representative government toward a more "economic democracy" model, where laissez-faire economics—i.e., free markets—comes to dominate policymaking and the culture. The neoliberalism or market-based philosophy that dominates much of American thinking these days—especially privatization and deregulation—is represented more so in this model than a traditional "republic." While this has been the dominant trend in American democracy for the past thirty to forty years, we are moving into uncharted territory with the development of all-encompassing and physically pervasive information technologies.

Where will we go from here? It is clear that we should consider other approaches to mitigate the risks of digital manipulation inherent in our online information technologies. The other novel technology-based models proposed by Hilbert look at a more citizen-based control of information systems. Yet each one has their distinct advantages coupled with foreseeable drawbacks. "Cyber democracy" is one such model. The model is characterized by its focus on "liberalistic and individualistic decision making," meaning that people are making decisions for their own locally based good, and not necessarily the good of a wider society (Hilbert, 2007). The primary benefit to this way of devising a democracy would be that it reduces centralized bureaucracies, making government more efficient and dynamic. It mirrors, in many ways, how the Internet itself is set up, as decentralized nodes that bypass the middlemen who might control or distort direct messaging. Yet it could lead, as we have seen with Facebook, Reddit, Twitter, and so on, to a "tyranny of the majority," and a significant marginalization of minority viewpoints that become drowned out by the Internet mob. The rise of the Internet as a "pretty hate machine" is fueled by this type of decentralized system that is unable to discourage negative behaviors or reward positive ones.

Another new model, known as "Push-button" democracy, favors a slightly different approach than cyber democracy. It is "a variation of direct democracy in which all public power is exercised by referendums among the elector-

Table 13.1. Various types of democratic systems, both in historical and theoretical models, and their potential as digital technology-driven systems. *Hilbert (2007)*

Government Type	Characteristics	Opportunities	Risks
Polis Democracy	All the power with the people through direct decision-making and weak central institutions	Direct participation and deliberation of issues; more involvement and satisfaction; like-minded can band together	Tribalization of the public sphere, minimal integration, and less social stability
Cyber Democracy	Focus on liberalistic individual decision-making	Optimizes the "subsidiarity" principle to separate public/private conduct	Tyranny of the majority; discrimination against the minority view
Plebiscitarian Leadership Democracy	Legitimization of political leaders through those who are led	Constant contact and checks between people and their political representatives	Shift from free mandate to imperative mandate and populism
Big Brother Democracy	State uses ICT as a surveillance instrument	Facilitation of e-gov services; focus on antiterrorism, crime, and public safety	Manipulation of individual and public will; an "informational dictatorship"
Economic Democracy	Marketplace of ideas	Diminished information "asymmetry"	Theatralization of politics; fragmentation of public
Push-Button Democracy	Optimization of direct voting and referendums	Constant involvement of people voting from home via ICT	Unequal access to digital public sphere; threat to the secret ballot; crude/emotional decision-making
Roman Republic	Publicity principle; representative government; not direct	Optimization of freedom of information; legislation; participative policy making	Tendency to elitist approach; gap between opinion of people and the implementation of the real power
Deliberationware Democracy	Digital intermediation of public consideration and decision-making	Transparent identification of consensus; value neutral intermediation; fine-tuned collective opinions	Investments necessary to develop ICT

ate" (Hilbert, 2007). The technology needed for this type of democracy would be a home-based e-voting system that allows people to vote directly on "all aspects of social life," such as a hospital, the government's budget, or going to war. However, this model would depend upon all citizens having universal Internet access, especially problematic for the poorer and rural areas in the United States. It is also assumed that everyone would be educated enough to make informed and reasonable decisions. It is hard to imagine, though, that people would be motivated enough to vote on every referendum or proposal that crosses their virtual desks. Indeed, many already in the United States do not participate in national presidential elections (only 55.5 percent of eligible public in 2016, which means roughly 110 million people *did not vote*), let alone minor elections concerning more prosaic issues. Governments would be especially vulnerable to groupthink and other whims of groups of people who decided to vote together on certain issues. One of the issues of political parties, too, is that people tend to vote for the (R) or the (D) next to someone's name or go by the policy recommended by their party without spending much time reflecting on the issue. This tendency could be exacerbated with this model. Finally, the expense of ensuring everyone has Internet access would likely be prohibitive—though if carried out it would serve as a public good and could spur at least a somewhat greater share of participation.

Within that list of models, "Deliberationware" democracy is probably the most "futuristic" vision of a democracy fully engaged in an information society, one that is fully digitalizing the way that people make decisions for their public life. The system would rely upon neutral software that serves to mediate conflicting views, aiding the reconciliation of opposing or contradictory viewpoints. The system would function based on an artificial intelligence that provides various sorting and classification of ideas and issues to help derive a consensus from participants. Somehow—and this is not clearly explained—neutrally constructed algorithms would find ways to mediate various positions to measure and help determine "the people's will." It would function more like a republic (with representatives replaced by AI *algorithm*) than a polis (with individual voters confronting and negotiating conflicting viewpoints).

As revolutionary as this new system sounds, it relies on a number of assumptions that might not work in the real world. First, the assumption of neutrality in an algorithm may be somewhat overstated. As we saw in chapter 11, algorithms are dependent upon their makers. Illusions of neutrality would only make the problem worse, as inherent deceptions would go unnoticed. If partisan creators were to tinker with the AI to favor specific viewpoints or ideals, then we would be living through a "digital gerrymander," controlled by the forces that favor specific ideas or certain demographics. Physical gerrymanders are bad enough. We've all seen how they negatively impact our politics in real life by reducing the impact of some people's votes while increasing the impact of others'. This could further marginalize minority or non-mainstream views, removing any possibility of equality while functioning under the misleading banner of neutrality. Second, the assumption that an AI would be able to perform the complex sorting of ideas to reach consensus among nuanced ideas is a bit far-fetched. It is unclear how this would occur and whether such results would be reasonable or could even be trusted. People may find the fact that we are being nudged by an AI to reach a compromise quite disturbing. People have destroyed things for far less.

An "AI code of conduct" being developed by the Department of Defense shows how difficult it may be for people to both accept and come to trust an AI system. (See figure 13.1.) As they explain it, "Democratic societies can

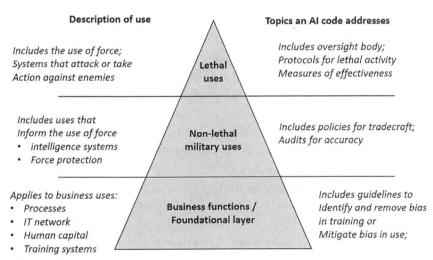

A proposed AI code of conduct

Description of use | Topics an AI code addresses

Includes the use of force;
Systems that attack or take
Action against enemies

Lethal uses

Includes oversight body;
Protocols for lethal activity
Measures of effectiveness

Includes uses that
Inform the use of force
- *intelligence systems*
- *Force protection*

Non-lethal military uses

Includes policies for tradecraft;
Audits for accuracy

Applies to business uses:
- *Processes*
- *IT network*
- *Human capital*
- *Training systems*

Business functions / Foundational layer

Includes guidelines to
Identify and remove bias
in training or
Mitigate bias in use;

FIGURE 13.1
Description of a potential AI "Code of Conduct" from the Department of Defense.
Weinbaum (2019); redrawn by author

make decisions that are representative of their citizens' values and stand up to public scrutiny. It is these values that distinguish the U.S. from its adversaries" (Weinbaum, 2019). It is certainly commendable that the Pentagon is starting to consider how artificial intelligence should be dealt with, especially with mitigating bias in both business and societal functions. But there are some problems with this reasoning. If government agencies choose not to listen to their citizens' values (or if citizen values change for the worse)— especially in areas of "national security"—then it blurs the distinction between us and our adversaries. We cannot assume the pose of exceptionalism if we are secretly doing what everyone else is doing. Furthermore, it is not very comforting to see the government's potential responses for the other uses proposed. Non-lethal *military* uses may be hard to swallow for some, especially if we're working with intelligence systems that serve to spy on foreign adversaries and U.S. citizens alike.

But even worse, at the top of their pyramid are the potential *lethal* uses of an AI system. It is likely that many, if not most of us will be extremely uncomfortable with the level of harm these systems might potentially wreak on others—even our perceived enemies. The issue remains whether people will reach a level of comfort with this, similar to how people felt uncomfortable with video surveillance systems at traffic lights, but now generally rationalize them as reasonable safety measures. Or will they find relying on an algorithm ultimately strange and threatening and be unable and unwilling to cross that "uncanny valley" of the not-quite-human?

Finally, it is unclear whether an AI system would be able to replace the concept of the elected "representative" in a republic like ours. Perhaps if there were a system employed like a blockchain, built upon truly unhackable and unassailable technologies (and not ones *assumed* to be so), people might come to trust and buy into the neutral ledger. They might come to see this digital tool as their ultimately reasonable and unassailable representative. But that is also a bit far-fetched to me as it requires an implicit and unwavering trust in the creators behind the AI system.

Given the way that governments are struggling to adapt to digital technologies, perhaps the time has come to seriously look at new models. However, this change must come with a word of caution. Hilbert (2007) concludes that "there is an *abundance of undemocratic features* in the digitization of democratic processes." All the models proposed provide distinct benefits and definite drawbacks both in real life and in a digitalized environment. The problems seem exacerbated by the introduction of digital technologies. It is hoped that an understanding of the equally beneficial and negative roles that information technology plays in our society can help us to devise an appropriate political environment or system that meets the needs of advanced societies with a minimum of disruption.

Aside from being cognizant of how digital information systems are impacting our governments, and altering them accordingly, there are other things we can do to improve our societies. As the Digital Public Library of American has pointed out, "As a society, we are wrestling with the fact that our online platforms have been weaponized to actively undermine our democracy" (Johnson, 2019). Current American models of government and policy implementation have failed in significant ways, not least of which is the protection of elections from hacking and the manipulation of public opinion through social media, leading us into populist politics, polarized opinions, and eroded democratic ideals.

The ongoing problem of people voting against their own interests seems to be a symptom of political manipulations that spur the rise of "outgroup hate" and encourage "ingroup love" (Piore, 2015). Think red vs. blue, fascist vs. anti-fascist, immigrants vs. citizens, and so on. Fear mongering in our political discourse clearly drives this behavior. People are sadly more willing "to sacrifice money to punish an outgroup . . . when subjects were made to feel that an outgroup posed an active threat to the needs of the ingroup" (Piore, 2015). In other words, people were more willing to forgo their own best interests (e.g., cut welfare spending or medical insurance) if doing so harmed another group *more*!

Fear mongering through online targeted ads on Facebook or through bots retweeting hateful rhetoric on Twitter exacerbates the polarization of our politics and public life and heightens the level of fear within our society. It is therefore imperative for us to find the right way forward, where fear and hate are not allowed to spread without a fight. We need to make sure that the terms of online life are not altered *for* us without our own input, just because we are unaware of how the technology disrupted our previously reliable democratic norms, practices, and systems. We also need to make sure that the flaws and fault lines that already exist in our societies (as well as our general psychological tendencies to fear others) are not exacerbated or exploited further by those seeking control and power. It becomes clear that not only does digitization impact our society at-large in cultural and behavioral ways, it also impacts our ability to administer and protect our political landscape.

Advocating for a Stronger Digital "Information Commons" — A Public Good Worth Protecting

Over the past few hundred years, one of the central pillars of public life has been the concept of "the commons," which allows all people in a society to share something—whether it be land, information, or services—for the betterment of all. It is in many ways a counterpoint to the spiteful austerity movements that stem from outgroup hate and fear mongering. Over time, though, the problem with this public arrangement became clear. Without clear incentives to maintain the commons, people invariably let them fall into decline through overuse, misuse, or abandonment. The "tragedy of the commons," as it is called, stems from people using their common areas without the sense of direct stewardship necessary for long-term sustainability.

In some ways, this tragedy of the commons has happened with the Internet as well. The original utopian vision of open, worldwide communication has morphed into a very polluted infosphere, rife with discord, manipulation, and fraud. Many have adapted to this, getting what they can from it, charging fees for unsullied, quality information. While others have abandoned the open web completely, preferring to spend all their time on just one or two sites.

Some are trying to change this situation, however, by creating and maintaining the "information commons," which asserts that "people collectively own certain public resources (e.g., the broadcast airwaves, the Internet, physical public spaces), and that they therefore ought to have the legal authority and social norms for controlling those resources" (Brollier, 2002). We aren't always owners of all online content, but we do have a stake in how it is regulated, controlled, and parceled out. In that regard, a robust "information commons" remains an essential concept for a viable Internet.

One of the most concerning aspects of the Internet has been the walling-off of content, especially through copyright restrictions and subscription access models (aka "paywalls"). While this is not a call to abolish copyright in any sense or to bypass legitimate publishers, there is a lot of confusion about who can use what content online and in what situations. Creative Commons licensing was developed to help alleviate some of this confusion. Creators can apply any number of flexible and changeable licenses to their works upon their publication in order to let their readers or consumers know what can or cannot be done with the work. The more restrictive licenses spell out the exact conditions for someone to use a work, while other licenses leave few restrictions or none at all, allowing most people to use or reuse content with little fear of litigation. The licensing has also helped to provide a much clearer line of demarcation between usable works and non-usable works, further strengthening the public domain, as well as the information commons, by eliminating much of the ambiguity that often arises with intellectual property rights.

While the creative commons license helps to demarcate newly created works for the information commons, other entities have made it their mission to improve online life with the development of digital collections and digital libraries that provide restriction-free access to important, previously published cultural works. The Digital Public Library of America (DPLA), the Internet Archive, and the HathiTrust all function as pillars of this "open web," reflecting the original utopian instincts and public-service roles that physical libraries have provided for centuries. As these new massive digital libraries have grown in size, their positive impact on the online digital commons has been profound, adding tens of millions of digital versions of works that exist in the public domain or are free of copyright restrictions (Weiss, 2014).

In the case of the Internet Archive, for example, they provide a wide range of content types, including videos of Grateful Dead concerts, emulated video games from the 1980s, recordings from old or defunct record labels, and, of course, two million digitized books. Best of all, the Internet Archive also provides the Wayback Machine, a site that has archived more than 200 million web sites (380 billion pages; 25 petabytes of data!), so that people can check how the information displayed in them has changed over the years, from the earliest era of the Internet to the latest. Additionally, Wikipedia and the Wiki Commons movement also look to improve the information commons by providing factual information for free on all possible subjects. In contrast to the *Encyclopedia Britannica*, Wikipedia doesn't charge money for access and relies on both crowd-sourcing for financing and crowd-editing for verifying information. In one notable study, it was found to have a comparable amount of errors to *Britannica*, long considered the gold standard in encyclopedias. It "fared well in comparison" to the more traditional publication and "scored significantly higher on accuracy, references and overall judgment" (Casebourne et al., 2012). What this tells us is that traditional publishing methods do not automatically equate superior results, especially in regard to quickly changing, large-scale information resources.

These open online institutions have one thing in common: a shared mission for a transparent and equal Internet paired with freely accessible information. This utopian vision of providing the world's knowledge to all gives us a great counterexample to the extreme hate and conspiracy swamps of the online world of 8chan, Reddit, and the like. It is imperative that these institutions remain strong and vital forces in online life. Without them, the Internet will be a bleak "pay-to-play" landscape, where the best content is hidden behind paywall gardens and the worst is openly polluting our information streams. The good news, however, is that they are still going strong. Even though the DPLA is relatively new, it has quickly grown in size since it began in 2013. The HathiTrust and Internet Archive have been around for more than two decades. Their efforts may often go unnoticed, but their impacts are pervasive and continue to preserve the utopian ideals that the Internet started under.

Information Literacy: Teaching to Combat Untruths, Re-Learning *How* to Learn

A robust information commons, paired with an appropriately designed digital democratic system, could be stronger still with the development of education programs designed to create an informed e-citizenry. One of the best ways to help people navigate the new information society that has developed over the past ten to fifteen years has been to focus on the concept of "information literacy." To be information literate, according to the American Library Association (2019), "a person must be able to recognize when information is needed and have the ability to locate, evaluate, and use effectively the needed information." In simpler terms, such people "have learned how to learn," by their understanding of the ways in which information is organized, their ability to find information, and their practice in using information to help others learn from them (ALA, 2019). This concept has been widely adopted in education circles, but especially by libraries, as they exist on the fault lines between information users, societal and market systems, and information content providers.

These fault lines have unfortunately become more fragmented, jagged, and complex in the Internet age, to the point where the negative consequences of this fragmentation may be significant if not addressed quickly. According to Peter Singer and Emerson Brooking (2018), in their book *LikeWar: The Weaponization of Social Media*, "Information literacy is no longer merely an education issue but a *national security imperative*" (p. 264) because of the malicious nature of how certain information—especially misinformation and disinformation—is spread in order to sow confusion or dissent. The domain for information literacy needs to extend much further out from libraries and education departments in academia to all aspects of public life. We need to be better at getting the message out about educating people on the best practices of using digital information and the threat of being manipulated, nudged, and surveilled.

Transforming Information into Knowledge

But here's the rub: what the American Library Association is proposing as information literacy may be confused partly with what we see as knowledge. One of the problems with information is that it is like a sharpened double-edged knife. Used in the wrong hands for the wrong purposes, information can become harmful. Not all information can or should be made available. Not everyone should know how to develop and produce a nuclear weapon! Used in the right hands for the appropriate purpose, though, information becomes a beneficial tool. Information literacy is designed to help with this process, but the singular focus on merely information is misguided. We need to focus instead on the generation of *knowledge*—which in all aspects is superior to and more useful than the generic, all-purpose "information."

While information literacy certainly helps people to combat things like information overload or with basic search retrieval or even the basic principles of information organization, it doesn't always help with comprehension or developing new understanding. Indeed, people are likely reading more now and encountering more information than ever in history, "100,000 words a day," according to one estimate (Beck, 2018), yet they are no more informed than they were decades ago. Indeed, the way that technology now presents information to us may be leading to a "misinformation effect," which is characterized by people taking in "information that they know to be false, but use . . . later anyway" (Beck, 2018). And the rest of the information has no chance of becoming knowledge as it is merely discarded and forgotten. It may be important, then, to look at all aspects of the human reading experience, starting with the technology aspect, to help eliminate distraction and foster slower and more paced reading, while also advocating for the library-centric ideas of being aware of how information is organized. This meta-literacy will lead to more knowledge creation and less information abuse.

Fostering Trusted and Socially Responsible Online Social Media

For the most part, social media companies have attempted to remain as outwardly neutral as they can get away with in the current online climate. Over the years, the major social media companies have been quite strong in their policy of allowing controversial ideas to flow through their websites, while at the same time trying to avoid rocking the boat in order to preserve advertising revenues. However, as we saw in chapter 11, social media companies have also struggled to meet the content moderation needs of a large-scale, universally adopted platform, especially as it comes at the expense of their main revenue sources: people viewing advertisements. Sometimes they have responded by being too lenient or lax in their responses to egregious content, as in the case of the New Zealand shooter, and other times they have been too heavy-handed (Newton, 2019). But this may be about to change for the better.

First, some social media companies have recently pushed back against the misinformation campaigns run by the Chinese during their conflict with Hong Kong protesters. YouTube eliminated nearly two hundred channels devoted to sowing discord and sharing misinformation against the city's protesters; these efforts were discovered when it was noticed that these channels "behaved in a coordinated manner while uploading videos related to the months-long unrest in Hong Kong" (Romm and Bensinger, 2019). Similarly, Twitter claims to have eliminated close to a thousand Chinese accounts that appeared suspicious; they also cut off advertising revenues from China's state-owned media companies. Facebook seems to have made the lightest response by removing just a "handful" of sites that seemed to favor China over the Hong Kong protesters. This is only one instance, but it may become an effective response over time if the companies remain cognizant of how their platforms manipulate opinion and distort fact.

Second, there is a greater awareness among many users that information is being mishandled or misused online, and as a result, people are "voting with

their feet" and drifting away from these sites. Overall growth in the use of social media sites, according to the Pew Research Center, has stagnated. All but
Instagram have either remained the same or declined over the past two years
(Perrin and Anderson, 2019). Many users have canceled and closed their
accounts. Others have gone to social media platforms that are more heavily
regulated or much more specific in their purpose. LinkedIn, for example,
focuses much more on career networking and therefore user behavior is far
less controversial. Users tend to be more cautious in their interactions on the
website, as negative impressions from controversial ideas and behaviors could
have the real-world consequence of losing out on a job opportunity.

Third, a trusted and socially responsible social media has become a matter of national and international importance. There is currently a greater
awareness of the need for "digital diplomacy," which might apply some of the
traditional rules of statecraft within the context of information technology
and social media (Lichtenstein, 2010). While this movement started in 2009,
just as Twitter and Facebook were getting big, the need for improved communications among nations has only grown. These technologies have "theo-
retically given a voice to the anonymous and formerly powerless," but require
management within a clear political philosophy of construction rather than
destruction. It must be acknowledged that our shrinking, networked world
"exists above the state, below the state and through the state," and that we
have a responsibility to enforce equality through our social media interactions
(ibid.) Guidelines must be further developed to make sure that the implementation of social media by all governments is applied in an even-handed,
rational, and reasonable manner. The Twitter ban on political advertising for
the 2020 presidential election is a good start, and hopefully an effective deter-
rent of disinformation and negativity during the election cycle (Romm, 2019).
But this is merely one platform. The frequent divisive tweets of the current
president of the United States as well as the misinformation campaigns of
China and Russia clearly underline the severity of this need for all platforms
to perform a similar ban.

Countering the "Tragedy of Scale"

The tragedy of the commons often pointed toward a singular cause: too
many people with too little oversight or too few incentives to preserve a common resource resulted in the overall decline and abandonment of their shared

resource. The decline impacted more than just the primary users, extending to the overall environs and the quality of life in that region. We might say the same for the Internet. Like any other common resource, it needs oversight for the common good. But its massive scale has turned its decentralized nature (one of its best features) into a growing problem of effective maintenance. It is this problem of growth and universal adoption that we might call the "tragedy of scale." The Internet has grown far beyond its current capacity to provide a common, well-tended, and well-regulated cyberspace for all. It has also grown far beyond its ability to curtail the negative, antisocial tendencies of the more negative and abusive users.

One proposal to counteract a tragedy of scale is to find ways to centralize and standardize the web, providing more regulation and control over how people interact on it. Certainly, this may help with the moderation of online forums, especially if users' anonymity is managed better and their sense of personal responsibility is increased. Yet curtailing privacy would likely turn off too many people; there is protection in anonymity and an appealing sense of freedom. And, frankly, as we saw with social credit systems in China, the cure may be worse than the disease.

Is It Time to Break Up the Tech Monopolies?

Another solution to the problem of scale is to fight against the domination of the Internet by the major social medial and online content companies. Shoshana Zuboff (2019)argues that consumers and users of the Internet are subjected to asymmetrical power relationships and essentially now use the Internet on the terms set up and enforced by corporations. This vast network of imbalance, she argues, will have long-term negative impacts on our personal well-being for the sake of short-term shareholder gain. She writes, it "is not OK for every move, emotion, utterance, and desire to be catalogued, manipulated, and then used to surreptitiously herd us through the future tense for the sake of someone else's profit" (ibid.). She proposes that people become more assertive in their roles in order to return some of the balance in our capitalist society that had developed over centuries. She admits this may not be enough, but it doesn't have to be "inevitable" that we give it all up (Zuboff, 2019, p. 524).

One of the founders of Facebook, Chris Hughes (not Mark Zuckerberg), took things a step further and proposed that social media be curtailed in a much more radical way: break up Facebook to remove its damaging monopoly on the Internet. "Facebook," he argues, "should be separated into multiple companies. The F.T.C., in conjunction with the Justice Department, should enforce antitrust laws by undoing the Instagram and WhatsApp acquisitions and banning future acquisitions for several years. The F.T.C. should have blocked these mergers, but it's not too late to act" (Hughes, 2019). The problem with Facebook is that it has gone from a relatively minor niche web service to an all-encompassing web experience.

Some people never leave the confines of Facebook. Their online lives are dominated by logging in and checking Facebook multiple times daily, at the expense of all other web uses. Facebook owns not only the Facebook Platform, but also WhatsApp, Messenger, and Instagram. Up to 2.3 billion users in addition to the multiple billions of unique and overlapping users in the other platforms are registered with the company. In comparison, YouTube, owned by Google, is heavily used by nearly two billion, and the world's most-used search engine remains Google Search. The damage that monopolies and oligarchies wreak upon societies is well-documented. The gilded ages of the 1880s and the 1920s show the damage that income inequality incurred upon American society. Similar rates of income inequality now dominate American life. The U.S. government in the 1890s and 1950s had attempted to rectify these conglomerations of power but has taken a more laissez-faire approach over the past forty years to the mergers and acquisitions of companies as they consolidate their power, market share, and advertising revenues. It seems the hard lessons need to be relearned every few generations or so.

Add to this growing inequality the outsized influence in terms of how the current dominant IT and online social media companies have weaved themselves into the fabric of our economies, cultures, and governments, and we have the makings of very a damaging online monopoly. By Hughes's (2019) estimation, Facebook "is worth half a trillion dollars and commands . . . more than 80 percent of the world's social networking revenue. It is a powerful monopoly, eclipsing all of its rivals and erasing competition from the social networking category." The power and influence it wields has made it nearly impervious to punishment. Despite the difficult year Facebook had in 2018 with the numerous scandals that rocked it (i.e., Cambridge Analytica and data breaches), Facebook's value still increased by 40 percent!

Hughes's solution to break up the monopoly of Facebook would, in his estimation, reduce its current excessive influence and force it to become more honest in its approach to business. The issue, of course, is that its business is *people and their data*. Without a curb on Facebook, we will not only be in danger of being dominated by a single corporation for social networking—and by implication the information we use and reuse, share and broadcast—but our very identities and personal agencies will be compromised by the power held in their hands. We are forced with a difficult decision: either trust the powerful men whom history has shown again and again to be easily corrupted ("Absolute power corrupts absolutely") or weaken their power for the benefit of all.

What this tragedy of scale ultimately teaches us about the concentrations of power in the few, over millions and possibly billions of people spread out and weakened by a declining quality of life, is that it is dangerous. It leads to abuses or violence when minority voices choose to dissent against the powers that be. When organizations become too big to fail, they also become too cocooned to see the dangers around them. *Hubris*, in other words. The public good can only serve all so long as proper oversight ensures that power is diffuse and remains equally distributed.

AN ENDING, OF SORTS: TOWARD A THEORY OF INFORMATION ETHICS TO COMBAT INFORMATION PATHOLOGIES

Sometimes it feels like the world has gone crazy; that it has lost its collective mind; that, online at least, reason, community, compassion, companionship, friendship, and a satisfactory life have disappeared. But this is not true. The Internet, as compelling and real as it *seems*, is not reality. It is an image, and a distorted one at that, of what represents reality. People unfortunately tend to take this digital funhouse mirror at face value. It is all an illusion, of course. It is a grand illusion of universal communication devolving into babble *and* Babel, rooted in our easily fooled perceptions, our unknown and known internal biases, and the blinkered personal beliefs we harbor about other people and ourselves. It is also an ancient desire, like that ancient tower, a dream of universal communication that hints at humanity's deepest hopes for lasting peace and prosperity.

It is clear from the topics covered throughout this book that information pathologies have come to define the Internet experience for many, if not most users. Whether we are aware of these pathologies or not, we will need to find ways to bring them to the attention of others so we can better counteract them. The realization that information itself—especially in its digital form—is merely a tool to be used for good or ill makes it necessary that we develop a set of best practices and a theory of information ethics to help deal with our problem, just as we would with any tool adopted by a society.

How we create this grand theory of information ethics is the challenge for the next decades. It will require that we look back to our predecessors in order to relearn some of what we may have forgotten in our rush toward the digital utopia that became, instead, a no-holds-barred free-for-all. It will also require us to "unlearn" some of the worst habits of the digital age: instant gratification, unearned trust in the written but *rewritable* digital word (and world), multitasking to our own cognitive decline, skimming for speed, indulging in unfounded conspiracies, giving in to the flash and nudge of distraction, and exchanging our basic freedoms and autonomy for short-term, minimal gain.

We have been gradually losing the accretions of wisdom from our oldest civilizations as we shift to the future. We may currently live in a so-called information society, but that is no guarantee that knowledge will reach everyone or that wisdom will grow. If the future is here, to paraphrase William Gibson, it's not very evenly (or fairly) distributed. And in our haste to get here, we also threw out some of the best tools and practices (e.g., vetting information, privacy, truth, the rule of law, reasonably short copyright terms, a robust public domain and commons, antitrust, meta-literacy, and so on) that had been developing over centuries, even millennia. It is high time to bring them back.

REFERENCES

American Library Association. (2019). Information literacy—Evaluating information. LibGuides. libguides.ala.org/InformationEvaluation/Infolit.

Beck, J. (2018). Why we forget most of the books we read. *Atlantic*. www .theatlantic.com/science/archive/2018/01/what-was-this-article-about -again/551603/.

Brollier, D. (2002). Why we must talk about the information commons. American Library Association. www.ala.org/aboutala/offices/oitp/publications/ infocommons0204/brollier.

Casebourne, I., Davies, C., Fernandes, M., and Norman, N. (2012). *Assessing the accuracy and quality of Wikipedia entries compared to popular online encyclopaedias: A comparative preliminary study across disciplines in English, Spanish and Arabic.* Brighton, UK: Epic. commons.wikimedia.org/wiki/File:EPIC_Oxford_report.pdf.

Hilbert, M. (2007). Digital processes and democratic theory: Dynamics, risk and opportunities that arise when democratic institutions meet digital information and communication technologies. www.martinhilbert.net/democracy.html.

Hughes, C. (2019). It's time to break up Facebook. *New York Times.* Gale General OneFile: link.gale.com/apps/doc/A585131331/ITOF?u=csunorthridge&sid=ITOF&xid=2fd8c6ea.

Johnson, B. (2019). DPLA and the fight to preserve American democracy. Information Today, Inc. newsbreaks.infotoday.com/NewsBreaks/DPLA-and-the-Fight-to-Preserve-American-Democracy-133604.asp.

Lichtenstein, J. (2010). Digital diplomacy. *New York Times Magazine.* Gale General OneFile: link.gale.com/apps/doc/A231922797/ITOF?u=csunorthridge&sid=ITOF&xid=461fe16f.

Newton, C. (2019). The secret lives of Facebook moderators in America. *Verge.* www.theverge.com/2019/2/25/18229714/cognizant-facebook-content-moderator-interviews-trauma-working-conditions-arizona.

Perrin, A., and Anderson, M. (2019). Share of U.S. adults using social media, including Facebook, is mostly unchanged since 2018. Pew Research Center. www.pewresearch.org/fact-tank/2019/04/10/share-of-u-s-adults-using-social-media-including-facebook-is-mostly-unchanged-since-2018/.

Piore, A. (2015). Could patriotism be genetic? *Nautilus.* nautil.us/issue/30/identity/why-were-patriotic.

Romm, T. (2019). Twitter to ban all political ads amid 2020 election uproar. *Washington Post.* www.washingtonpost.com/technology/2019/10/30/twitter-ban-all-political-ads-amid-election-uproar/.

Romm, T., and Bensinger, G. (2019). YouTube disables more than 200 channels for inauthentic activity around Hong Kong protests. *Washington Post.* www.washingtonpost.com/technology/2019/08/22/youtube-disables-more-than-channels-inauthentic-activity-around-hong-kong-protests/.

Singer, P., and Brooking, E. (2018). *LikeWar: The weaponization of social media.* Boston: Houghton Mifflin Harcourt.

Weinbaum, C. (2019). Here's what an AI code of conduct for the Pentagon might look like. C4ISRNET. www.c4isrnet.com/opinion/2019/06/21/heres-what-an-ai -code-of-conduct-for-the-pentagon-might-look-like/.

Weiss, A. (2014). *Using Massive Digital Libraries.* Chicago: Neal-Schuman.

Zuboff, S. (2019). *The age of surveillance capitalism: The fight for a human future at the new frontier of power.* New York: PublicAffairs.

Index

Note: Page references for figures are italicized.

Twitter: and bullying, 178–179; and conspiracy theories, 91, *92, 93*; and content moderation, 203; and disinformation, 12, 149–151; and e-democracy measures, 242 ; and nudging, 49; and real-world violence, 183; and social responsibility, 252–253; and surveillance capitalism, 60

Twitter and Tear Gas, 53

"uncanny valley," *161*, 162–163, 246
United States President's Commission on CIA Activities within the United States, 134
United States Senate Intelligence Committee, 172, 227, 228, *229*
USA PATRIOT ACT, 9, 135

vaccine skepticism, 93–94
"Vault 7," 137–138
voyeurism, 22–23

Wakefield, Andrew, 94
Whelan, Ed, 91, *92, 93*
Wikileaks, 9, 136–139, 167–168

YouTube: and disinformation, 156, 196–197, 252; and terrorism, 167, 186; use of content moderation, 203, 206–207, *208*

Zuboff, Shoshana, 58, 60, 66, 131, 138, 193, 241, 254
Zuckerberg, Mark, 32, 53, 195–197, 222, 254

About the Author

Andrew Weiss is a digital services librarian at California State University, Northridge, with more than twelve years of experience working in academic libraries. He focuses primarily on scholarly communication issues, especially open access, copyright policy in academia, institutional repositories, and developing better strategies for data curation. His current and prior research examines fake news and disinformation; the impact of Massive Digital Libraries such as Google Books, the HathiTrust, and the Internet Archive; the future developments of open access publishing; the impact of big data; and, last but not least, information ethics. He lives in Los Angeles with his family.